The characteristics of the writings of Saint John of the Cross, greatest of all mystical theologians, are so striking that his major works, *Ascent of Mount Carmel, Dark Night of the Soul, Spiritual Canticle,* and *Living Flame of Love,* have received the highest critical acclaim from literary scholars, poets, theologians, and spiritual directors. The saint's luminous spirituality, evangelical zeal, poetic brilliance, and profound spiritual wisdom shine through his writings and have led countless thousands of readers to see in his treatises the inspiration of divine illumination.

Saint John of the Cross' contributions to mystical theology have been equated with the magnificent contribution made by Saint Thomas Aquinas to dogmatic theology. Through Saint Thomas we have received the ecclesiastical tradition of the Church on questions of religious belief; through Saint John we have inherited an equally venerable tradition on questions of divine love. Both writers combined sainthood with genius—and, in the case of Saint John, astonishing poetic fervor.

The verse and prose works of Saint John of the Cross have, through the ages, moved and inspired all who have sought a closer intimacy with God. From the profound spiritual insights of the *Ascent* and *Dark Night,* to the exalted vision and beauty of *Spiritual Canticle* and *Living Flame,* Saint John speaks to us of the most compelling of human hopes: the triumph of the soul through the ineffable mercy of divine love.

The late Professor E. Allison Peers was one of the greatest authorities on Spanish mystical literature. His translation of the works of Saint John of the Cross, profusely annotated with references to the various texts and to the contemporary history of the Spanish Carmelites, is based on the critical five-volume edition in Spanish edited by P. Silverio de Santa Teresa, late General of the Discalced Carmelites. It is a monument of scholarship and devoted research which has long been recognized as the definitive English translation.

LIVING FLAME OF LOVE

by

Saint John of the Cross

DOCTOR OF THE CHURCH

Translated, edited, and with an introduction
by E. ALLISON PEERS
from the critical edition of
P. SILVERIO DE SANTA TERESA, C. D.

IMAGE BOOKS
A Division of Doubleday & Company, Inc.
Garden City, New York

IMAGE BOOKS EDITION 1962
by special arrangement with the Newman Press

Image Books Edition published February 1962

NIHIL OBSTAT: GEORGIVS SMITH, S.T.D., PH.D.
CENSOR DEPVTATVS

IMPRIMATUR: E. MORROGH BERNARD
VICARIVS GENERALIS

WESTMONASTERII: DIE XXIV SEPTEMBRIS MCMLII

PRINCIPAL ABBREVIATIONS

A.V.—Authorized Version of the Bible (1611).

D.V.—Douay Version of the Bible (1609).

C.W.S.T.J.—*The Complete Works of Saint Teresa of Jesus*, translated and edited by E. Allison Peers, from the critical edition of P. Silverio de Santa Teresa, C. D. London: Sheed and Ward, 1946. 3 vols.

H.—E. Allison Peers: *Handbook of the Life and Times of St. Teresa and St. John of the Cross*. London: Burns Oates & Washbourne, 1953.

LL.—*The Letters of Saint Teresa of Jesus*, translated and edited by E. Allison Peers from the critical edition of P. Silverio de Santa Teresa, C. D. London: Burns Oates & Washbourne, 1951. 2 vols.

N.L.M.—National Library of Spain (Biblioteca Nacional), Madrid.

Obras (P. Silv.)—*Obras de San Juan de la Cruz*, Doctor de la Iglesia, editadas y anotadas por el P. Silverio de Santa Teresa, C. D. Burgos, 1929-31. 5 vols.

S.S.M.—E. Allison Peers: *Studies of the Spanish Mystics*. Vol. I, London: Sheldon Press, 1927; 2nd ed., London: S.P.C.K., 1951. Vol. II, London: Sheldon Press, 1930.

Sobrino.—Jose Antonio de Sobrino, S.J.: *Estudios sobre San Juan de la Cruz y nuevos textos de su obra*. Madrid, 1950.

INTRODUCTION

ONE of the Carmelite followers of St. John of the Cross whose depositions at the Segovian process of 1627 are still extant remarks that the teaching of the Saint so far transcends that of other mystical writers that where they leave off, there it may be said to begin. The reader of the *Spiritual Canticle*, may well subscribe to this statement. Beyond such sublimity of description, one would suppose, there can only lie the ineffable. Yet it must be agreed that in the *Living Flame of Love*—the shortest of his four great treatises—St. John of the Cross takes us still farther into the mysteries of which he is so rare an exponent and presents us with a work, less tenderly appealing, no doubt, than the *Spiritual Canticle*, but written with greater eloquence and ardour, impetuosity and lyrical fervour, telling of a love more completely refined and of a soul nearer than ever to God.

The poem expounded in the treatise consists of but four stanzas and the preface describes the author's attitude to his own exposition of them.

I have felt some unwillingness . . . to expound these four stanzas . . . for they relate to things so interior and spiritual that words commonly fail to describe them, since spirit transcends sense and it is with difficulty that anything can be said of the substance thereof. For it is hard to speak of that which passes in the depths of the spirit if one have not deep spirituality; wherefore, having little thereof myself, I have delayed writing until now. But now that the Lord appears to have opened knowledge somewhat to me and given me some fervour . . . I have taken courage, knowing for certain that out of my own resources I can say

9

naught that is of any value, especially in things of such sublimity and substance.[1]

These words indicate that a special preparation has been undergone by one whose writing was habitually of exceptional sublimity, and who, furthermore, was unusually reticent about anything which might redound to his own praise. From the outset of the treatise, therefore, we should be prepared to find that the Saint had reached a point as near as possible to perfection. Although 'in the stanzas which we expounded above' (i.e. the *Spiritual Canticle*), he tells us, in fact, 'we spoke of the most perfect degree of perfection to which a man may attain in this life, which is transformation in God, nevertheless these stanzas treat of a love which is even more completed and perfected within this same state of transformation.' 'There is no reason for marvelling,' he remarks, meeting an objection which might easily be raised by a reader,' that God should grant such high and rare favours to those souls on whom He bestows consolations. . . . For God said that the Father, the Son and the Holy Spirit would come to him that loved Him and make Their abode in him, and this would come to pass by His making him live and dwell in the Father, the Son and the Holy Spirit, in the life of God.'[2]

In the first stanza, the soul is already transformed in God, and is 'adorned with such a marvellous wealth of gifts and virtues,' and so near to eternal bliss, that it is separated from such bliss only by a frail and delicate web which it entreats God to sunder so that its glorification may be completed.[3] Fit theme for the pen of one who, like St. John of the Cross, could rejoice in what he happily terms 'exercises of love.' Within the soul thus transformed there is held, as it were, a 'feast of the Holy Spirit'; and, now that purgation is past, the soul's intimacy is so 'secure,

---

[1] [Cf. p. 27, below.]
[2] Cf. p. 28, below.
[3] [Cf. p. 32, below.]

substantial and delectable' that the devil cannot enter and impede its joy.[4]

Having expressed its desire to be united with God in glory, the soul passes, in the second stanza, to a consideration of the perfections of the Most Holy Trinity, dwelling upon its ineffable happiness as it is cauterized, wounded and touched by that gentle hand. So exquisite is the 'savour of eternal life' which this experience produces that the soul desires to escape, by means of death, that it may know that life in its fullness. 'I die,' it exclaims in the words of St. John of the Cross's own poem, 'because I do not die.'[5]

'May God be pleased to grant me His favour here!' exclaims the Saint before entering upon the commentary to his third stanza, for he felt its 'profound meaning' to be as difficult to convey as to understand. The soul now 'gives deepest thanks to its Spouse for the great favours which it receives from union with Him, for by means of this union He has given it great and abundant knowledge of Himself wherewith the faculties and senses . . . have been enlightened and enkindled with love, and can now be illumined, as indeed they are, and through the heat of love can give light and love to Him Who enkindled and enamoured them and infused into them such Divine gifts.' This is so for many reasons—among others because 'the true lover is content only when all that he is, and all that he is worth and can be worth, and all that he has and can have, are employed in the Beloved; and the more of this there is, the greater is the pleasure that he receives in giving it.'[6] Sublime and profound indeed is the application which follows of the similitude of the lamp, which, with its double office of giving light and burning, represents the wonderful effects of the love of God within purified souls—that is, where the

[4] [Cf. p. 38, below.]
[5] Cf. *The Complete Works of St. John of the Cross*, ed. by E. Allison Peers, Vol. II, p. 428.
[6] Cf. p. 82, below.

terrible purgations of sense and spirit have formed the 'deep caverns of sense.'

When St. John of the Cross reaches this point, his ardour abates for a time, and he follows, rather sadly, a line of thought suggested by an abuse of too frequent occurrence in the world of the spirit—the unskilled direction of souls that have reached the highest stages of Christian perfection. So greatly was he oppressed by this impediment to sanctity that he allows himself to discuss it in a long digression which fills no less than one-fifth of his entire treatise.[7] Concurrently with his exposure of the harm caused by unskilful direction—a theme which is also treated by St. Teresa—he makes a rapid synthesis, on the lines laid down in the *Ascent* and the *Dark Night*, of the progress of the soul from the moment of its initiation into the spiritual life to its transformation in God through love.

The commentary on the fourth stanza finds the author once more immersed in the theme of Divine love. With ineffable tenderness the soul describes to the Beloved His awakening within it and His secret indwelling. After developing at some length the various manners of this awakening, the Saint passes to the delectable aspiration of God within the soul, but here at length words fail him and he breaks the strings of his lyre, leaving the last lines of the poem practically without commentary.

The period at which the *Living Flame of Love* was written can be fixed within narrow limits—i.e. between May 1585 and April 1587, a period during which the Saint was Vicar-Provincial of the Order in Andalusia.[8] This we know from P. Juan Evangelista, who tells us that the author composed the treatise in a fortnight, without abandoning any of his

---

[7] For the reader's convenience, the *editio princeps* divided this commentary into seventeen paragraphs, which, however, we do not observe, as in this edition the whole treatise is divided into numbered paragraphs.

[8] Cf. *The Complete Works of St. John of the Cross*, ed. by E. Allison Peers, Vol. I, p. xxviii.

obligations or duties as Vicar-Provincial. There seems no reason to doubt the exactness of this statement. Difficulty has been found in the fact that the *Canticle* contains a reference to the *Living Flame*,[9] while the *Living Flame* mentions the *Canticle*.[10] But, if we admit the authenticity of both redactions of the *Canticle*, this is easily explained, for it is in the second redaction of that commentary that we find the former of the two quotations. The first redaction, as we have said, was written in 1584, some months before the *Living Flame* could possibly have been begun, while the second redaction must have been completed by August 1586, a date which not only falls well within the limits for the composition of the *Living Flame*, but gives us the likelier of the two possible years in which it might have been composed, since during the second year of his vicariate the Saint travelled much more widely than during the first, which saw him in Granada almost continuously.

Both the stanzas known as the *Living Flame* and the commentary upon them were composed, as we learn from the Prologue, at the repeated entreaty of the Saint's spiritual daughter, Doña Ana de Peñalosa, a Segovian widow living in Granada with her brother and a generous benefactress of the Discalced Reform in her native city.[11] Not unnaturally, considering the scanty leisure which he had had for writing it, St. John of the Cross revised it some time after it was written and thus gave us the second redaction which is included in this edition with the first. There is ample external evidence for the authenticity of this second redaction, which was made during the last months of his life at La Peñuela.[12] Here he lived for about

[9] Stanza XXXI, Second Redaction [Image Books edition, p. 454].

[10] Prologue [p. 28, below].

[11] Cf. Letters XXIV, XXVIII [*The Complete Works of St. John of the Cross*, Vol. III], which are addressed to Doña Ana del Mercado y Peñalosa.

[12] Cf. *The Complete Works of St. John of the Cross*, Vol. I, p. xxviii.

six weeks before illness overtook him, and for some two months altogether. Both P. Jerónimo de San José[13] and P. José de Jesús María[14] refer to the Saint's being occupied there with the revision of 'the last of his mystical treatises,' and Francisco de San Hilarión, who lived with him at this time, describes how he would go out daily to pray in the garden before sunrise, then come in to say Mass and finally return to his cell for prayer or 'the writing of some small books (*libricos*) which he left upon certain stanzas.'[15] Although the name of this commentary is not given, the use of the diminutive termination and the fact that the Saint's other commentaries are earlier in date makes it probable that the *Living Flame* is referred to. Nor does the evidence end here. The existence of some very early copies of this treatise, which we shall describe later, enables us to judge, from internal as well as from external testimony, the genuineness of the second redaction, the probability of which, in our view, is so great as to amount practically to certainty.

The revision is chiefly concerned with the commentary upon the first three stanzas, which varies considerably in the two versions; the commentaries on the fourth stanza are almost identical until near the end. In the original Spanish, the second version is almost exactly one-seventh longer than the first. The doctrinal content of the book is unaffected; the additions are chiefly designed to amplify or clarify; of omissions there are very few. Occasionally a new paragraph (such as the fifteenth of the commentary on the first stanza) seems to have been inserted to meet some particular difficulty caused by the sublimity of the Saint's instruction. No new stanzas are introduced, nor is the order of the stanzas changed as in the *Spiritual Canticle*.

The principal critic to combat the genuineness of the

[13] *Historia*, etc., Bk. VII, chap. iii, p. 709.
[14] *Vida*, Bk. III, chap. xiv.
[15] N.L.M., MS. 12,738, fol. 17.

second redaction of the *Living Flame* is M. Baruzi,[16] who holds that 'certains affadissements d'ordre littéraire sont assez troublants,' and then proceeds to discuss what he considers graver objections. He cites, for example, the phrase '(endeavouring to persuade love to set it free) from the knot of this life,' which in the second redaction becomes 'from mortal flesh.'[17] In the first phrase he finds 'energy,' which disappears in the second. We do not ourselves see any great improvement in the alteration, but we certainly fail to find any great *affadissement* in it. In any case, M. Baruzi has been unfortunate in his example, for the 'energetic' words 'from the knot of this life' are an addition of the *editio princeps* to the reading of the manuscripts, and only two manuscripts have 'from mortal flesh.' Further-more, it may be added that the Saint did, to our certain knowledge, make numerous corrections as insignificant as this in his own manuscripts. So much is proved by the Sanlúcar codex of the *Spiritual Canticle*, where we find frequent marginal emendations made in what is beyond all doubt St. John of the Cross's own hand.

A more serious objection made by M. Baruzi to the genuineness of the second redaction is what he alleges to be its weakening of the thought and expression of the first. Before the objection could be considered valid it would be necessary to show that the changes made are not in con-formity either with his thought or with the form which he gives to his writings, and this we believe to be impossible. To our own mind the majority of the changes strengthen the original rather than weaken it, as, for example, with the two passages beginning 'For in this preparatory state of purgation . . .'[18] which the reader can compare for himself. In the original text the Saint had explained only why the flame was 'not sweet, but grievous'; in the revised

16 *Saint Jean de la Croix*, Paris, 1924, pp. 35–42; 1931 (2nd edition), pp. 33–40.
17 Stanza I, § 2 [pp. 33, 154, below].
18 [Cf. pp. 44, 165, below.]

text he enlarges upon other of its qualities. There are many similar examples of this type of treatment.

M. Baruzi considers, further, that in the second redaction he finds 'le souci de diminuer en quelque sorte l'ardeur mystique et de rappeler le plus souvent possible que les états humains, même les plus hauts, ne sont qu'une très imparfaite image de la vie de gloire.' He cites two examples of this, both taken from the commentary on the line: 'That tenderly woundest my soul in its deepest centre.'

'The centre of the soul,' says the first redaction, 'is God; and, when the soul has attained to Him according to the whole capacity of its being . . .'[19] The second redaction omits the word 'whole,' which, according to M. Baruzi, disfigures the passage. Once again, his example is not happily chosen, for both Codex 17,950 (S), which we normally follow, and Codex 8,795 (Bz) have the word 'whole,' which will be found in our edition.[20] The other MSS. omit the word, and P. Gerardo, whose edition is used by M. Baruzi, follows them. In any case, no part of the sense is strictly lost in Spanish by the omission of the word: 'the capacity of its being' means 'the whole capacity of its being'; the adjective simply gives emphasis.

No better founded is the objection that the second redaction continually insists that even the highest human states are only an imperfect image of the life of bliss. We reproduce the passages chosen by M. Baruzi from Stanza I, §§ 12–13, in illustration of this thesis.

FIRST REDACTION

The centre of the soul is God; and, when the soul has attained to Him according to the whole capacity of its being, and according to the force of its operation, it will have reached the last and the deep centre of the soul, which will be when with all its powers it loves and understands

[19] [Pp. 39–40, below.]
[20] [Pp. 159–60, below.]

and enjoys God; and so long as it attains not as far as this, although it be in God, Who is its centre by grace and by His own communication, still, if it has the power of movement to go farther and strength to do more, and is not satisfied, then, although it is in the centre, it is not in the deepest centre, since it is capable of going still farther.[21]

SECOND REDACTION

The centre of the soul is God; and, when the soul has attained to Him according to the whole capacity of its being, and according to the force of its operation and inclination, it will have reached its last and deepest centre in God, which will be when with all its powers it understands and loves and enjoys God; and, so long as it has not attained as far as this, *as is the case in this mortal life, wherein the soul cannot attain to God with all its powers,* then, although it be in this its centre, which is God, by grace and by His own communication which He has with it, still, inasmuch as it has the power of movement and strength to go farther, and is not satisfied, then, although it may be in the centre, it is nevertheless not in the deepest centre, since it is capable of going to the deepest centre of God.[22]

M. Baruzi's second example, taken from the same commentary (§ 13), runs thus:

FIRST REDACTION

And thus, when the soul says that the flame wounds it in its deepest centre, it means that it wounds it in the farthest point attained by its own substance and virtue and power. This it says to indicate the copiousness and abundance of

---

21 § 12, pp. 39–40, below.
22 Pp. 159–60, below. The italics are M. Baruzi's.

its glory and delight, which is the greater and the more tender when the soul is the more fervently and substantially transformed and centred in God. This is something much greater than comes to pass in the ordinary union of love. . . . For this soul, which is now in such sweetness and glory, and the soul that enjoys only the ordinary union of love, are in a certain way comparable respectively to the fire of God, which, says Isaias, is in Sion, and which signifies the Church Militant, and to the furnace of God which was in Jerusalem and which signifies the vision of peace.[23]

SECOND REDACTION

And thus, when the soul says here that the flame *of love* wounds it in its deepest centre, it means that the Holy Spirit wounds and assails it in the farthest point attained by its own substance, virtue and power. *This it says, not because it desires to indicate here that this flame wounds it as substantially and completely as it will do*[24] *in the beatific vision of God in the life to come.* . . . And thus these two kinds (of union)—that is, of union alone, and of love and union with enkindling of love—are in a certain way comparable respectively to the fire of God, which, says Isaias, is in Sion, and to the furnace of God which is in Jerusalem. The one signifies the Church Militant . . . and the other signifies the vision of peace, *which is the* (*Church*) *Triumphant.*[25]

We can see no such fundamental divergence as M. Baruzi finds in these passages. The author of the additions and emendations does no more than adapt the commentary to the aim set down in the exposition to the stanza, in order to make it clearer and more definite, possibly with the less instructed of his readers in view who would otherwise find

[23] P. 41, below.
[24] [*Lit.*, 'that this is as substantial and complete as.']
[25] Pp. 161–63, below. The italics are M. Baruzi's.

it obscure. In the Exposition the Saint describes, so clearly that he who runs may read, how the soul that sees itself 'adorned with . . . a marvellous wealth of gifts and virtues' longs to achieve union with God in glory, the only obstacle to which is its earthly life; to which end it entreats 'this flame, which is the Holy Spirit,' to 'break the web of this sweet encounter.'[26] This is the theme of the whole of the *Living Flame*: it is only natural that, in revising his own work, the Saint should try to bring it out more clearly.

Finally, M. Baruzi remarks upon a few modifications of detail, which, taken together with the fundamental changes already noted, he considers of cumulative significance. The figure of fire and flame, he says, in itself so natural and simple, is of frequent occurrence in the first redaction, but to the author of the second seemed insufficiently clear. So we find in the first (Stanza I, § 15) 'for it must be known that this flame,'[27] which the second amplifies to read, 'for it must be known that this flame, which is God.'[28] In the next paragraph, again, the second redaction reminds the reader that 'this flame' of the first redaction 'is the Holy Spirit.'[29] Once more, in the second of the longer passages cited above, the Holy Spirit is quite unnecessarily introduced into the later redaction.

But if, in the first redaction, and at the very beginning of his commentary, St. John of the Cross had made this formal comparison between the flame and the Holy Spirit, why should it be considered unnatural that, in revising his work, he should repeat it for the better understanding of his doctrine? Such modifications appear to us to be an argument in favour of the authenticity of the second redaction rather than against it.

But why, it may be asked (as M. Baruzi has asked), was the *Living Flame* published according to the first redaction

---

26 Pp. 32–33, below.
27 P. 43, below.
28 [*Lit.*, 'this flame of God.' P. 164, below.]
29 [Pp. 43, 164, below.]

rather than according to the second? It is undeniable, as the most superficial comparison of the second redaction with the *editio princeps* will suffice to show, that there is no kind of relation between these. But the answer casts no reflection on the authenticity of the second redaction—it is simply that it was unknown until P. Andrés de la Encarnación discovered it in collating the various copies of the commentary with a view to preparing his own projected edition. P. Andrés himself held it to be genuine and would certainly have published it had his edition ever been completed.[30]

It will be relevant here to quote a few lines copied by P. Andrés on a blank sheet at the end of MS. P of the second redaction:

This manuscript has revealed the fact that our father St. John of the Cross wrote a second time, or revised, the book of the *Flame of Love*, for there are found in it many things which are not to be seen either in the work as printed or in many old manuscripts which agree with it, and also many additions and things set down at greater length and more clearly, which it is evident cannot be the work of any other hand than that of the glorious father. . . .[31]

From this note it is clear that nothing was previously known about the second redaction of the *Living Flame*, and also that the examination of it made by P. Andrés, who, as we have seen, was no mean critic, led him to think very highly of it. The editors who followed immediately upon P. Salablanca were content to reproduce his edition, for the most part quite uncritically. If the second redaction of the *Spiritual Canticle* escaped attention for so long, despite its additional stanza, its annotations and additional passages of commentary, it is easy to understand how that of the *Living Flame* should have been overlooked, its additions and modifications being, relatively speaking,

---

[30] [Cf. *Ascent of Mount Carmel* (Image Books), pp. lxxix ff.]
[31] [The remainder of the note, which is not relevant to the discussion, will be found in P. Silverio, Vol. IV, pp. xxii–xxiii.]

so few. There are fewer copies extant of the second redaction of the *Living Flame* than of the *Spiritual Canticle*, nor are these copies as satisfactory. We now describe the manuscripts of each redaction.

MANUSCRIPTS OF THE FIRST REDACTION

Toledo. The Codex belonging to the Discalced Carmelite nuns of Toledo which contains the *Dark Night* [cf. *Dark Night of the Soul*, Image Books, p. 28] also contains a copy of the *Living Flame*. It is written in several hands and probably dates from the end of the sixteenth century.

Sacro Monte. At the end of the *Canticle* as it appears in this manuscript [*Spiritual Canticle*, Image Books, p. 23] is a copy of the *Living Flame* with the title 'Exposition of the stanzas which treat of the very intimate and perfected union and transformation of the soul in God, (made) at the request of Sra. Doña Ana de Peñalosa by him who composed them.' With few and unimportant exceptions, this copy, which was made at the same time as that of the *Canticle* in the same Codex, agrees with the foregoing, even in the infrequent phrases which it omits.

Córdoba. This fine copy, which belongs to the Discalced Carmelite nuns of Córdoba, is entitled 'Exposition of the stanzas which treat of the very intimate and perfected union of the soul with God, composed and expounded by the holy father Fray John of the Cross, religious of the Order of Our Lady of Carmel, the first man to assume the Discalced habit.' The copy dates from the Saint's own time, and is in a large, clear hand; there are a good many copyist's slips but few variants of importance.

MS. 18,160. An early copy in a legible hand, containing also the *Ascent* and the *Dark Night* [cf. *Ascent*, Image Books edition, p. 8, *Dark Night*, Image Books, p. 30]. The Prologue is missing from this copy, as are also the note referring to Boscán [p. 31, below] and III, § 53, together with various shorter passages. The copy also has numerous variants.

MS. 6,624. This MS., dated 1755, we have described in the Introduction, *Ascent of Mount Carmel* [Image Books], p. 7; cf. also the Introduction, *Dark Night* [Image Books], p. 29. The copy of the *Living Flame* agrees almost exactly with that of the Toledo MS.

Alba de Tormes. Described in the Introduction, *Ascent of Mount Carmel* [Image Books], pp. 6–7; Introduction, *Dark Night* [Image Books], pp. 28–29. The copy of the *Living Flame* follows that of the *Spiritual Canticle* and is prefaced only by the words 'Via illuminativa.' It is in a much more unsatisfactory condition than that of any of the other three treatises which with it comprise the Codex. Long passages of the commentary on each stanza are omitted, and only the first and the last paragraphs are copied of the seventeen into which the editions divide the commentary on the line 'The deep caverns of sense.' The impression which the copy gives is that the amanuensis was anxious to complete his work at the first possible moment.

Pamplona. Described in the Introduction, *Ascent of Mount Carmel* [Image Books], p. 8; Introduction, *Dark Night* [Image Books], p. 31. On p. 230 of this Codex, under the title 'Of how the soul must behave which God sets in the dark night of the spirit,' we read: 'The same holy father, Fray John of the Cross, explaining certain stanzas which he composed on the intimate union of the soul with God which begin "O, living flame of love,"' says as follows in his explanation of the third stanza on that line 'The deep caverns of sense.' The copy then begins at III, § 27 of our edition, and continues, with slight variants and numerous long omissions, as far as III, § 58. It thus has no critical value.

Manuscripts of the Second Redaction

MS. 17,950 (N.L.M.). The copy of the *Living Flame* begins: 'I.H.S. Exposition of the Stanzas which treat of the very intimate and perfected union and transformation of the soul in God, by the father Fray John of the Cross, Discalced Carmelite, at the request of Doña Ana de Peñalosa, composed in prayer in the same year 1584.' The copy is in a woman's hand and has no corrections. P. Andrés tells us that it belonged to the Discalced Carmelite nuns of Seville; no doubt the copyist (certainly an Andalusian) was one of the nuns. A peculiarity of this MS. is that the Prologue is signed by St. John of the Cross. The transcription, which dates from the time of the Saint, is well done; there are practically no omissions; and the copyist's errors are easily rectified. On the whole, the copy is a very satisfactory one and may well serve as basis for the edition of this second redaction.

Cordoba. A fine copy in a man's hand and of the same period as MS. 17,950. It originally belonged to a Discalced Carmelite *desierto* in the Sierra of Córdoba and in the eighteenth century came into the possession of the Discalced Carmelite nuns of Córdoba. Besides having a title similar to that of MS. 17,950, but rather shorter, it has a sub-title of contemporary date: 'Stanzas made by the soul in the last union in God.' The copy agrees closely with that of Seville and has scarcely any serious errors.

MS. 8,795. Described in the Introduction, *Dark Night* [Image Books], p. 29. The *Living Flame* is reproduced substantially as in the two preceding MSS., under the title 'Stanzas made by the soul in the last union with God, made and commented by the father Fray John of the Cross.' The first eighteen folios are in a small and bad hand and the remainder in a much better hand. In the commentary on the third stanza are added some late corrections. This is one of the MSS. recommended by P. Andrés for his edition of the *Living Flame*.

Palencia. A well-written copy in an excellent state of preservation, but unsatisfactory from the critical standpoint, as P. Andrés noted. It is contemporary with, or perhaps rather later than, the last years of the Saint's life.

Burgos. A generally correct MS. dating from the late eighteenth century. The version of the *Living Flame* follows the Palencia MS., from which it seems to be copied. The title is identical with that of the Sacro Monte MS. (first redaction) save that there are added the words 'namely the father Fray John of the Cross, Discalced Carmelite.'

A note may be added on the principal editions of the *Living Flame*. The *editio princeps* introduces many variants, and occasionally omits passages, and even whole paragraphs, though normally short ones. It also regularly omits the Latin texts of the Scriptural quotations. But many of the changes it makes aim at clarifying the Saint's exposition and the editions which follow it depart from it very little.

P. Gerardo's edition (1912) gave precedence to the second redaction over the first, which it printed as an appendix. Our own proceeding is to give both redactions their full weight; as a basis for the first we have used the Toledo MS., and, for the second, that of Seville.

The following abbreviations are used in the footnotes:

First Redaction

A=MS. of the Discalced Carmelite Friars of Alba de Tormes.
B=MS. 6,624 (N.L.M.).
C=MS. of the Discalced Carmelite Nuns of Córdoba.
G=MS. 18,160 (N.L.M.).
Gr=MS. Sacro Monte, Granada.

P=MS. of the Discalced Carmelite Nuns of Pamplona.
T=MS. of the Discalced Carmelite Nuns of Toledo.

Second Redaction

Bg=MS. of the Discalced Carmelite Friars of Burgos.
Bz=MS. 8,795 (N.L.M.).
C=MS. of the Discalced Carmelite Nuns of Córdoba.
P=MS. of the Discalced Carmelite Nuns of Palencia.
S=MS. 17,950 (N.L.M.).

The *editio princeps* (Alcalá, 1618) is referred to throughout as e.p.

Exposition of the stanzas which treat of the most intimate and perfected union and transformation of the soul in God, written at the request of Doña Ana de Peñalosa by the author of the stanzas themselves.[1]

PROLOGUE[2]

I HAVE felt some unwillingness, most noble and devout lady,[3] to expound these four stanzas which you have[4] requested me to explain, for they relate to things so interior and spiritual that words commonly fail to describe them, since spirit transcends sense and it is with difficulty that anything can be said of the substance thereof. For it is hard to speak of that which passes in the depths of the spirit[5] if one have not deep spirituality; wherefore, having little thereof myself, I have delayed writing until now. But now that the Lord appears to have opened knowledge somewhat to me and given me some fervour[6] (which must arise from your devout desire, for perhaps, as these words have

---

[1] The MSS. vary greatly here. We follow Gr. B and T have neither title nor subtitle. A has only the words: 'Unitive Way.' The same is true of the MSS. of the second redaction (cf. p. 149, below). E.p. reads: 'Living Flame of Love and Exposition of the stanzas which treat of the most intimate union and transformation of the soul with God, by the venerable Father Fray John of the Cross, first discalced friar of the Reform of our Lady of Carmel and coadjutor of the blessed Mother St. Teresa of Jesus, foundress of the same Reform.'

[2] G omits the prologue.

[3] E.p. omits: 'most noble and devout lady.'

[4] E.p. substitutes 'they' for 'you.'

[5] E.p. abbreviates: 'since spirit transcends sense and it is hard to speak of the depths of the spirit.'

[6] E.p.: 'some fervour of spirit.' [Cf. the 'certain degree of fervour' of *Spiritual Canticle*, Prologue (Image Books edition, p. 39).]

been written for you, His Majesty desires them to be expounded for you)[7] I have taken courage, knowing for certain that out of my own resources I can say naught that is of any value, especially in things of such sublimity and substance. Wherefore my part herein will be limited to the defects and errors that this book may contain, for which reason I submit it all to the better judgment and understanding of our Mother[8] the Roman Catholic Church, under whose guidance no man goes astray. And, with this preamble, relying upon Divine Scripture, and making clear that all which is said herein is as far removed from all that there is to say as is a picture from a living person, I shall make bold to say that which I know.[9]

2. And there is no reason for marvelling that God should grant such high and rare favours[10] to those souls on whom He bestows consolations. For if we consider that He is God, and that He bestows them as God, with infinite love and goodness, it will not seem to us unreasonable. For God said that the Father, the Son and the Holy Spirit would come to him that loved Him and make Their abode in him,[11] and this would come to pass by His making him live[12] and dwell in the Father, the Son and the Holy Spirit, in the life of God, as the soul explains in these stanzas.

3. For although in the stanzas which we expounded above[13] we spoke of the most perfect degree of perfection to which a man may attain in this life, which is transformation in God, nevertheless these stanzas treat of a love which

[7] E.p. omits the parenthesis.
[8] E.p.: 'our holy Mother.'
[9] E.p. modifies thus: 'relying upon Divine Scripture, and observing that all which is said herein is much less than that which happens in that intimate union with God, I shall make bold to say that which I know.'
[10] Gr: 'such high and great and rare favours.'
[11] St. John xiv, 23.
[12] A: 'making him come.'
[13] [i.e., in the 'Spiritual Canticle.']

is even more completed[14] and perfected within this same state of transformation. For, although it is true that both these stanzas and those speak of a state of transformation beyond which, as such, a soul cannot pass, yet none the less, with time and practice, as I say, the soul may become more completely perfected and grounded in love. Even so, when a log of wood has been set upon the fire, it is transformed into fire and united with it; yet, as the fire grows hotter and the wood remains upon it for a longer time, it glows much more and becomes more completely enkindled, until it gives out sparks of fire and flame.

4. And it is of[15] this degree of enkindled love that the soul must be understood as speaking when it is at last transformed and perfected interiorly in the fire of love; not only is it united with this fire[16] but it has now become one living flame within it. Such the soul feels itself to be, and as such it speaks in these stanzas, with an intimate and delicate sweetness of love, burning in the flame thereof, and extolling in these stanzas certain effects thereof which are wrought in itself.[17] These I shall expound in the same order as with the other stanzas, setting them down first all together, then setting down each stanza and expounding it briefly, and finally setting down each line and expounding it by itself alone.

[14] C: 'treat of that which is greater and more completed.'
[15] [*Lit.*, 'in.']
[16] [*Lit.*, 'in this fire.'] E.p.: 'with this Divine fire.'
[17] E.p.: 'burning in the flame thereof and considering here certain marvellous effects thereof which are wrought in itself.'

END OF THE PROLOGUE

STANZAS OF THE SOUL

IN THE INTIMATE COMMUNICATION OF UNION OF THE LOVE OF GOD

1. Oh, living flame of love   That tenderly woundest my
   soul in its deepest centre,
   Since thou art no longer oppressive, perfect me now if it
   be thy will,   Break the web of this sweet encounter.

2. Oh, sweet burn!   Oh, delectable wound!   Oh, soft
   hand!   Oh, delicate touch
   That savours of eternal life and pays every debt!   In
   slaying, thou hast changed death into life.

3. Oh, lamps of fire,   In whose splendours[1] the deep caverns of sense which were dark and blind
   With strange brightness   Give heat and light together to
   their Beloved!

4. How gently and lovingly thou awakenest in my bosom,
   Where thou dwellest secretly and alone!
   And in thy sweet breathing, full of blessing and glory,
   How delicately thou inspirest my love![2]

---

[1] A, B, T: 'Of whose splendours.'
[2] The MSS., with the exception of G, here add the following
note, which is omitted from e.p. [and from all later editions until
that of 1912]: 'The arrangement of these *liras* resembles that of
those which in Boscán are adapted in a divine [i.e., spiritual]
sense [*vueltas a lo divino*], and which say:

> La soledad siguiendo,
> Llorando mi fortuna,
> Me voy por los caminos, que se ofrecen, etc.

In these there are six feet [i.e. lines], of which the fourth rhymes
with the first, the fifth with the second, and the sixth with the
third.'

[The reference is to an adaptation *a lo divino* made by Sebastián de Córdoba (*Las Obras de Boscán y Garcilaso trasladadas en materias cristianas y religiosas*, Granada, 1575) of the first lines of Garcilaso's 'Canción segunda.' On this, see J. Baruzi, *Saint Jean de la Croix*, etc., Paris, 1924, pp. 108–12, Dámaso Alonso, *La Poesía de San Juan de la Cruz*, Madrid, 1942, pp. 47–90, and Emeterio G. S. de Jesús María, O.C.D., *Las Raíces de la poesía sanjuanista y Dámaso Alonso*, Burgos, 1950, pp. 80–6. In his *Poesía española*, Madrid, 1950, Sr. Alonso returns to the subject (pp. 287–9), and also (pp. 229 ff.) makes some interesting remarks on these adaptations *a lo divino* in general.]

STANZA THE FIRST

Oh, living flame of love   That tenderly woundest my soul
   in its deepest centre,
Since thou art no longer oppressive, perfect me now if it be
   thy will,   Break the web of this sweet encounter.

EXPOSITION

THE soul feels itself to be at last wholly enkindled[1] in
Divine union, its palate to be wholly bathed in glory and
love, and from the very inmost part of its substance to be
flowing veritable rivers of glory, abounding in delights,
for it perceives[2] that from its belly are flowing the rivers of
living water which the Son of God[3] said would flow from
such souls.[4] It seems to this soul that, since it is transformed in God with such vehemence and is in so lofty a
way possessed of Him, and is adorned with such a marvellous wealth of gifts and virtues, it is very near to bliss, from
which it is divided only by a slender web.[5] And, seeing
that that delicate flame of love that burns within it is, as
it were, glorifying it with a glory both gentle and powerful[6]
whensoever it assails it, to such a degree that, whensoever
it is so absorbed and assailed, it believes that it is about
to enter upon eternal life and that this web of mortal life
will be broken, and that there remains but a very short space
of time, yet during this space it cannot be perfectly
glorified in its essence, the soul addresses[7] this flame, which

[1] A: 'transformed.'
[2] E.p. abbreviates: 'in Divine union and transformed through
love in God, for it perceives.'
[3] E.p.: 'which Christ Our Lord.'
[4] St. John vii, 38.
[5] E.p.: 'slender and delicate web.' A: 'thin web.'
[6] E.p.: 'with gentle foretastes of glory.'
[7] E.p. abbreviates: 'will be broken, the soul addresses.'

is the Holy Spirit, with great yearning, begging Him now to break this its mortal life in that sweet encounter, so that of a truth He may communicate to it perfectly that which it believes Him to be about to give to it and to work in it whensoever He meets it[8]—namely, complete and perfect glory. And thus the soul says:

Oh, living flame of love

2. In order to extol the fervour and delight wherewith it speaks in these four stanzas, the soul begins each of them with the word 'Oh' or 'How,' which words signify affectionate exultation. Each time that they are used they show that something is passing within the soul beyond that which can be expressed by the tongue. And the word 'Oh' serves also to express a deep yearning and earnest supplication with the aim of persuasion; for both these reasons the soul uses that word in this stanza, intimating and extolling its great desire, and endeavouring to persuade love to set it free.[1]

3. This flame of love is the Spirit of its Spouse—that is, the Holy Spirit. And this flame the soul feels within it, not only as a fire that has consumed and transformed it in sweet love, but also as a fire which burns within it and sends out flame, as I have said, and that flame bathes the soul in glory and refreshes it with the temper of Divine life.[2] And this is the operation of the Holy Spirit in the soul that is transformed in love, that the acts that He performs within it cause it to send out flames, which are the enkindling of love,[3] wherein the will of the soul is united, and it loves most deeply,[4] being made one with that flame in love.[5]

[8] E.p. omits: 'and to work in it whensoever He meets it.'

[1] E.p. adds: 'from the knot of this life.'

[2] E.p.: 'of eternal life.'

[3] [*Lit.*, 'enkindlings.'] C omits: 'which are the enkindling of love.'

[4] C: 'most sweetly.'

[5] [*Lit.*, 'being made one love.'] E.p.: 'being made one thing with that flame through love.'

And thus these acts of love of the soul are most precious, and even one of them is of greater merit and worth than all that the soul may have done in its life apart from this transformation, however much this may be.[6] Like to the difference that exists between a habit and an act is that which exists between transformation in love and the flame of love; it is the same difference as that between the log of wood that is enkindled and the flame which it sends forth, for the flame is the effect of the fire that burns there.

4. Wherefore the soul that is in a state of transformation of love may be said to be, in its ordinary habit, like to the log of wood that is continually assailed by the fire; and the acts of this soul are the flame that arises from the fire of love: the more intense is the fire of union,[7] the more vehemently does its flame issue forth. In the which flame the acts of the will are united and rise upward, being carried away and absorbed in the flame of the Holy Spirit, even as the angel rose upward to God in the flame of the sacrifice of Manue.[8] In this state, therefore, the soul can perform no acts, but it is the Holy Spirit that moves it to perform them; wherefore all its acts are Divine, since it is impelled and moved to them by God.[9] Hence it seems to the soul that whensoever this flame breaks forth, causing it to love with the Divine temper and sweetness, it is granting it eternal life, since it raises it to the operation of God in God.[10]

5. This is the language[11] used and employed by God

[6] [The Spanish adds: 'etc.'] E.p. abbreviates: 'is of greater merit than many more that the soul may have done.'

[7] C: 'the fire of the love of union.'

[8] [Judges xiii, 20.]

[9] G: 'since they are impelled and moved by God.' E.p.: 'In this present state, therefore, the soul cannot perform these acts save if the Holy Spirit move it very specially thereto; wherefore all its acts are Divine, inasmuch as it is moved in this special way by God.'

[10] E.p.: 'to a Divine operation in God.'

[11] [Lit., 'the language and the words.']

34

when He speaks to souls that are purified and clean: these words are wholly enkindled, even as David said: 'Thy word is vehemently enkindled.'[12] And the Prophet asked: 'Are not my words as a fire?'[13] These words, as God Himself says through Saint John, are spirit and life,[14] and are felt to be such by souls[15] that have ears to hear them, who, as I say, are souls that are pure and enkindled with love. But those that have not a healthy palate, and desire other things, cannot relish the spirit and life that these words contain; for which reason, the loftier were the words spoken by the Son of God, the more they displeased certain persons because of those persons' impurity,[16] as when the Lord preached that sweet and loving doctrine of the Holy Eucharist, and many of His hearers turned back.[17]

6. Because such persons are not attracted by this language of God, which He speaks inwardly, they must not think that others will not be attracted by it. On the occasion here mentioned it greatly attracted Saint Peter, so that he said to Christ: 'Lord, whither shall we go, for Thou hast the words of eternal life?'[18] And the Samaritan woman forgot her water and her pitcher, because of the sweetness of the words of God. And thus, when this soul is so near to God that it is transformed in the flame of love, wherein Father, Son and Holy Spirit communicate Themselves to it, how is it a thing incredible that it should be said to enjoy a foretaste of eternal life,[19] though this cannot be perfectly so, since that is not permitted by the conditions of this life? But the delight caused in the soul by that

12 [Psalm cxviii, 140: *Ignitum eloquium tuum vehementer.*]

13 Jeremias xxiii, 29.

14 [St. John vi, 64.]

15 E.p.: 'and their virtue and efficacy are felt by souls.'

16 E.p.: 'the more insipid did certain persons find them because of the impurity of those who heard them.'

17 St. John vi, 67.

18 St. John vi, 69.

19 G: 'commune with it, it can certainly be said that it enjoys eternal life.'

flaming of the Holy Spirit is so sublime that it teaches the
soul what is the savour of eternal life. For that reason it
speaks of the flame as living;[20] not that it is not always
living, but because its effect is to make the soul live
spiritually in God, and experience the life of God, even
as David says: 'My heart and my flesh have rejoiced in the
living God.'[21] There was no necessity for him to use the
word 'living,' since God is ever living; he uses it to show
that spirit and sense had a living experience of God, being
wrought in God—which is to have experience[22] of the
living God, that is to say, the life of God and life eternal.
David spoke in that passage of the living God because he
had had experience of Him in a living manner, albeit not
perfectly, but he had had as it were a foretaste of eternal
life.[23] And thus in this flame the soul has so living a
perception of God and experiences Him with such great
sweetness and delight that it says: 'Oh, living flame of
love!'

That tenderly woundest

7. That is, that touchest me tenderly with Thy love.
For, inasmuch as this flame is a flame of Divine life, it
wounds the soul with the tenderness of the life of God; and
so deeply and profoundly does it wound it and fill it with

[20] E.p. abbreviates: 'how is it a thing incredible to say that
in this flaming of the Holy Spirit it enjoys a foretaste of eternal
life, though this cannot be perfectly, since that is not permitted
by the conditions of this life? For this reason it speaks of this
flame as living.'

[21] Psalm lxxxiii, 3 [A.V., lxxxiv, 2].

[22] [The word translated 'have experience of' is that rendered
'be attracted by' at the beginning of this paragraph, and 'relish'
near the end of the preceding one.]

[23] E.p. gives the Scriptural text in Latin only; then continues
with only the slightest variation as far as 'experience of God'; and
finally, substitutes for 'being wrought in God' 'and this is to rejoice in the living God.' C has: 'experience of God, which is to
have experience of [see last note] the living God—that is, the life
of God and eternal life.'

tenderness that it causes it to melt in love, so that there may be fulfilled in it that which came to pass to the Bride in the Song of Songs. She conceived such great tenderness that she melted away, wherefore she says in that place: 'When the Spouse spake, my soul melted.'[1] For this is the effect that the speaking of God causes in the soul.

8. But how can we say that this flame wounds the soul, when there is nothing in the soul to be wounded, since it is wholly consumed by the fire of love? It is a marvellous thing: for, as love is never idle, but is continually in motion, it is ever throwing out sparks, like a flame, in every direction; and, as the office[2] of love is to wound, that it may enkindle with love and cause delight, so, when it is as it were a living flame, within the soul, it is ever sending forth its arrow-wounds, like most tender sparks of delicate love, joyfully and happily exercising the arts and playings[3] of love. Even so, in his palace, at his marriage, did Assuerus show forth his graces to Esther his bride, revealing to her there his riches[4] and the glory of his greatness.[5] Thus that which the Wise Man said in the Proverbs is now fulfilled in this soul, namely: 'I was delighted every day as I played before him at all times,[6] playing over the whole earth, and my delight is to be with the children of men, namely, by giving myself to them.'[7] Wherefore these wounds, which are the playings of God,[8] are the sparks of these tender touches of flame which touch the soul intermittently and proceed from the fire of love, which is not idle, but whose flames, says the stanza, strike and wound

[1] Canticles v, 6.
[2] G: 'the effect.'
[3] E.p.: 'the arts and devices.'
[4] G abbreviates: 'show forth his riches to Esther his bride.' E.p.: 'show forth his riches to the fair Esther.'
[5] [Esther ii, 17–18.]
[6] G, T, e.p. omit: 'as I played before him at all times.'
[7] [Proverbs viii, 30–1.]
[8] E.p.: 'of Divine knowledge.'

My soul in its deepest centre,

9. For this feast of the Holy Spirit takes place in the substance of the soul, where neither the devil nor the world nor sense can enter;[1] and therefore the more interior it is, the more is it secure, substantial and delectable; for the more interior it is the purer is it, and the more of purity there is in it, the more abundantly and frequently and widely does God communicate Himself. And thus the delight and rejoicing of the soul and the spirit is the greater herein because it is God that works all this and the soul of its own power does naught therein;[2] for the soul can do naught of itself,[3] save through the bodily senses and by their help, from which in this case the soul is very free and very far removed, its only business being the reception of God, Who alone can work in the depth of the soul, without the aid of the senses, and can move the soul in that which it does.[4] And thus all the movements of such a soul are Divine; and, although they come from Him, they belong to the soul likewise, for God works them in the soul, with its own aid, since it gives its will and consent thereto.[5] And, since to say that He wounds the soul in its deepest centre is to imply that the soul has other centres which are less deep, it is necessary to explain in what way this is so.

10. In the first place, it must be known that the soul, inasmuch as it is spirit, has not height and depth, nor greater nor lesser degrees of profundity in its own being, as

[1] Thus e.p.: The MSS. [and P. Silverio] read: 'where neither the centre of sense nor the devil can enter.'

[2] E.p. adds: 'in the sense that we shall presently describe.'

[3] E.p.: 'can do naught naturally and by its own industry.'

[4] [Lit., 'in itself in the work.'] G: 'He alone can make the soul work, and can move, etc.' A, B, omit 'in itself.' C has: 'in itself and in the work.'

[5] E.p.: 'He alone, without the aid of the senses, can work and move the soul and work within it, in its own depth; and thus all the movements of such a soul are Divine; and, although they come from God, they belong likewise to the soul.'

have bodies that can be measured.[6] For, since there are no parts in the soul, there is no difference between its inward and its outward being; it is all the same, and it has no depths of greater or lesser profundity in a way that can be measured;[7] for it cannot be more enlightened in one part than in another, as is the case with physical bodies, but the whole of it is enlightened in one manner, either to a greater or to a lesser degree, in the same way as the air is enlightened or unenlightened to a greater or a lesser degree.[8]

11. We term[9] the deepest centre of a thing the farthest point to which its being and virtue and the force of its operation and movement can attain, and beyond which they cannot pass. Thus fire or a stone has natural movement and power, and strength to reach the centre of its sphere, and cannot pass beyond it, neither can help remaining in it, save by reason of some contrary impediment. Accordingly, we shall say that a stone, when it is within the earth, is in[10] its centre, because it is within the sphere of its activity and movement, which is the element of earth; but it is not in the deepest part of that element, which is the middle of the earth, because it still has power and force to descend and to attain thither if that which impedes it be taken away; and when it attains to its centre and there remains to it no more power of its own to move farther, we shall say that it is in the deepest centre.

12. The centre of the soul is God; and, when the soul

6 [*Lit.*, 'quantitative bodies,' i.e. bodies that contain matter, have bulk.]

7 E.p. omits: 'in a way that can be measured.'

8 G omits: 'and it has no depths . . . measured' and from 'but the whole' to the end of the paragraph. A omits from 'and it has no depths' to the end of the paragraph.

9 E.p.: 'in the same way as the air. But, setting aside this acceptation of the measurable [*cuantitativa*] and material depth and centre, we term.'

10 E.p.: 'is, as it were, in.'

has attained to Him according to the whole capacity of its being,[11] and according to the force of its operation, it will have reached the last and the deep centre of the soul, which will be when with all its powers it loves and understands and enjoys God; and so long as it attains not as far as this, although it be in God, Who is its centre by grace and by His own communication, still, if it has the power of movement to go farther and strength to do more, and is not satisfied, then, although it is in the centre, it is not in the deepest centre, since it is capable of going still farther. Love[12] unites the soul with God, and, the more degrees of love the soul has, the more profoundly does it enter into God and the more is it centred in Him;[13] and thus[14] we can say that, as are the degrees of love of God, so are the centres, each one deeper than another,[15] which the soul has in God; these are the many mansions which, He said, were in His Father's house.[16] And thus the soul which has one degree of love is already in its centre in God,[17] since one degree of love suffices for a soul to abide in Him through grace. If it have two degrees of love, it will have entered into[18] another and a more interior centre with God; and, if it attain to three, it will have entered into the third. If it attain to the last degree, the love of God will succeed in wounding the soul even in its deepest centre—that is, in transforming and enlightening it as regards all the being and power and virtue of the soul, such as it is capable of receiving, until it be brought into such a state

[11] E.p.: 'according to its being.'

[12] C adds: 'which is the strength and virtue of the soul.'

[13] G: 'and finds itself with Him.'

[14] E.p.: 'and thus, according to this way of speaking which we are following.'

[15] [Lit., 'one more than another.'] G: 'some more interior than others.'

[16] [St. John xiv, 2.]

[17] E.p.: 'is already in God, Who is its centre.'

[18] [Lit., 'will have centred itself in,' and similarly in the following clause.]

that it appears to be God.[19] In this state the soul is like the crystal that is clear and pure; the more degrees of light it receives, the greater concentration of light there is in it, and this enlightenment continues to such a degree that at last it attains a point at which the light is centred in it with such copiousness that it comes to appear to be wholly light, and cannot be distinguished from the light, for it is enlightened to the greatest possible extent and thus appears to be light itself.

13. And thus, when the soul says that the flame wounds it in its deepest centre, it means that it wounds it in the farthest point attained by its own substance[20] and virtue and power. This it says to indicate the copiousness and[21] abundance of its glory and delight, which is the greater and the more tender when the soul is the more fervently and substantially transformed and centred in God. This is something much greater than comes to pass in the ordinary union of love, because of the greater fervency of the fire, which here, as we say, gives forth living flame. For this soul, which is now in such sweetness and glory, and the soul that enjoys only the ordinary union of love, are in a certain way comparable respectively to the fire of God[22] which, says Isaias, is in Sion, and which signifies the Church Militant, and to the furnace of God which was in Jerusalem and which signifies the vision of peace.[23] For the soul in this state is like a furnace enkindled, the

---

[19] E.p.: 'into the third. And if it attain to a very profound degree of love, the love of God will succeed in wounding that which we call the deepest [or "profoundest"] centre of the soul, and the soul will be transformed and enlightened in a very lofty degree, according to its being, power and virtue, until it be brought into such a state that it is very like to God.'

[20] E.p.: 'that it wounds it by touching most deeply its own substance.'

[21] E.p.: omits 'copiousness and.'

[22] G abbreviates: 'This is something much greater than in the communion of love, and thus these souls are comparable [respectively] to the fire of God.'

[23] [Isaias xxxi, 9.]

vision whereof is, as we say, the more peaceful and glorious and tender in proportion as the flame of this furnace is more vehemently enkindled than common fire. And thus, when the soul feels that this living flame is communicating all blessings to it after a living manner, because this Divine love brings everything with it, it says: 'Oh, living flame of love, that tenderly woundest.' This is as though it were to say: Oh, love enkindled, that art tenderly glorifying me with thy loving movements in the greatest capacity and power of my soul, that is to say, art giving me Divine intelligence according to the entire capacity of my understanding, and communicating love to me according to the utmost power of my will, and delighting me in the substance of the soul with the affluence and copiousness of the sweetness of Thy Divine contact and substantial union, according to its utmost purity and the capacity of my memory.[24] This comes to pass in a greater degree than it is possible for the soul to describe at the time when this flame uprises in it.

14. Now, inasmuch as the soul has been purged with respect to its faculties and to its substance,[25] and has been made most pure, Wisdom absorbs it, in a profound and subtle and sublime manner, by means of its flame; the which Wisdom reacheth from one end even to another by reason of her purity.[26] And in that absorption of wisdom the Holy Spirit brings to pass the glorious vibrations of His flame, of which we have spoken; wherefore, since it is so sweet, the soul then says:

Since thou art no longer oppressive,[1]

[24] B, Gr, T: 'of my memory and freedom' [anchura: lit., 'breadth']. E.p.: 'according to the utmost freedom of my will: that is, by raising to the greatest height, through the Divine intelligence, the capacity of my understanding, in the most intense fervour of my will, and in a substantial union, as has already been described.'

[25] E.p.: 'Now, inasmuch as the soul has been wholly purged.'

[26] [Wisdom vii, 24.]

[1] [The word esquiva cannot be rendered by a single word. Its commonest meanings fall into two categories: (1) shy, reserved,

15. That is to say, since thou dost no longer afflict or oppress or weary as thou didst aforetime. For it must be known that this flame, when the soul was in the state of spiritual purgation[2]—that is, when it was entering upon contemplation—was not as friendly[3] and sweet to it as it now is in this state of union. And we must tarry here a little in order to explain how this comes to pass.[4]

16. Here it must be known that, before this Divine fire of love is introduced into the substance of the soul, and is united with it, by means of a purity and purgation which is perfect and complete,[5] this flame is wounding the soul, and destroying and consuming in it the imperfections of its evil habits; and this is the operation of the Holy Spirit, wherein He prepares it for Divine union and the transformation of its substance[6] in God through love. For the same fire of love which afterwards is united with the soul and glorifies it[7] is that which aforetime assailed it in order to purge it; even as the fire that penetrates the log of wood is the same that first of all attacked and wounded it with its flame, cleansing and stripping it of its accidents of ugliness,[8] until, by means of its heat, it had prepared it to such a degree that it could enter it and transform it into itself. In this operation the soul endures great suffering and experiences grievous afflictions in its spirit, which at times

---

disdainful; (2) harsh, unsociable, rough-mannered. Apart from the difficulties in the metaphorical use of the second group of these words, however, the definition at the beginning of § 15 suggests the employment of an adjective corresponding to one of the three verbs given which are similar in sense.]

[2] C: 'spiritual perfection.'

[3] E.p.: 'as peaceful.' A reads: 'entering upon contemplation, did not deal with it sweetly as now it does in this state of union.'

[4] E.p. omits this last sentence.

[5] E.p.: 'into the inmost depth of the soul, and is united with it, by means of a perfect purity and purgation.'

[6] E.p.: 'for Divine union and transformation.'

[7] E.p.: 'is united with the soul in this glory of love.'

[8] [Lit., 'its ugly accidents.'] E.p.: 'its cold accidents [fríos for feos].'

overflow into the senses, at which times this flame is very oppressive. For in this preparatory state of purgation the flame is not bright to it, but dark. Neither is it sweet to it, but grievous; for, although at times it kindles within it the heat of love, this is accompanied by torment and affliction. And it is not delectable to it, but arid; it brings it neither refreshment nor peace, but consumes and proves it; neither is it glorious to it, but rather it makes it miserable and bitter, by means of the spiritual light of self-knowledge which it sheds upon it, for God sends fire, as Jeremias says, into its bones,[9] and tries it by fire, as David says likewise.

17. And thus at this time the soul also suffers great darkness in the understanding, many aridities and afflictions in the will and grievous knowledge of its miseries in the memory, for the eye of its spiritual self-knowledge is very bright. And in its substance the soul suffers profoundly from its poverty and abandonment. Dry and cold, and at times hot, it finds relief in naught, nor is there any thought that can console it, nor can it raise its heart to God, since this flame has become so oppressive to it. Even so, says Job, did God treat him in this operation, where he says: 'Thou art changed to be cruel to me.'[10] For, when the soul suffers all these things together, they become like purgatory to it and any description of this falls short of the reality. At times it is indeed very little less terrible than purgatory and I can think now of no way to describe this state of oppression, and that which the soul feels and suffers in it, save by using these words of Jeremias which refer to it: 'I am the man that see my poverty by the rod of His indignation; He hath threatened me and brought me into darkness and not into light; so greatly is He turned against me and turneth His hand. My skin and my flesh He hath made old: He hath broken my bones. He hath builded a wall round about me and hath compassed me with gall

[9] [Lamentations i, 13.]
[10] Job xxx, 21.

and labour. He hath set me in dark places as those that are dead for ever. He hath builded against me round about, that I may not get out. He hath made my imprisonment heavy; yea, and when I have lifted up my voice and cried, He hath shut out my prayer. He hath surrounded my ways with square stones and hath turned my steps and paths upside down.'[11]

18. All this says Jeremias; and he continues at much greater length. Now, since this is the remedy and medicine which God gives to the soul for its many infirmities, that He may bring it health, the soul must needs suffer in the purgation and remedy, according to the nature of its sickness. For here its heart is laid upon the coals, so that every kind of evil spirit is driven away from it;[12] and here its infirmities are continually brought to light and are laid bare before its eyes that it may feel them, and then they are cured. And that which aforetime was hidden and set deep within the soul is now seen and felt by it, in the light and heat of the fire, whereas aforetime it saw nothing. Even so, in the water and smoke that the fire drives out of the wood, are seen the humidity and the frigidity which it had aforetime, though this was realized by none. But now, being brought near to this flame, the soul clearly sees and feels its miseries, for—oh, wondrous thing!—there arise within it contraries against contraries, some of which, as the philosophers[13] say, become visible in reacting to others; and they make war in the soul, striving to expel each other in order that they may reign within it. For, as this flame is of brightest light, and assails the soul, its light shines in the darkness of the soul, which is as dark as the light is bright; and then the soul is conscious of its natural darkness, which opposes itself to the supernatural light, and it is not conscious of the supernatural light, because the darkness comprehends it not. And thus it will be conscious

---

[11] Lamentations iii, 1–9.
[12] G: 'so that every kind of torment is wrought within it.'
[13] G: 'the physicists.'

of this its natural darkness for so long as the light beats upon it, for souls can have no perception of their darkness until they come near to the Divine light, and only when the darkness has been driven out is the soul illumined and able to see the light, its eye having been cleansed and strengthened. For, to sight that is weak and not clear, infinite light is total darkness and the faculty suffers deprivation through excess of sense.[14]

19. And thus this flame was oppressive to the soul in the sight of its understanding, for, being both loving and tender, the flame assails the will in a loving and a tender manner; and the hardness of the one is felt by comparison with the tenderness of the other and the aridity of the one by comparison with the love of the other. The will is conscious of its natural hardness and aridity with respect to God and is not conscious of love and tenderness; for hardness and aridity cannot comprehend these other contrary things until they are driven out by them and love and tenderness of God reign in the will, for two contraries cannot co-exist in one subject. And in the same way, since this flame is very extensive, the will is conscious of its littleness by comparison with it, and thus it suffers great affliction until it acts upon it and dilates it and gives it greater capacity. And in this way the flame has been oppressive to it according to the will, since the sweet food of love is insipid to a palate that is not weaned from other affections. And finally, since this flame is of vast wealth and goodness and delight, the soul, which of itself has great poverty and has no good thing of its own, nor can give any satisfaction, is clearly conscious of its poverty and misery and wickedness by contrast with this wealth and goodness and delight of the flame (for wickedness comprehends not goodness, and so forth) until this flame

---

[14] [The phrase *el excelente sensible* is difficult, and P. Gurdon suggests to me an emendation *excedente*. That this is the sense of the phrase I have little doubt, but the *eminente* of the second redaction hardly justifies a change in the original text.]

succeeds in purifying the soul, and together with transformation gives it riches, glories and delights. In this way
the flame was at first oppressive to it, and in this way the
soul has ordinarily to endure the worst possible suffering
in its substance and faculties, experiencing great anguish
and affliction from the battle which is being waged by the
contrary forces within its suffering self. God, Who is all
perfection, wars against all the imperfect habits of the soul,
and, purifying the soul[15] with the heat of His flame, He
uproots these habits from it, and prepares it, so that at last
He may enter it and be united with it by His sweet,
peaceful and glorious love, as is the fire when it has entered
the wood.

20. This severe purgation comes to pass in few souls—
in those alone whom He desires to raise to some degree
of union by means of contemplation; and those who are
to be raised to the highest degree of all are the most severely
purged. This happens as follows. When God desires to bring
the soul forth from its ordinary state—that is, from its
natural way and operation—to a spiritual life, and to lead
it from meditation to contemplation, which is a state
rather heavenly than earthly, wherein He communicates
Himself through union of love, He begins at once to
communicate Himself to the spirit, which is still impure
and imperfect, and has evil habits, so that each soul suffers
according to the degree of its imperfection; and at times
this purgation is in some ways as grievous to the soul whom
it is preparing for the reception of perfect union here
below as is that of purgatory, wherein we are purged in
order to see God in the life to come.

21. As to the intensity of this purgation—when it is
greater and when less, and when it is according to the will
and when according to the understanding or the memory,
and when and how it is according to the substance of the

---

[15] C: 'and, shedding Himself upon the soul.' [The word translated 'purifying' is normally applied to leather, and means 'tan-
ning,' 'dressing.']

soul, and likewise when it affects the entire soul and when its sensual part only, and how it may be known when it is each of these—we have treated this in the *Dark Night* of the *Ascent of Mount Carmel* and it affects not our purpose here, wherefore I say no more of it.[16] It suffices here to know that God Himself,[17] Who desires to enter the soul by union and transformation of love, is He that aforetime was assailing it and purging it with the light and heat of His Divine flame, even as the fire that enters the wood is the same fire that has prepared it before entering it. And thus that very flame[18] that is here sweet to the soul was aforetime bitter[19] to it. It is therefore as if the soul were to say: Since not only art thou not dark to me as thou wert aforetime, but art the Divine light of my understanding,[20] wherewith I can look upon thee, and dost not only not cause my weakness to faint,[21] but art rather the strength of my will wherewith I can love thee and enjoy thee, now that it is wholly converted into Divine love, and since thou art not pain and affliction to the substance of my soul,[22] but art rather its glory and delights and boundless freedom, therefore may there be said of me that which is sung in the Divine Songs,[23] in these words: 'Who is this that cometh up from the desert, abounding in delights, leaning upon her Beloved and scattering love on every side?'[24]

Perfect me now if it be thy will,

[16] E.p. omits the whole of § 20, the latter part of § 19, and this first sentence of § 21.

[17] A abbreviates: 'from meditation to contemplation, wherein He communicates Himself through union of love. And finally, abbreviating as much as is possible, it suffices that God Himself.'

[18] E.p. abbreviates: 'of His Divine flame. And thus that very flame.'

[19] [*esquiva.*]

[20] A omits 'of my understanding.'

[21] A, G omit 'my weakness.'

[22] A, e.p.: 'and affliction to my soul.'

[23] A, G: 'in the Songs.' E: 'which is said in the Songs.'

[24] [Canticles viii, 5. The quotation ends at the word 'Beloved.']

22. That is to say: Perfect and consummate the spiritual marriage in me with the beatific vision of Thyself. For, although it is true that in this state that is so lofty, the more completely transformed is the soul the more conformed is it, for it knows nothing of itself, neither is able to ask anything for itself, but all is for its Beloved; for charity seeks nothing of its own, but only the things of the Beloved;[1] nevertheless, since it still lives in hope, and thus cannot fail to be conscious of something that is lacking, it sighs deeply, though with sweetness and joy,[2] in proportion as it still lacks complete possession of the adoption of God's sonship, wherein, when its glory is consummated, its desire will be at rest. This desire, although here below the soul may have closer union[3] with God, will never be satisfied until this glory shall appear,[4] especially if it has already tasted the sweetness and delight thereof,[5] which it has in this state. This sweetness is such that, had God not granted a favour to its flesh, and covered its natural being with His right hand (as He did to Moses in the rock, that he might see His glory and not die,[6] for from this right hand the natural being receives refreshment and delight rather than harm), it would have died at each touch of this flame, and its natural being would have been corrupted, since its lower part would have no means of enduring so great and sublime a fire.[7]

23. Wherefore this desire and the soul's entreaty for it

---

[1] 1 Corinthians xiii, 5. E.p.: 'for it knows nothing, neither seeks to ask anything, and it looks not for itself, but for its Beloved in everything, for charity seeks nothing save the good and glory of the Beloved.'

[2] A omits 'though with sweetness and joy.'

[3] G: 'may be more [closely] united.' E.p.: 'may be more [closely] joined.'

[4] Psalm xvi, 15 [A.V., xvii, 15].

[5] E.p.: 'the delight and the expectation thereof.'

[6] [Exodus xxxiii, 22.]

[7] E.p.: 'it seems that it would have died at each touch of this flame, since its lower part would not have the strength to endure so great and sublime a fire.'

are not accompanied by pain, for the soul in this state is no longer capable of pain, but its entreaty is made with great sweetness and delight and conformity of the reason and the senses.[8] It is for this reason that it says: 'If it be Thy will.' For the will and desire are to such an extent united with God[9] that the soul regards it as its glory that it should fulfil the will of God in it. Such are the glimpses of glory and such is the love that filters through the crevices of the door, in order that it may enter, though it cannot do so because of the smallness of our earthly house,[10] that the soul would have little love if it entreated not to be allowed to enter into that perfection and consummation of love. Furthermore, the soul now sees that in the power of that delectable communication the Holy Spirit is impelling and inviting it, by wondrous ways and with sweet affections, to that boundless glory which He is setting before its eyes, saying that which is said to the Bride in the Songs, namely: 'See (she says) that which my Spouse is saying to me: "Arise[11] and make haste, my love, my dove, my fair one, and come; for winter is now past and the rain is over and gone and the flowers have appeared in our land. And the time of pruning has come and the voice of the turtle is heard in our land,[12] and the fig tree has put forth her figs and the vines in flower have yielded their fragrance. Arise, my love, my fair one, and come, my dove, into the holes of the rock, into the cavern of the wall; show me thy face; let thy voice sound in my ears; for thy voice is sweet, and thy face comely." '[13] All these things the soul most clearly[14] perceives that the

---

[8] E.p.: 'Wherefore this desire is not accompanied by pain, for the soul in this state is no longer in a condition of pain, but its entreaty is made with great sweetness and delight and conformity.'

[9] E.p. adds: 'each in its own way.'

[10] E.p. omits: 'the crevices . . . earthly house.'

[11] E.p. abbreviates: 'in the Songs: Arise.'

[12] E.p. omits: 'And the time . . . in our land.'

[13] Canticles ii, 10–14.

[14] E.p. omits: 'most clearly.'

Holy Spirit is saying to her in that sweet and tender flame.[15] Wherefore the soul here makes answer: 'Perfect me now if it be Thy will.' Herein she makes Him those two petitions which in Saint Matthew He[16] commanded us to make: *Adveniat regnum tuum. Fiat voluntas tua.*[17] This is as much as to say: Give me this kingdom perfectly, as is Thy will, and, that this may come to pass:

Break the web of this sweet encounter.

24. For it is this web which hinders so important a business as this, since it is easy to reach God once the separating obstacles and webs are taken away. These webs which must be broken if we are to possess God perfectly are reduced to three, namely: the temporal, which comprises every creature; the natural, which comprises the operations[1] and inclinations that are purely natural; and the sensual, which comprises only union of the soul in the body, which is sensual and animal life, whereof Saint Paul says: 'We know that if this our earthly house be dissolved we have a dwelling-place of God in the heavens.'[2] The first two webs must of necessity be broken in order that we may attain to this possession of the union of God through love,[3] wherein all things of the world are put aside and renounced,[4] and all the natural affections and appetites are mortified, and the operations of the soul become Divine. All this was broken by the encounters of the soul with this flame when it was oppressive to it; for, in spiritual purgation, as we have said above,[5] the soul succeeds in breaking these two webs and in being united, as it now is, and there remains to be broken only the third web of the life of sense. For

15 [*Lit.*, 'flaming.'] E.p. has 'flame.'
16 E.p.: 'which Christ our Saviour.'
17 St. Matthew vi, 10.
1 E.p.: 'which comprises all the operations.'
2 [2 Corinthians v, 1.]
3 E.p.: 'this possession of God through the union of love.'
4 Gr: 'denounced.'
5 E.p. omits: 'as we have said above.'

this reason the soul here speaks of a web and not of webs; for there is now no other web than this, which, being already so delicate and fine and so greatly spiritualized by this union, is attacked[6] by the flame, not in a severe and oppressive way, as were the others, but sweetly and delectably. And thus the death of such souls is ever[7] sweeter and gentler than was their whole life; for they die amid the delectable encounters and impulses of love, like the swan, which sings most sweetly when it is about to die and is at the point of death.[8] For this reason David said: 'Precious is the death of the just';[9] for at such a time the rivers of love of the soul are about to enter the sea,[10] and they are so broad and dense and motionless[11] that they seem to be seas already. The beginning and the end[12] unite together to accompany the just man as he departs and goes forth to his kingdom, and praises are heard from the ends of the earth, which are the glory of the just man.[13]

25. When, at that time, amid these glorious encounters, the soul feels itself very near to[14] going forth in abundance to the perfect possession of its kingdom, since it sees itself to be pure and rich[15] and prepared for this, God permits it in this state to see His beauty,[16] and entrusts it with the gifts and virtues that He has given it, and all this turns into love and praise, since there is no leaven to corrupt the

---

[6] E.p. abbreviates: 'no other web than this, which is attacked.'

[7] E.p. omits: 'ever.'

[8] E.p. omits: 'and is at the point of death.' [The phrase rendered 'is about to die' may also mean 'wishes to die.']

[9] Psalm cxv, 15 [A.V., cxvi, 15].

[10] E.p.: 'the sea of loving.'

[11] [The word translated 'dense and motionless' is represados, 'restrained,' 'dammed up.']

[12] [P. Silverio's text has: 'the first and the last.' E.p. reads: 'the beginning and the end, the first and the last.']

[13] [Cf. Isaias xxiv, 16.]

[14] E.p.: 'and on the very point of.'

[15] E.p.: 'pure and rich, in so far as is in conformity with the faith and with the state of this life.'

[16] [Or, 'its (own) beauty.']

mass. And when it sees that it has only now to break the frail web of this human condition of natural life wherein it feels itself to be enmeshed and imprisoned, and its liberty to be impeded, it desires to be loosed and to see itself with Christ,[17] and to burst these bonds of spirit and of flesh, which are of very different kinds, so that each may receive its deserts, the flesh remaining upon the earth and the spirit returning to God that gave it.[18] For the flesh[19] profiteth nothing, as Saint John says,[20] but has rather been a hindrance to this spiritual good; and the soul grieves that a life which is so high should be obstructed by another that is so low, and therefore begs that this web may be broken.[21]

26. This life is called a web for three reasons: first, because of the bond that exists between spirit and flesh; second, because it makes a division between God and the soul; third, because even as a web is not so opaque and dense but that the light can shine through it, even so in this state this bond appears to it to be a very fine web, since it is greatly spiritualized and enlightened and refined, so that the Divinity cannot but shine through it. And when the soul becomes conscious of the power of the life to come, it feels keenly the weakness of this other life, which appears to it as a very fine web—even as a spider's web, which is the name that David gives to it, saying: 'Our years shall be considered as a spider.'[22] And it is much less still in the eyes of a soul that is so greatly enlarged; for, since this soul has entered into the consciousness of God, it is conscious of things in the way that God is; and in the sight of God, as David also says, a thousand years are as yesterday when it is past.[23] And according to Isaias all nations are as

17 Philippians i, 23.
18 Ecclesiastes xii, 7.
19 E.p.: 'For mortal flesh.'
20 St. John vi, 64 [A.V., vi, 63].
21 A omits from 'and entrusts it' to the end of the paragraph, and also the whole of the next paragraph.
22 Psalm lxxxix, 9 [A.V., xc, 9]. E.p. omits this quotation.
23 Psalm lxxxix, 4 [A.V., xc, 4].

if they were not.[24] And they have the same importance to the soul—namely, all things are to it as nothing, and to its own eyes it is itself nothing: to it its God alone is all.

27. But here one point should be noticed. Why does the soul beg that the web may be broken, rather than be cut or allowed to wear itself out, since all these things would seem to have the same result? We may say that this is for four reasons. First, in order to use language of greater propriety, for in an encounter it is more proper to say that a thing is broken than that it is cut or wears away. Second, because love delights in the force of love and in forceful and impetuous contacts, and these are produced by breaking rather than by cutting or wearing away. Third, because love desires that the act should be very brief, since it will then be the more quickly concluded; the briefer and more spiritual is it, the greater is its power and worth. For virtue in union is stronger than virtue that is scattered; and love is introduced as form is introduced into matter, namely, in an instant, and until then there has been no act but only dispositions for an act; and thus spiritual acts which are done in an instant are for the most part dispositions of successive affections and desires, very few of which succeed in becoming acts. For this cause the Wise Man said: 'Better is the end of a prayer than the beginning.'[25] But those that so succeed instantly become acts in God, for which reason it is said that the short prayer penetrates the Heavens. Wherefore the soul that is prepared[26] can

---

[24] Isaias xl, 17.

[25] [Ecclesiastes vii, 9.]

[26] E.p.: 'Second, because love delights in force and in forceful and impetuous contacts, and these are produced by breaking rather than by cutting or wearing away. Third, because the soul has so much love that it desires that this act of breaking the web should be very brief so that it may be quickly concluded; the briefer and more spiritual is it, the greater is its power and worth. For the virtue of love is here more united and stronger, and the perfection of transforming love is introduced [into the soul] as form is introduced into matter, namely, in an instant, and until then

perform more acts, and acts of greater intensity, in a short time than the soul that is not prepared can perform in a long time; for the latter wastes its strength in the preparation of the spirit, and, even when this is done, the fire has not yet penetrated the wood. But into the soul that is prepared love enters continuously, for the spark seizes upon the dry fuel at its first contact; and thus the soul that is kindled in love prefers the short act of the breaking of the web to the duration of the act of cutting it or of waiting for it to wear away. The fourth reason is so that the web of life may the more quickly come to an end, for cutting a thing and allowing it to wear away are acts performed after greater deliberation when the thing is riper, and seem to require more time and a stage of greater maturity, whereas breaking needs not to wait for maturity or for anything else of the kind.

28. And this the soul desires—namely, that it may not have to wait until its life come naturally to an end[27] nor even to tarry until it be cut[28]—because the force of love, and the propensities which it feels, make it desire and entreat that its life may be broken[29] by some encounter and supernatural assault of love. For the soul in this state knows very well that it is the habit of God to take away such souls before their time in order to give them good things and to remove them from evil things, perfecting them in a short time by means of that love and giving them that which they might have gained gradually in a long time, even as the Wise Man says, in these words: 'He that is pleasing to God is made beloved, and living among sinners he was translated and taken away, lest wickedness

---

there has been no act of transformative informing, but only dispositions thereto of desires and affections successively repeated, which in very few attain to the perfect act of transformation. Wherefore the soul that is prepared, etc.'

[27] A omits all the rest of the chapter except for the final lines ('and since my petitions . . . for ever').

[28] E.p. omits: 'nor even . . . cut.'

[29] E.p.: 'incline it with resignation to the breaking of its life.'

should alter his understanding or deceit beguile his soul. Being made perfect in a short space, he fulfilled a long time; for his soul was pleasing to God, therefore hastened He to take him out of the midst.'[30] For this reason it is a great thing for the soul to exercise itself constantly in love, so that, when it is perfected here below, it may not stay long, either in this world or in the next, before seeing God face to face.

29. But let us now see why the soul calls this interior assault of the Holy Spirit an encounter rather than by any other name. It is because, as we have said, the soul in God is conscious of an infinite desire that its life may come to an end so that it may have the consummation thereof in glory; yet, because the time is not yet come, this is not accomplished[31]; and thus, so that the soul may be the more completely perfected and raised up above the flesh, God makes certain assaults upon it that are glorious and Divine and after the manner of encounters—indeed, they are encounters—wherewith He penetrates the soul continually, deifying its substance and making it Divine.[32] Herein He absorbs the soul, above all being, in the Being of God, for He has encountered it[33] and pierced it to the quick in the Holy Spirit, Whose communications are impetuous when they are full of fervour, as is this communication. This encounter, since it has a lively taste of God, the soul calls sweet; not that many other touches and encounters which it receives in this state are not also sweet and delectable, but rather that this is eminently so above all the rest; for God effects it, as we have said, in order to

[30] Wisdom iv, 10–11, 13–14. E.p. has 'from the world' for 'out of the midst.'

[31] E.p. reads: '. . . of the Holy Spirit an encounter. The reason is that, although the soul is conscious of a great desire that its life may come to an end, yet, because the time is not yet come, this is not accomplished.'

[32] E.p.: 'making it as it were Divine.'

[33] E.p.: 'Herein the soul absorbs the Being of God, for He has encountered it.'

loose the soul and glorify it.[34] Wherefore the soul takes courage to say: 'Break the web of this sweet encounter.'

30. And thus this whole stanza is as though the soul were to say: Oh, flame of the Holy Spirit, that so intimately and tenderly[35] dost pierce the substance of my soul and cauterize it with Thy heat! Since Thou art now so loving as to show Thyself with the desire of giving Thyself to me in perfect and eternal life; if formerly my petitions did not reach Thine ears, when in their weakness my sense and spirit suffered with yearnings and fatigues of love by reason of the great weakness and impurity and the little strength of love that they had, I entreated Thee to loose me, for with desire did my soul desire Thee when my impatient love would not suffer me to be conformed with the condition of this life that Thou desiredst me to live, and the past assaults of love sufficed not in Thy sight, because they had not sufficient substance; now that I am so greatly strengthened in love that not alone do my sense and spirit[36] not fail before Thee, but rather my heart and my flesh are strengthened in Thy sight, they rejoice in the living God with a great conformity between their various parts. Therefore do I entreat that which Thou desirest me to entreat, and that which Thou desirest not, that desire I not, nor can I desire it,[37] nor does it pass through my mind to entreat it; and, since my petitions are now more effective and more reasonable in Thine eyes (for they go forth from Thee and Thou desirest them, and I pray to Thee with delight and rejoicing in the Holy Spirit, and my judgment comes forth from Thy countenance,[38] which comes to pass when Thou esteemest and hearest my prayers), do Thou break the slender web of this life, and let it not come to pass that age and years cut it after a

---

[34] E.p. adds: 'perfectly.'
[35] C: 'so tenderly and intimately.' G: 'so tenderly.'
[36] E.p.: 'my spirit and sense.'
[37] E.p.: 'nor does it seem that I can desire it.'
[38] [Psalm xvi, 2.]

natural manner,[39] so that I may be able to love Thee with the fullness and satisfaction which my soul desires, without end, for ever.[40]

STANZA II

Oh, sweet burn!   Oh, delectable wound!   Oh, soft hand! Oh, delicate touch
That savours of eternal life and pays every debt!   In slaying, thou hast changed death into life.

Exposition

In this stanza the soul explains how the three Persons of the Most Holy Trinity, Father, Son and Holy Spirit, are They that effect within it this Divine work of union. Thus the 'hand,' the 'burn' and the 'touch' are in substance one and the same thing; and the soul gives them these names, inasmuch as they describe the effect which is caused by each. The 'burn' is the Holy Spirit, the 'hand' is the Father and the 'touch' is the Son. And thus the soul here magnifies the Father, the Son and the Holy Spirit, dwelling upon[1] three great favours and blessings which They work within it, since They have changed its death into life, transforming it in Themselves. The first is the delectable wound, which the soul attributes to the Holy Spirit, wherefore it is called a burn. The second is the desire for eternal life, which it attributes to the Son, and therefore calls a delicate touch. The third is a gift wherewith the soul is right well pleased, and this it attributes to the Father, and therefore calls it a soft hand. And although the soul here names the three things,[2] because of the properties of their effects,

[39] E.p. omits: 'and let . . . manner.'
[40] C adds: 'And here the first verse [copla] comes to an end.'
[1] G: 'magnifying.'
[2] G, e.p.: 'names the three Persons.' G adds: 'by reason of the effects which they cause.'

it addresses only one of them, saying: 'Thou hast changed death into life.' For they all work in one, and the soul attributes the whole of their work to one, and the whole of it to all of them. There follows the line:

Oh, sweet burn!

2. In the Book of Deuteronomy Moses says that our Lord God is a consuming fire[1]—that is to say, a fire of love. This fire, as it is of infinite power, is able to consume to an extent which cannot be measured, and by burning with great vehemence to transform into itself that which it touches. But it burns everything according to the degree of the preparation thereof; some things more and others less; and likewise according to its own pleasure, and after the manner and at the time which it pleases. And since God is an infinite fire of love, when therefore He is pleased to touch the soul with some severity, the heat of the soul rises to such a degree that the soul believes that it is being burned with a heat greater than any other in the world. For this reason it speaks of this touch as of a burn, for it is experienced where the fire is most intense[2] and most concentrated, and the effect of its heat is greater than that of other fires. And when this Divine fire has transformed the substance of[3] the soul into itself, not only is the soul conscious of the burn, but it has itself become one burn of vehement fire.

3. And it is a wondrous thing, worthy to be related,[4] that, though this fire of God is so vehement and so consuming that it would consume a thousand worlds more easily than natural fire[5] consumes a straw of flax,[6] it consumes not the spirits wherein it burns, neither destroys them; but rather,

1 Deuteronomy iv, 24.
2 C: 'where the fire is brightest and most intense.'
3 E.p. omits: 'the substance of.'
4 E.p. omits: 'worthy to be related.'
5 [Lit., 'than fire.']
6 G: 'a little flax.'

LIVING FLAME OF LOVE

in proportion to its strength and heat, it brings them delight and deifies them, burning sweetly in them by reason of the purity of their spirits.[7] Thus did it come to pass, as we read in the Acts of the Apostles, when this fire descended with great vehemence and enkindled the disciples;[8] and, as Saint Gregory says, they burned inwardly with sweetness.[9] And it is this that the Church says, in these words: 'There came fire from Heaven, burning not but giving splendour; consuming not but enlightening.'[10] For, in these communications, since their object is to magnify the soul, this fire afflicts it not but rather enlarges it; it wearies it not, but delights it and makes it glorious and rich, for which cause the soul calls it sweet.

4.[11] And thus the happy soul that by great good fortune attains to this burning knows everything, tastes everything, does all that it desires, and prospers, and none prevails against it or touches it. For it is of this soul that the Apostle says: 'The spiritual man judgeth all things, and he himself is judged of no man.'[12] *Et iterum:* 'The spiritual man searcheth all things,[13] yea, the deep things of God.'[14]

5. Oh, the great glory of you souls that are worthy to attain to this supreme fire, which, while it has infinite power to consume and annihilate you, consumes you not, but grants you a boundless consummation[15] in glory! Marvel not that God should bring certain souls to such a state;

---

[7] E.p.: 'burning sweetly, according to the strength which He has given them.'
[8] [Acts ii, 3.]
[9] Hom. XXX, in Evang.
[10] In officio feriæ 2ᵃᵉ Pent.
[11] A omits § 4 and § 5 down to the words 'three manners.'
[12] 1 Corinthians ii, 15.
[13] E.p.: '. . . of no man, and, in another place, that he penetrateth all things.'
[14] 1 Corinthians ii, 10.
[15] [The play upon the words *consumir* ('consume') and *consumar* ('consummate,' 'perfect') cannot be exactly rendered in English.]

for in certain ways the sun[16] is conspicuous for the marvellous effects which it causes; as the Holy Spirit says, it burns the mountains of the just after three manners.[17] Since, then, this burn is so sweet, as we have here explained, how delectable, may we believe, will it not be in one that is touched by such fire? Of this the soul would fain speak, but speaks not, limiting itself to expressing its wonder and esteem in this word 'Oh,' saying:

Oh, delectable wound!

6. This wound is inflicted by the same burn that cures it,[1] and, as it is made, it is healed; for it is in some ways similar to a burn caused by natural fire, which, when it is applied to a wound, makes a greater wound, and causes the first, which has been produced by iron or in some other way, to be turned into a wound inflicted by fire; and the more it is subjected to the burning, the greater is the wound caused by the fire, until the whole of the matter is destroyed.[2] Even so this Divine burn of love heals the wound which has been inflicted in the soul by love, and with each application it becomes greater. For the healing of love is to hurt and wound once more that which has been hurt and wounded already, until the soul comes to be wholly dissolved in the wound of love. And in this way, when it is now completely turned into a wound of love, it regains its perfect health,[3] and is transformed in love and wounded in love. So in this case he that is most severely wounded is most healthy, and he that is altogether wounded is altogether healthy. Yet, even if this soul be altogether wounded and altogether healthy, the burning still performs its office, which is to wound with love; but

---

16 [*el sol.*] E.p. has 'He alone': *él solo.*

17 [Ecclus. xliii, 4.] E.p. omits: 'as . . . manners.'

1 E.p.: 'is cured by Him Who inflicts it.'

2 [*Lit.,* 'dissolved'—a word repeated below.]

3 A omits the rest of § 6 and § 7 down to the words: 'Oh, then, thou delectable wound!'

then it has also to relieve[4] the wound which has been healed, after the manner aforementioned. Wherefore the soul says: 'Oh, delectable wound!' The loftier and the more sublime is the fire of love that has caused the wound, the more delectable is the wound. For, as the Holy Spirit inflicted the wound in order to relieve it, and as He has a great desire and will to relieve it, the wound, therefore, is great, in order that it[5] may be greatly relieved.

7. Oh, happy wound, inflicted by One Who cannot but heal![6] Oh, fortunate and most happy wound, inflicted only for the relief[7] and delight of the soul! Great is the wound, since great is He that has inflicted it; and great is the relief, since the fire of love is infinite and is measured according to its capacity.[8] Oh, then, thou delectable wound! So much the more sublimely delectable art thou in proportion as the burn of love has touched the inmost centre of the substance of the soul,[9] burning all that was capable of being burned, that it might relieve all that was capable of being relieved. This burn and this wound, in my opinion, represent the highest degree to which the soul can attain in this state. But there are many other ways[10] wherein the soul attains not so far as this, nor are they like this; for this is a touch of the Divinity in the soul, without any form or figure whether formal or imaginary.

8. But there is another and a most sublime way wherein the soul may be cauterized, which is after this manner. It will come to pass that, when the soul is enkindled in this love, although not so perfectly[11] as in the way of which

---

[4] [The past participle of this verb (*regalar*) has also the meaning 'delectable,' and is so translated in the verse-line above, and elsewhere in the text.]

[5] E.p.: 'in order that the soul that receives it.'

[6] C: 'Who can do naught else than comfort.'

[7] [*regalo.*]

[8] E.p. omits: 'and is measured according to its capacity.'

[9] E.p.: 'touches the inmost centre of the soul.'

[10] C adds: 'in which God cauterizes the soul.'

[11] Gr: 'although it is not so much cauterized.'

we have spoken (though it is most meet that it should be so with a view to that which I am about to describe), the soul will be conscious of an assault upon it made by a seraph armed with a dart[12] of most enkindled love, which will pierce that enkindled coal of fire, the soul, or, to speak more exactly, that flame, and will cauterize it in a sublime manner; and, when it has pierced and cauterized it thus, the flame will rush forth and will rise suddenly and vehemently, even as comes to pass in a white-hot furnace or forge; when they stir and poke the fire,[13] the flame becomes hotter and the fire revives, and then the soul is conscious of this wound, with a delight which transcends all description. For, not only is it moved through and through by the stirring and the impetuous motion given to its fire,[14] wherein the heat and melting of love are great, but the keen wound[15] and the healing herb wherewith the effect of the dart was being greatly assuaged[16] are felt by it in the substance of the spirit, even as in the heart of him whose soul has been thus pierced.

9. Who can speak fittingly of this grain of mustard seed which now seems to remain in the centre of the heart of the spirit, and which is the point of the wound and the refinement of its delight?[17] For the soul feels that there

12 [*dardo*. The same word is used by St. Teresa in her description (*Life*, Chap. xxix) of the transverberation of her heart, though the pictorial representations of that event generally show the seraph armed with a long spear.]

13 E.p.: 'when they disturb the fuel and turn it over.'

14 E.p.: '. . . moved when they turn the fuel over and by the motion given to its fire.'

15 E.p.: 'the keen and efficacious wound.'

16 [This seems the most probable of various interpretations. The literal translation would read: 'the herb wherewith the iron was being intensely (*or* keenly) tempered.']

17 C: 'of this intimate point of the wound which seems to remain in the centre of the heart of the spirit, which is where the refinement of its delight is felt?' E.p. (from the end of § 8) has: 'are felt by the soul [which also feels] the depth of its spirit pierced and the refinement of the delight [of this], whereof none can speak fittingly.'

has remained within it, as it were, a grain of mustard seed, most minute, highly enkindled and wondrous keen;[18] keen also and enkindled even to the circumference to which its substance extends, and the virtue of that point of the wound. Thence the substance and the virtue of the herb are subtly diffused through all the spiritual and substantial[19] veins of the soul, according to its potentiality and the strength of the heat.[20] And the soul feels its love to be increasing and to be growing in strength and refinement to such a degree that it seems to have within it seas of fire which reach to the farthest heights and depths of the spheres, filling it wholly with love.[21]

10. And that whereof the soul now has fruition cannot be further described, save by saying that the soul is now conscious of the fitness of the comparison of the Kingdom of Heaven with the grain of mustard seed made in the Gospel; which grain, because of its great heat, small as it is, grows into a great tree.[22] For the soul sees that it has become like a vast fire of love[23] and the point of its virtue is in the heart of the spirit.

11. Few souls attain to this state, but some have done so, especially those whose virtue and spirituality was to be transmitted to the succession of their children. For God bestows spiritual wealth and strength upon the head of a house according as He means his descendants to inherit the first-fruits of the Spirit.

12. Let us return, then, to the work done by that seraph, which in truth is to strike and to wound. If the effect of

---

[18] E.p. adds here: 'in the inmost heart of the spirit, which is the point of the wound' and continues: '[Here] is the substance and virtue, etc.'

[19] E.p. omits: 'and substantial.' G: 'through all the spiritual veins, nerves and arteries of the soul.'

[20] A omits the rest of this paragraph and the whole of the two paragraphs following.

[21] E.p.: 'seas of fire which fill it wholly with love.'

[22] St. Matthew xiii, 31–2.

[23] G and e.p. end the sentence here.

the wound should sometimes be permitted to pass outward to the bodily senses, to an extent corresponding to the interior wound, the effect of the impact and the wound will be felt without, as came to pass when the seraph wounded the soul of Saint Francis with love, and in that way the effect of those wounds became outwardly visible. For God bestows no favours upon the body without bestowing them first and principally upon the soul. And then, the greater is the delight and strength of love which causes the wound within, the greater is the pain of that wound without,[24] and if the one grows, the other grows likewise. This comes to pass because, since these souls have been purged and made strong in God, all that pertains to God and is strong and sweet is a delight[25] to them in their spirits, which are strong and healthy; to their weak and corruptible flesh, however, it causes pain and torture; wherefore it is a wondrous thing to feel the pain growing with the pleasure. This wonder Job perceived in his wounds, when he said to God: 'Turning to me, Thou tormentest me wonderfully.'[26] For it is a great marvel and a thing worthy of the abundance of God and of the sweetness which He has laid up for them that fear Him,[27] that, the greater is the pain and torment of which the soul is conscious, the greater is its pleasure and delight.

13. Oh, immeasurable greatness, in all things showing thyself omnipotent! Who but Thou, Lord, could cause sweetness in the midst of bitterness and pleasure in torment? How delectable a wound, then, art thou, since the deeper is thy mark, the greater delight dost thou cause! But when the wound is within the soul, and is not communicated without, it can be far more intense and sublime;[28]

---

[24] A omits the rest of this paragraph and the first two sentences of the paragraph following.

[25] E.p.: '. . . strong in God, the strong and sweet Spirit of God is a delight.'

[26] Job x, 16.

[27] Psalm xxx, 20 [A.V., xxxi, 19].

[28] G: 'and solid.'

for, as the flesh is the bridle of the spirit, so, when the blessings of the spirit are communicated to it, the flesh draws in the rein and curbs this fleet steed and restrains its great energy;[29] for the body, being then corrupted, presses down the soul, and the habits of life oppress the spiritual sense when it muses upon many things.[30] Wherefore, he that will place great reliance upon bodily sense will never become a very spiritual person.

14. This I say for those who think that they can attain to the powers and the height of the spirit by means of the power and operation of sense alone, which is low. They cannot attain thereto save when bodily sense is left without. It is quite different when the affection of feeling overflows from spirit into sense, for herein, as Saint Paul says, there may be much spirituality;[31] for, when the intensity of his realization of the sufferings of Christ was so great that it overflowed into his body, he writes to the Galatians, saying: 'I bear in my body the marks of my Lord Jesus.'[32] As the wound and the burn, therefore, are such as this, what will be the hand that takes part therein, and what will be the touch that causes it? This the soul describes, extolling it rather than expounding it, in the following line,[33] saying:

Oh, soft hand!   Oh, delicate touch

15. Oh, hand, as generous as thou art powerful and rich, richly and powerfully dost thou give me thy gifts! Oh, soft hand, the softer for this soul, and softly laid upon it, for if thou wert to lean hardly upon it the whole world would perish; for at Thy glance alone the earth

[29] C: 'its grace and energy.'

[30] Wisdom ix, 15.

[31] G: 'I will not for this reason exclude the feeling which overflows from spirit into sense, as is seen in Saint Paul.'

[32] Galatians vi, 17.

[33] E.p.: 'And thus, as are the wound and the burn, so will be the hand that takes part therein, and as is the touch, so will be He that causes it. This the soul describes in the following line.'

shakes,[1] and the nations are undone,[2] and the mountains crumble to pieces.[3] Once more, then,[4] I say: 'Oh, soft hand!' For whereas thou wert harsh and severe to Job,[5] since thou didst touch him so very heavily,[6] thou art laid very firmly but very lovingly and graciously upon my soul, and art as soft and as gentle to me as thou wert hard to him, touching me firmly with sweet love even as thou didst touch him with severity. For Thou slayest and Thou givest life and there is none that can flee from Thy hand. But Thou, oh, Life Divine, never slayest save to give life, even as Thou never woundest save to heal. Thou hast wounded me, oh, hand Divine, in order to heal me, and thou hast slain in me that which would have slain me, but for the life of God wherein now I see that I live. And this Thou didst with the liberality of Thy habitual[7] grace, through the touch wherewith Thou didst touch me—namely, the splendour of Thy glory and the image of Thy substance, which is Thy only begotten Son;[8] in Whom, since He is Thy wisdom, Thou reachest from one end to another mightily through His purity.[9]

16. Oh, then, thou delicate touch, Thou Word, Son of God, Who, through the delicateness of Thy Divine Being, dost subtly penetrate the substance of my soul, and, touching it wholly and delicately, dost absorb it wholly in Thyself in Divine ways of sweetness which have never been heard of in the land of Chanaan, nor seen in Theman![10]

[1] Psalm ciii, 32 [A.V., civ, 32].
[2] E.p.: 'the nations tremble.'
[3] Habakkuk iii, 6.
[4] G abbreviates: 'softer still for this soul, as thou touchest me more firmly. Once more, then, etc.'
[5] Job xix, 21.
[6] E.p.: 'since thou didst touch him so heavily.'
[7] [*Lit.*, 'general.'] So A, B, C, G, Gr. E.p.: 'generous.' The MSS. of the second redaction vary between 'generous' and 'gracious.' See p. 190, below.
[8] Hebrews i, 3.
[9] Wisdom [vii, 24] viii, 1.
[10] Baruch iii, 22.

Oh, delicate touch of the Word, delicate, yea, wondrously delicate, to me, which, having overthrown the mountains and broken the stones in Mount Horeb with the shadow of Thy power and strength that went before Thee, didst reveal Thyself to the Prophet with the whisper of gentle air.[11] Oh, gentle air, that art so delicate and gentle![12] Say, how dost Thou touch the soul so gently and delicately when Thou art so terrible and powerful? Oh, blessed, twice blessed, the soul whom Thou dost touch so gently[13] though Thou art so terrible and powerful! Tell it out to the world. But nay, tell it not to the world, for the world knows naught of air so gentle, and will not feel Thee, because it can neither receive Thee nor see Thee.[14]

17. Oh, my God and my life! They whom Thou refinest[15] shall know Thee and behold Thee when Thou touchest them, since purity corresponds with purity.[16] Thou dost touch them the more delicately because Thou art hidden in the substance of their souls, which have been beautified and made delicate,[17] and because they are withdrawn from all creatures and from all traces of creature, and Thou hidest them in the hiding-place of Thy presence,[18] which is Thy Divine Son, and dost conceal them from the disturbance of men.[19] Once again, then, oh, delicate touch, and again most delicate, that with the strength of Thy delicacy dost melt

[11] 3 Kings [A.V., 1 Kings] xix, 11–12.

[12] A, G, e.p. omit: 'that art so delicate and gentle.' A also omits the rest of the paragraph.

[13] C: 'so delicately.' B: 'so happily and delicately.'

[14] E.p.: 'because it cannot receive these lofty things.' [St. John xiv, 17.]

[15] [Lit., 'They who become delicate': the word 'delicate' is also used below, where I render 'purity,' but the sense is evidently 'refined,' 'purified.']

[16] [Lit., 'delicacy . . . delicacy.']

[17] E.p.: 'in their souls, made delicate.'

[18] [Lit., 'Thy face.' Cf. Psalm xxx, 21 (A.V., xxxi, 21).]

[19] E.p.: 'Thou hidest them in the hidden place of Thy presence, from the disturbance of men.' A omits the remainder of this paragraph and the first sentence of the paragraph following.

the soul and removest it from all other touches and makest it Thine own alone. So delicate an effect and impression dost Thou leave in the soul that every other touch, of everything else, whether high or low, will seem to it rude and gross if it touches the soul, and even the sight of other things will offend it, and to have to do with them and touch them will cause it trouble and grievous torment.

18. The more delicate is a thing, the broader and more capacious it is; and the more delicate it is, the more it becomes diffusive and communicative. Oh, then, thou delicate touch, that dost infuse Thyself the more by reason of Thy delicacy, while the vessel of my soul, through this Thy touch, becomes the simpler, purer, more delicate and more capacious! Oh, then, thou delicate touch, so delicate that, when naught[20] is felt in the touch, Thou dost touch the soul the more, and, by penetrating deeply within it, Thou dost make it at Thy touch the more Divine, according as Thy Divine Being[21] wherewith Thou dost touch the soul is far removed from the way and manner thereof and free from all outward seeming[22] of form and figure! Oh, then, at last, Thou delicate, most delicate touch, that touchest not the soul save with Thy most pure and simple Being, which is infinite, and therefore infinitely delicate! Wherefore it is a touch

That savours of eternal life

19. Although this is not so in a perfect degree, there is indeed a certain savour herein of life eternal, as has been said above, which the soul tastes in this touch of God. And it is not incredible that this should be so if we believe, as

20 [*Lit.*, 'when no bulk.']
21 E.p.: 'while the vessel of my soul, through this Thy touch, is simple and pure and has capacity to receive Thee. Oh, then, Thou delicate touch, that feelest naught material within Thyself, yet dost touch the soul the more and the more deeply, changing it from the human into the Divine, according as Thy Divine Being.'
22 [*Lit.*, 'from all husk.']

we must believe, that this touch is substantial, that is to say, is a touch of the Substance of God in the substance of the soul;[1] and to this many holy men have attained in this life. Wherefore the delicacy of the delight which is felt in this touch is impossible of description; nor would I willingly speak thereof, lest it should be supposed that it is no more than that which I say; for there are no words to expound and enumerate such sublime things of God as come to pass in these souls; whereof the proper way to speak is for one that knows them to understand them inwardly and feel them and enjoy them and be silent concerning them. For the soul in this state sees that these things are in some measure like the white stone which Saint John says will be given to him that conquers, and on the stone a name shall be written, which no man knoweth saving he that receiveth it.[2] This alone can be said of it with truth, that it savours of eternal life.[3] For, although in this life we may not have perfect fruition of it, as in glory, yet nevertheless this touch, being of God, savours of eternal life. And in this way the soul in such a state tastes of all the things of God,[4] and there are communicated to it fortitude, wisdom, love, beauty, grace and goodness, and so forth. For as God is all these things, the soul tastes them in one single touch of God, and thus the soul has fruition of Him according to its faculties and its substance.

20. And of this good which comes to the soul a part sometimes overflows into the body through the union of the spirit, and this is enjoyed by all the substance of sense and all the members of the body and the very marrow and bones, not as feebly as is usually the case, but with a

[1] E.p.: 'that this touch is most substantial and that the Substance of God touches the substance of the soul.'

[2] Apocalypse ii, 17.

[3] A omits the rest of this paragraph and all of the paragraph following except the last sentence.

[4] E.p.: 'tastes in a wondrous manner, and by participation, of all the things of God.'

feeling of great delight and glory, which is felt even in the remotest joints of the feet and hands. And the body feels such glory in the glory of the soul that it magnifies God after its own manner, perceiving that He is in its very bones,[5] even as David said: 'All my bones shall say, "God, who is like to Thee?"'[6] And since all that can be said concerning this matter is less than the truth, it suffices to say of the bodily experience, as of the spiritual, that it savours of eternal life.[7]

And pays every debt!

21. Here it behoves us to explain what debts are these which the soul now recognizes as paid. It must be known that the souls which attain to this lofty kingdom have commonly passed through many trials and tribulations, since it behoves us to enter through many tribulations into the kingdom of the heavens;[1] which things have in this state already passed, for henceforth there is no more suffering.[2] That which has to be suffered by those who are about to attain to union with God is trials and temptations of many kinds in sense, and trials and tribulations and temptations and darknesses and perils in the spirit, so that both these parts may be purged together, as we said in the exposition of the fourth line of the first stanza.[3] And the reason for these trials is that the delight and knowledge of God cannot well find a home in the soul if sense and spirit be not thoroughly purged and toughened and purified.

---

[5] E.p. abbreviates: 'in one single touch of God, in a certain eminent way. And of this good which comes to the soul some of the unction of the spirit sometimes overflows into the body, and it seems to penetrate to its very bones.'

[6] Psalm xxxiv, 10 [A.V., xxxv, 10].

[7] E.p. abbreviates: 'it suffices to say that it savours of eternal life.'

[1] Acts xiv, 21 [A.V., xiv, 22].

[2] E.p. omits: 'for . . . suffering.'

[3] E.p.: 'as we said in the Ascent of Mount Carmel and in the Dark Night.'

And thus, since trials and penances purify and refine the soul and tribulations and temptations and darknesses and perils refine and prepare the spirit, it behoves the soul to pass through them to attain to transformation in God, even as those beyond the grave must do, by going through purgatory, some with greater intensity and others with less, some spending more time therein and others less, according to the degrees of union to which God is pleased to raise them and the degree of purgation which they have to undergo.

22. By means of these trials whereinto God leads the soul and the senses, the soul gradually acquires virtues and strength and perfection, together with bitterness, for virtue is made perfect in weakness,[4] and is wrought by the experience of sufferings. For iron cannot be subservient to the intelligence[5] of the artificer, unless he use fire and a hammer, which do harm to the iron if it be compared with what it was in its former state. Even so Jeremias says that God taught him, saying: 'He sent fire into my bones and taught me.'[6] And he likewise says of the hammer: 'Thou hast chastised me, Lord, and I was instructed and became wise.'[7] Even so the Preacher says: 'He that is not tried, what does he know and whereof has he knowledge?'[8]

23. And here it behoves us to note why it is that there are so few that attain to this lofty state. It must be known that this is not because God is pleased that there should be few raised to this high spiritual state—on the contrary, it would please Him if all were so raised—but rather because He finds few vessels in whom He can perform so high and lofty a work. For, when He proves them in small things

[4] 2 Corinthians xii, 9.
[5] E.p.: 'to the plan.'
[6] Lamentations i, 13.
[7] Jeremias xxxi, 18.
[8] Ecclesiasticus xxxiv, 9. [The two verbs have different senses in the original. We might bring out this difference by paraphrasing: 'what wisdom has he and what thing can he recognize?']

and finds them weak and sees that they at once flee[9] from labour, and desire not to submit to the least discomfort or mortification, or to work with solid patience, He finds that they are not strong enough to bear the favour which He was granting them when He began to purge them,[10] and goes no farther with their purification, neither does He lift them up from the dust of the earth, since for this they would need greater fortitude and constancy. To these, then, who would fain make progress, yet cannot suffer the smallest things nor submit themselves to them, can be made the reply which we find in Jeremias in these words: 'If thou hast run with those who went on foot and hast laboured, how canst thou contend with horses? And as thou hast had quietness in the land of peace, how wilt thou do in the pride of Jordan?'[11] This is as though he were to say: If in the trials which commonly and ordinarily afflict all those who live this human life thy pace was so slow that thou didst run and countedst all as labour, how wilt thou be able to keep pace with the step of a horse —that is to say, to leave these ordinary and common trials and pass from them to others of greater strength and swiftness? And if thou has been loth to make war against the peace and pleasure of this land of thine, which is thy sensual nature, but seekest to be quiet and to have comfort therein, what wilt thou do in the pride of Jordan? That is, how wilt thou suffer the impetuous waters of spiritual tribulation and trial, which are more interior?

24.[12] Oh, souls that seek to walk in security and comfort! If ye did but know how necessary it is to suffer and endure in order to reach this lofty state, and of what great benefit it is to suffer and be mortified in order to reach

[9] E.p. abbreviates: 'to this lofty state. The reason is that in this lofty and sublime work which God begins there are many weak souls; as these at once flee.'

[10] E.p.: 'began to carve (or 'form') them.'

[11] Jeremias xii, 5.

[12] A omits this and the two following paragraphs.

such lofty blessings, ye would in no way seek consolation, either from God or from the creatures,[13] but would rather bear the cross, together with pure vinegar and gall, and would count this a great happiness, for, being thus dead to the world and to your own selves, ye would live to God in the delights of the spirit; and, bearing outward things with patience, ye would become worthy for God to set His eyes upon you to cleanse and purge you more inwardly by means of more interior spiritual trials.[14] For they to whom God is to grant so notable a favour[15] as to tempt them more interiorly must have rendered Him many services, and have had much patience and constancy for His sake, and be very acceptable in their lives in His sight. This we read of the holy man Tobias, to whom Raphael said that, because he had been acceptable to God, He had granted him this favour of sending him a temptation that should prove him more in order that he might give him more.[16] And even so, says the Scripture, all that remained to him of life, after that time, caused him joy. In the same way we read of Job that, when God accepted him as His servant, as He did in the presence of the good and the evil spirits, He then granted him the favour of sending him those heavy trials, that He might afterwards exalt him, as indeed He did, both in spiritual and in temporal things, and much more so than before.[17]

25. Even so acts God to those whom He desires to exalt with the chiefest exaltation; He causes them to be tempted to the highest degree possible, that He may also deify them to the highest degree possible, by granting them

[13] E.p.: 'seek consolation in aught.'

[14] Gr: 'more inward spiritual trials, in order to give you more inward blessings.' B: 'more inward spiritual trials.' C: 'inward spiritual trials, in order to give you inward blessings.'

[15] E.p.: 'such a favour.'

[16] Tobias xii, 13. E.p. begins the sentence: 'And thus the angel spake to the holy man Tobias, saying that, etc.'

[17] [Job i, 8; xlii, 12.]

union[18] in His wisdom, which is the highest state, and purging them first of all in this wisdom to the highest possible degree, even as David observes, where he says: 'The wisdom of the Lord is silver tried by the fire, proved in the earth of our flesh and purged seven times,'[19] which is the greatest purgation possible.[20] And there is no reason to tarry here any longer in order to show how each of the seven purgations leads us to this communion with God,[21] which here below is like silver, for, however high it be, it is not yet as gold.[22]

26. But it greatly behoves the soul to have much constancy and patience in these tribulations and trials, whether they come from without or from within, and are spiritual or corporeal, greater or lesser. It must take them all as from the hand of God for its healing and its good, and not flee from them, since they are health to the soul. This the Wise Man counsels, in these words: 'If the spirit of him that is powerful descend upon thee, leave not thy place' (that is, the place and abode of thy healing, by which is meant that trial); for the healing, he says, will cause great sins to cease.[23] That is, it will cut the thread of thy sins and imperfections, which is evil habit, that they go not farther. And thus interior perils and trials quench and purify the evil and imperfect habits of the soul. Wherefore we must count it a great favour when the Lord sends us interior trials, realizing that there are few who deserve to suffer that they may reach the goal of this lofty state of attainment to perfection through suffering.

18 E.p.: 'to exalt with the chiefest betterment, allowing them to be tempted, afflicted, tormented and purified, interiorly and exteriorly, as far as is possible, that He may deify them, by granting them union.'

19 Psalm xi, 7 [A.V., xii, 6].

20 E.p.: 'seven times—that is, greatly purged.'

21 [P. Silverio reads *eloquio*, an archaic word meaning literally 'speech.'] C has: 'this colloquy of God'; G: 'this union with God'; e.p.: 'this Divine wisdom.'

22 E.p.: 'as precious gold, which is kept for [the life of] glory.'

23 Ecclesiastes x, 4.

27. As the soul now remembers that it has been very well recompensed for all its past trials, since now *sicut tenebræ ejus, ita et lumen ejus*,[24] and, as the soul aforetime shared in tribulations, it now shares in consolations; and as all its trials, within and without, have been amply rewarded by Divine blessings of soul and body,[25] there is none of its trials that has not a correspondingly great reward. And thus the soul confesses that it is now well satisfied, when it says in this line: 'And pays every debt.' Even so David said in his own case, in these words: 'Many and grievous are the tribulations that Thou hast shown me, and Thou didst deliver me from them all, and from the depths of the earth hast Thou brought me out again; Thou hast multiplied Thy magnificence, and, turning to me, hast comforted me.'[26] And thus this soul that aforetime was without, at the gates of the palace (like Mardochai weeping in the streets of Susan, because his life was in peril, and clothed in sackcloth, refusing to receive the garments from Queen Esther, and having received no favour or reward for the services that he had rendered the King, and his faithfulness in serving the honour and life of the King),[27] is recompensed in a single day for all its trials and services, for not only is it made to enter the palace and stand before the King, clad in regal vesture, but likewise it is crowned, and given a sceptre, and a royal seat, and possession of the King's ring, so that it may do all that it desires, and need do naught that it desires not to do in the kingdom of its Spouse;[28] for those that are in this state receive all that they desire. It is well recompensed indeed for the whole debt, since its enemies are now dead—namely, the desires that were going about seeking to take away its

---

[24] Psalm cxxxviii, 12 [A.V., cxxxix, 12].

[25] E.p. omits: 'of soul and body.'

[26] Psalm lxx, 20 [A.V., lxxi, 20–1].

[27] Esther iv, 1–4.

[28] E.p.: 'but likewise a diadem is placed on its head and it is as another Esther in the possession of the kingdom, so that it may do all that it desires in the kingdom of its Spouse.'

life—and it now lives in God. For this cause the soul next says:

In slaying, thou hast changed death into life.

28. Death is naught else than privation of life, for, when life comes, there remains no trace of death. With respect to the spirit, there are two kinds of life; one is beatific, which consists in seeing God,[1] and this will be attained by means of[2] the natural death of the body, as Saint Paul says in these words: 'We know that if this our house of clay be dissolved, we have a dwelling of God in the heavens.'[3] The other is perfect spiritual life, which is the possession of God through the union of love, and this is attained through the complete mortification of all vices and desires and of the soul's entire nature.[4] And until this be done, the soul cannot attain to the perfection of this spiritual life of union with God, even as the Apostle says likewise in these words: 'If you live according to the flesh, you shall die; but if by the spirit you mortify the deeds of the flesh, you shall live.'[5]

29. It must be known, then, that that which the soul here calls death is all that is meant by the 'old man,' namely, the employment of the faculties—memory, understanding and will—and the use and occupation of them in things of the world, and the occupation of the desires in the pleasure afforded by created things. All this is the exercise of the old life, which is the death of the new, or spiritual, life. Herein the soul will be unable to live perfectly if it die not perfectly likewise to the old man, as the Apostle warns us when he says that we should put off the old man, and put on the new man, who according to God is created

---

[1] G adds: 'face to face.'
[2] E.p.: 'and this must be preceded by.'
[3] 2 Corinthians v, 1.
[4] E.p. omits: 'and of the soul's entire nature.'
[5] Romans viii, 13.

in justice and holiness.[6] In this new life, when the soul has reached the perfection of union with God, as we are saying here, all the desires of the soul, and its faculties and their operations, which of themselves were the operations of death and the privation of spiritual life, are changed into Divine operations.[7]

30. And as each living creature lives by its operation, as the philosophers say, having its operations in God, through the union that they have with God, the soul lives the life of God and its death has been changed into life.[8] For the understanding, which before this union understood in a natural way[9] with the strength and vigour of its natural light, is now moved and informed by another principle, that of the supernatural light of God, and has been changed into the Divine, for its understanding and that of God are now both one. And the will, which aforetime loved after the manner of death, that is to say, meanly and with its natural affection, has now[10] been changed into the life of Divine love; for it loves after a lofty manner with Divine affection and is moved by the Holy Spirit in Whom it now lives, since its will and His will are now only one.[11] And the memory, which of itself perceived only the forms and figures of created things, has become changed, so that it has in its mind the eternal years. And the desire, which enjoyed only creature food that wrought death, is now changed so that it tastes and enjoys Divine food, being now moved by another and a more living principle, which is the delight of God; so that it is now the desire of God.[12]

[6] Ephesians iv, 22–4.
[7] E.p.: 'all the affections of the soul, its faculties and operations, of themselves imperfect and mean, become Divine.'
[8] A omits almost all the rest of the commentary on this line.
[9] E.p.: 'understood inadequately [cortamente].'
[10] E.p.: 'by another principle and a higher light of God. And the will, which aforetime loved lukewarmly, has now, etc.'
[11] E.p. omits: 'since . . . only one.'
[12] E.p.: 'And the desire, which aforetime was inclined to the food of the creatures, now tastes and enjoys Divine food, being

And finally, all the movements and operations which the soul had aforetime, and which belonged to the principle of its natural life, are now in this union changed into movements of God. For the soul, like the true daughter of God that it now is, is moved wholly by the Spirit of God, even as Saint Paul says: 'That they that are moved by the Spirit of God are sons of God.'[13] So the understanding of the soul is now the understanding of God; and its will is the will of God; and its memory is the memory of God; and its delight is the delight of God;[14] and the substance of the soul, although it is not the Substance of God, for into this it cannot be changed, is nevertheless united in Him and absorbed in Him, and is thus God by participation in God, which comes to pass in this perfect state of the spiritual life, although not so perfectly as in the next life. And in this way[15] by 'slaying, thou hast changed death into life.' And for this reason the soul may here say very truly with Saint Paul: 'I live, now not I, but Christ liveth in me.'[16] And thus the death[17] of this soul is changed into the life of God, and the soul becomes absorbed in life, since within it there is likewise fulfilled the saying of the Apostle: 'Death is absorbed in victory.'[18] And likewise the words of Osee, the prophet, who says: 'O death, I will be thy death, saith God.'[19]

31. In this way the soul is absorbed in life, being withdrawn from all that is secular and temporal and freed from that which belongs to its own unruly nature, so that it is brought into the cellars of the King,[20] where it rejoices

now moved by another and a more living principle, which is the sweetness of God.'

[13] Romans viii, 14.
[14] E.p. omits: 'So the understanding . . . delight of God.'
[15] E.p. adds: 'he well says.'
[16] Galatians ii, 20.
[17] E.p.: 'the death and coldness.'
[18] 1 Corinthians xv, 54.
[19] Osee xiii, 14.
[20] C: 'into the streets of the King.' G: 'into the royal chamber.'

and is glad in its Beloved, and remembers His breasts more than wine, saying: 'I am black but beautiful, daughters of Jerusalem';[21] for my natural blackness is changed into the beauty of the heavenly King. Wherefore, oh burning of the fire that infinitely burnest above all fires else, the more thou burnest me the sweeter art thou to me! And oh, delectable wound, thou art to me most delectable health, more so than all other health and delights of the world! And oh, soft hand, that art infinitely soft above all softness,[22] the more thou art laid upon me and dost press upon me, the softer to me art thou! And oh, delicate touch, whose delicateness is more subtle and more curious than all the subtle beauties of the creatures, surpassing them infinitely, and sweeter and more delicious than honey and the honeycomb, since thou savourest of eternal life, the more intimately[23] thou dost touch me the greater is the delight that thou givest me; and infinitely more precious art thou than gold and precious stones, since thou payest debts which naught else could pay, turning death into life in a way most marvellous.

32. In this state of life, perfect as it is, the soul is, as it were, keeping festival, and has in its mouth[24] a great song of joy to God, and, as it were, a song new and ever new, turned into joy[25] and love, and having knowledge of its lofty state. At times it rejoices, saying within its spirit those words of Job, namely: 'My glory shall always be renewed and as a palm tree shall I multiply my days.'[26] Which is as much as to say: God Who, remaining within Himself unchangeably, makes all things new, as the Wise Man says, being united for ever in my glory, will make my glory ever new, that is to say, He will not suffer it to grow old as it was before; and I shall multiply my days—that is,

[21] Canticles i, 4.
[22] G: 'above all soft hands.'
[23] G, T: 'infinitely.'
[24] [Lit., 'palate.']
[25] C: 'into grace.'
[26] [Job xxix, 18, 20.]

my merits—unto Heaven, even as the palm tree multiplies its branches. And all that David says in the twenty-ninth Psalm the soul sings inwardly to God, particularly those last lines which say: 'Thou hast turned for me my mourning into joy, Thou hast cut my sackcloth, and hast compassed me with gladness, to the end that my glory may sing to Thee, and may not be ashamed (for here no pain reaches the soul). O Lord my God, I will praise Thee for ever.'[27] For the soul now feels God to be so solicitous in granting it favours and to be magnifying it with such precious and delicate and endearing words, and granting it favour upon favour, that it believes that there is no other soul in the world whom He thus favours, nor aught else wherewith He occupies Himself, but that He is wholly for itself alone. And, when it feels this, it confesses its feeling in the words of the Songs: 'My Beloved to me and I to Him.'[28]

STANZA III

Oh, lamps of fire, In whose splendours the deep caverns of sense which were dark and blind
With strange brightness Give heat and light together to their Beloved!

EXPOSITION

MAY God be pleased to grant me His favour here, for in truth it is very needful if I am to explain[1] the profound meaning of this stanza; great attention, too, is necessary in him that reads it, for, if he have no experience of this, it

---

27 Psalm xxix, 12–13 [A.V., xxx, 11–12].
28 Canticles ii, 16. E.p.: 'And it makes this confession in the Songs: "I wholly to my Beloved and my Beloved wholly to me." '
1 E.p. begins: 'Great is the need here of the favour of God in order that I may explain.'

will perhaps be somewhat obscure to him, though, if perchance he should have had such experience, it will be clear and pleasing.[2] In this stanza, the soul gives deepest thanks to its Spouse for the great favours which it receives[3] from union with Him, for by means of this union He has given it great and abundant knowledge[4] of Himself, wherewith the faculties and senses of the soul, which before this union were dark and blinded by other kinds of love,[5] have been enlightened and enkindled with love, and can now be illumined, as indeed they are, and through the heat of love can give light and love[6] to Him Who enkindled and enamoured them and infused into them such Divine gifts. For the true lover is content only when all that he is, and all that he is worth and can be worth, and all that he has and can have, are employed in the Beloved; and the more of this there is, the greater is the pleasure that he receives in giving it. In the first place, it must be known that lamps have two properties, which are to give light and to burn. There follows the line:

Oh, lamps of fire,

2. In order to understand this line, it must be known that God, in His one and simple Being, is all the virtues and grandeurs of His attributes;[1] for He is omnipotent, wise, good, merciful, just, strong and loving, and has other infinite[2] attributes and virtues whereof we have no knowl-

[2] E.p.: 'if he have no experience of this, that which is here treated will be very obscure, though, if perchance he should have had such experience, it will be clear and pleasing.'

[3] E.p.: 'which it has received.'

[4] E.p.: 'by means of this union abundant and most sublime knowledge.'

[5] E.p.: 'were dark and blind.'

[6] E.p.: 'and are illumined with the heat of love, in order that they may respond by offering that same light and love.'

[1] G: 'in His one and most simple Being, contains all the perfections and grandeurs of His attributes.'

[2] E.p. omits: 'infinite.'

edge here below; and, as He is all these things when He
is united with the soul, at the time when He is pleased to
reveal knowledge to it, it is able to see in Him all these
virtues and grandeurs, clearly and distinctly—namely,
omnipotence, goodness, wisdom, justice, mercy and so forth,
all in one simple Being. And, as each of these things is the
very Being of God in one sole reality, which is the Father
or the Son or the Holy Spirit, each attribute being God
Himself and God being infinite light and infinite Divine
fire, as we have said above, it follows from this that in
each of these attributes, which, as we say, are innumerable,
and are His virtues, He gives light and burns as God.[3]

3. And thus according to these kinds of knowledge of
God which the soul here possesses, actually distinct in one
single act, God Himself is to the soul as many lamps,
which give light to it each in a distinct way, for from
each lamp[4] the soul has knowledge and by each is given
the heat of love, in its own way and all in one simple being,
as we say; and all these are one lamp,[5] which is the Word,
which, as Saint Paul says, is the brightness of the glory of
the Father. This lamp[6] is all these lamps, since it gives
light and burns in all these ways; and this the soul is able
to see—namely, that this one lamp is many lamps to it.
For, as it is one, it can do all things, and has all virtues, and
comprehends all spirits,[7] and thus in one act it gives light
and burns according to all its grandeurs and virtues—in
many ways, we may say, yet in one way.[8] For it gives light

[3] E.p. omits: 'which . . . His virtues' and reads: 'as Very God.'
[4] G: 'And thus according to these distinct kinds of knowledge
of God which the soul here possesses, knowing all these perfections with one sole act, God Himself comes to be to the soul
as many lamps, etc.' E.p.: 'here possesses, in unity, God Himself
is to the soul as many lamps, for from each lamp.'
[5] A, C, Gr: 'and all one being and all one lamp.'
[6] E.p. abbreviates: 'and all these are one lamp, which lamp.'
[7] A omits the whole of what follows, down to the words 'well
of living waters' in § 7.
[8] E.p.: 'and thus we may say that it gives light and burns in
many ways, yet in one way.'

and burns as being omnipotent, and gives light and burns as being wise, and gives light and burns as being good, and gives light and burns as being strong, as being just, as being true, and as having each of the other Divine virtues and qualities which are in God, giving the soul intelligence and love concerning Him, both according to all these virtues distinctly and also according to each one. For when He communicates Himself, since He is all of them and each one of them, He gives the soul light and love Divine according to them all, and according to each one of them; for, wheresoever the fire is applied,[9] and whatever be the effect that it causes, it gives its heat and brightness; since this always happens in one manner.[10] For the brightness that this light gives inasmuch as it is omnipotence produces in the soul light and heat of the love of God inasmuch as He is omnipotent, and therefore God is now to the soul a lamp of omnipotence which gives it light and burns in it according to this attribute. And the brightness which this lamp gives inasmuch as it is wisdom produces the heat of the love of God in the soul inasmuch as He is wise and according to this God is to the soul a lamp of wisdom. And the brightness which this lamp of God gives inasmuch as it is goodness produces the heat of the love of God in the soul inasmuch as He is good, and accordingly God is then to the soul a lamp of goodness. In the same way He is a lamp of justice to it, and of fortitude, and of mercy, for the light[11] that He gives to the soul from each of these attributes and from all the rest produces in the soul the heat of the love of God inasmuch as He is such. And thus in this lofty communication and manifestation (which,

[9] G omits the rest of the paragraph except the final sentence and has many minor variations and omissions throughout the remainder of the chapter.

[10] E.p. abbreviates: 'giving the soul intelligence and love, and revealing itself to it, in a manner corresponding to its capacity, according to them all.'

[11] E.p. abbreviates: 'inasmuch as He is wise, and so of the remaining attributes, for the light.'

as I think, is the greatest that can come to the soul in this life), God is to the soul as innumerable lamps which give it light and love.[12]

4. These lamps gave light to Moses[13] on Mount Sinai, where God passed before him and he quickly fell prostrate on the ground, and proclaimed some of the grandeurs which he saw in God; and, loving Him according to those things which he had seen, he proclaimed them each separately, saying: 'Emperor, Lord, God that art merciful, clement, patient, of much compassion, true, that keepest mercy for thousands, that takest away sins and evil deeds and faults, and art so righteous that there is no man who of himself is innocent before Thee.'[14] Herein it is clear that the majority of the attributes and virtues of God which Moses then learned and loved were those of God's omnipotence, dominion, deity, mercy, justice, truth and uprightness; which was a most profound knowledge and a most sublime delight of love.

5. From this it follows that the delight and rapture of love which the soul receives in the fire of the light of these lamps is wondrous, boundless and as vast as that of many lamps, each of which burns with love, the heat of one being added to the heat of another, and the flame of one to the flame of another, as the light of one gives light to another, and all of them become one light and fire, and each of them becomes one fire. The soul is completely absorbed in these delicate flames, and wounded subtly in each of them, and in all of them more deeply and subtly wounded in love of life, so that it can see quite clearly that that love belongs to life eternal, which is the union of all blessings. So that the soul in that state knows well the truth of

[12] G: 'as innumerable lamps which enkindle it and illumine it in love of God Himself so that it knows Him and loves Him most ardently according to all His attributes.'

[13] [*Lit.*, 'gave light well to Moses.'] E.p.: 'allowed Moses to see Him.'

[14] Exodus xxxiv, 6–7.

those words of the Spouse in the Songs, where He says that the lamps of love were lamps of fire and flames. Beauteous art thou in thy footsteps and thy shoes, oh, prince's daughter! Who can recount the magnificence and rarity of thy delight in the love of thy lamps and thy wondrous splendour?[15] For if one single lamp of those that passed before Abraham caused him great and dark-some[16] horror, when God passed by, giving him knowledge of the rigorous justice which He was about to work upon the Chanaanites,[17] shall not all these lamps of the knowledge of God which give thee a pleasant[18] and loving light cause thee more light and joy of love than that single lamp caused horror and darkness in Abraham? And how great and how excellent and how manifold shall be thy light and joy, since in it all and from it all thou perceivest that He is giving thee His fruition and love, loving thee according to His virtues and attributes and qualities!

6. For he that loves another and does him good loves him and does him good according to his own attributes and properties. And thus since thy Spouse, Who is within thee, is omnipotent, He gives thee omnipotence and loves thee therewith; and since He is wise, thou perceivest that He loves thee with wisdom; since He is good, thou perceivest that He loves thee with goodness; since He is holy, thou perceivest that He loves thee with holiness; since He is just, thou perceivest that He loves thee justly; since He is merciful, thou perceivest that He loves thee with mercy; since He is compassionate and clement, thou perceivest that He loves thee with meekness and clemency; since His Being is strong and sublime and delicate, thou perceivest that He loves thee with strength, sublimity and delicacy; and since He is clean and pure, thou perceivest that He loves thee with cleanness and purity; and since He is true,

[15] Canticles vii, 1. E.p. omits: 'Beauteous . . . splendour.'
[16] E.p. omits 'and darksome.'
[17] [Genesis xv, 12–17.]
[18] [*Lit.*, 'a friendly.']

thou perceivest that He loves thee truly; and since He is liberal, thou perceivest likewise that He loves thee with liberality, without self-interest, and only that He may do thee good; as He is the virtue of the greatest humility, He loves thee with the greatest humility, and with the greatest esteem, making Himself thine equal and making thee His equal, joyfully revealing to thee, in these ways, His countenance, full of graces,[19] and saying to thee: I am thine and for thee, and I delight to be such as I am that I may give Myself to thee and be thine.

7. Who, then, can describe that which thou perceivest, oh, blessed soul, when thou seest thyself to be thus loved and to be exalted with such esteem? Thy belly, which is thy will, we shall describe as the heap of wheat which is covered and set about with lilies.[20] For in these grains of the wheat of the bread of life[21] which thou art tasting all together, the lilies of the virtues that surround thee are giving thee delight. For these daughters of the King, which are these virtues, are delighting thee wondrously with the fragrance of their aromatic spices, which are the knowledge that He gives thee; and thou art so wholly engulfed and absorbed therein that thou art also the well of living waters that run with vehemence from Mount Libanus, which is God,[22] in the which stream thou art become marvellously glad with all the harmony of thy soul and even of thy body. Thus may the words of the Psalm be accomplished in thee, namely: 'The vehemence of the river makes glad the city of God.'[23]

8. Oh, wondrous thing! At this time the soul is over-

---

[19] E.p., B abbreviate: 'that He loves thee with holiness, and so forth; and since He is liberal, thou perceivest likewise that He loves thee with liberality, without self-interest, and only that He may do thee good, joyfully revealing to thee this His countenance, full of graces.'

[20] Canticles vii, 2.

[21] [*Lit.*, 'grains of bread of life.']

[22] Canticles iv, 15.

[23] Psalm xlv, 5 [A.V., xlvi, 4].

flowing with Divine waters, which flow from it as from an abundant source,[24] whose waters gush in all directions. For, although it is true that this communication is light and fire from these lamps of God, yet this fire, as we have said, is here so sweet that, vast as it is, it is like the waters of life which quench the thirst of the spirit with the vehemence that it desires.[25] Thus, though these are lamps of fire, they are living waters of the spirit, even as were those that came upon the Apostles, which, though they were lamps of fire,[26] were also pure and clear water, as the prophet Ezechiel called them when he prophesied that coming of the Holy Spirit, saying: 'I will pour out upon you, saith God, clean water, and will put My spirit in the midst of you.'[27] And thus this fire is likewise water, since it is prefigured in the fire that Jeremias hid, which belonged to the sacrifice, which was water when it was hidden and fire when it was brought forth and used for the sacrifice.[28] And thus this spirit of God, while hidden in the veins of the soul, is like sweet and delectable water quenching the thirst of the spirit in the substance of the soul;[29] and, when the soul offers the sacrifice of love, it becomes living flames of fire,[30] which are the lamps of the act of love described, as we said, by the Spouse in the Songs, in these words: 'The lamps thereof are lamps of fire and of flames';[31] which the soul calls them here also. For not only does the soul taste them as waters of wisdom within itself, but likewise as fire of love, in an act of love, saying: 'Oh, lamps

[24] E.p. adds: 'that looks upon eternal life.'
[25] [Cf. here a poem attributed to St. John of the Cross, referred to in *The Complete Works of St. John of the Cross*, edited by E. Allison Peers, Vol. II, p. 413.]
[26] C: 'were tongues of fire.'
[27] Ezechiel xxxvi, 25-6.
[28] 2 Machabees i, 20-2. [The reference in this passage is to Nehemias. No doubt there is a scribal error here: a change of only two letters is involved.]
[29] E.p. omits: 'in the substance of the soul.'
[30] C: 'of fire of love.'
[31] [Canticles viii, 6.]

of fire.' And all that can be said of this matter is less than what there is to be said. If we consider that the soul is transformed in God, it will be understood in some wise how it is true that it has become a fountain of living waters, boiling and burning in the fire of love, which is God.

In whose splendours

9. It has already been explained that these splendours are the communications of these Divine lamps, wherein the soul that is in union shines forth in splendour with its faculties—memory, understanding and will—which are now illumined and united in this loving knowledge. It must be understood that this enlightenment of splendour is not like a material fire which, with its bursts of flame, enlightens and heats things that are outside it, but is like one that heats things that[1] are within it, as is the soul in this state. For this reason the soul says: 'In whose splendours': that is to say, it is 'within'—not 'near' but 'within'—its splendours, in the flames of the lamps, the soul being transformed into flame. And so we shall say that it is like the air which is within the flame and is enkindled and transformed into fire, for flame is naught else but enkindled air; and the movements made by this flame are not simply those of air nor simply those of fire, but of air and fire together, and the fire causes the air that is enkindled within it to burn.

10. And in this way we shall understand that the soul with its faculties is illumined within the splendours of God. And the movements of this flame, which are the flickerings and the flamings forth that we have described above, are not wrought only by the soul that is transformed in the flame of the Holy Spirit, neither are they wrought by Him alone; but by Him and by the soul together, the Spirit moving the soul, even as fire moves air that is en-

[1] So e.p. The other authorities [followed by P. Silverio] read: 'but is like those that.'

kindled. And thus these movements of God and the soul together are not only splendours, but also glorifications[2] which God works in the soul. For these movements or flickerings[3] are the fires[4] and the joyful festivals which we said, in the second line of the first stanza, the Holy Spirit brings to pass within the soul, wherein it seems that He is ever about to grant it eternal life. And thus those movements and bursts of flame are, as it were, provocations that the Spirit is causing the soul so that He may in the end remove it to His perfect glory and make it at last to enter truly within Himself. For all the blessings, both the early and the late, the great and the small, that God grants the soul He grants to it always with this motive, which pertains both to Him and to the soul, of bringing it to eternal life.[5] Just so is it when fire makes movements and motions in the enkindled air which it has within itself; the purpose of these is to bring it to the centre[6] of its sphere; and all these flickerings are attempts to bring it there, but, because the air is in its own sphere, this cannot be done. In the same way, although these movements of the Holy Spirit are most highly enkindled and are most effective in absorbing the soul into great glory, yet this is not accomplished perfectly until the time comes for the soul to leave the sphere of air—which is this life of the flesh—and to enter into the centre of its spirit, which is perfect life in Christ.

11. But it must be understood that these movements are movements of the soul rather than of God; for these glimpses of glory in God that are given to the soul are not stable, perfect and continuous, as they will be in the soul

[2] E.p.: '. . . together are as it were glorifications.'

[3] E.p.: 'movements and bursts of flame or flickerings.'

[4] A, C: 'the playing(s)'—i.e. of the fire: the general sense is the same as in the text. [The reading of the text, however, does not agree so well with the following substantive.]

[5] E.p. omits the whole of this sentence.

[6] E.p.: 'to the summit.'

hereafter, without any change[7] between greater and lesser, and without any intervening movements; and then the soul will see clearly how, although here below it appeared that God was moving in it, God moves not in Himself, even as the fire moves not in its sphere. But these splendours are inestimable graces and favours that God grants to the soul, which by another name are called overshadowings, and these, in my opinion, are among the highest favours that can be granted here on earth in this process of transformation.

12. To understand this it must be realized that 'overshadowing' means the casting of a shadow, and for a man to cast his shadow over another signifies that he protects him and grants him favours. When the shadow touches the person, this is a sign that he who overshadows him is now near to befriend and protect him. For this reason it was said to the Virgin, that the power of the Most High would overshadow her,[8] because the Holy Spirit was to approach her so nearly that He would come upon her. Herein it is to be noted that everything has and makes a shadow which corresponds to its nature and size. If the thing is dense and opaque, it will make a dark and dense shadow, and if it is clearer and lighter it will make a lighter shadow: this we see with a log of wood or with crystal; the one, being opaque, will make a dark shadow, and the other, being light, will make a light shadow.

13. Even so in spiritual matters. Death is the privation of all things. The shadow of death, then, will be darkness which in one sense deprives us of all things. This name was given to it by the Psalmist, where he said: *Sedentes in tenebris et in umbra mortis;*[9] whether the darkness be

---

[7] E.p. abbreviates (from the beginning of the paragraph) thus: 'These glimpses of glory in God that are here given to the soul are now more continuous than they used to be, and more perfect and stable; but in the next life they will be most perfect, without change.'

[8] St. Luke i, 35.

[9] Psalm cvi, 10 [A.V., cvii, 10].

spiritual, and relate to spiritual death, or bodily, and relate to bodily death. The shadow of life will be light: if Divine, Divine light; if human, natural light. What, then, will be the shadow of beauty? It will be other beauty, of the nature and proportions of that beauty. So the shadow of strength will be other strength, of the nature and quality of that strength. And the shadow of wisdom will be other wisdom; or, more correctly, it will be the same beauty and the same strength and the same wisdom in shadow, wherein will be recognized the nature and proportions of which the shadow is cast.[10]

14. What, then, will be the shadows that the Holy Spirit will cast upon the soul—namely, the shadows of all the grandeurs of His virtues and attributes? For He is so near to the soul that they not only touch it in shadow, but the soul is united with them in shadow, and experiences them in shadow,[11] and it understands and experiences the nature and proportions of God in the shadow of God —that is, by understanding and experiencing the nature of Divine power in the shadow of omnipotence; and it understands and experiences Divine wisdom in the shadow of Divine wisdom; understands and experiences infinite goodness in the shadow of infinite goodness which surrounds it; understands and experiences the delight of God infused in the shadow of the delight of God; and, finally,[12] experiences the glory of God in the shadow of glory which causes it to know and experience the nature and proportions of the glory of God when all these pass by in bright and enkindled shadows. For the attributes of God and His virtues are lamps which, resplendent and enkindled as they are, will cast shad-

[10] E.p. continues (after the Latin quotation): 'and thus the shadow of beauty will be as other beauty, of the proportions and properties of that beauty of which it is the shadow; and the shadow of strength will be as other strength, of its proportions and qualities. And the shadow of wisdom, etc.'

[11] E.p. omits: 'and experiences them in shadow.'

[12] E.p. abbreviates: 'of Divine wisdom; and finally.'

ows that are resplendent and enkindled according to His nature and proportions, and will cast a multitude of them in one sole being.

15. Oh, what this will be for the soul, when it experiences the power of that figure which Ezechiel saw in that beast with four forms, and in that wheel with four wheels, when he saw that its appearance was as the appearance of kindled coals and as the appearance of lamps! The soul will see the wheel, which is wisdom, full of eyes within and without, which are wondrous manifestations of wisdom, and will hear the sound that they made as they passed, which was like the sound of a multitude and of great armies, signifying in one number many different things of God, which the soul[13] here understands[14] in one single sound of God's passing through it. Finally, it will experience that sound of the beating of wings, which Ezechiel says was as the sound of many waters and as the sound of the Most High God;[15] this indicates the vehemence of the Divine waters, which, at the beating of the wings of the Holy Spirit, overwhelm the soul and make it to rejoice in the flame of love,[16] so that it now enjoys the glory of God in His protection and the favour of His shadow, even as this prophet says in that place that that vision was the similitude of the glory of the Lord.[17] And to what a height may this happy soul now find itself raised! How greatly will it know itself to be exalted! How wondrous will it see itself to be in holy beauty! How far beyond all telling! For so copiously does it become immersed in the waters of these Divine splendours that it is able to see the Eternal Father with bounteous hand pouring forth the upper and the lower

[13] E.p. abbreviates: 'which signifies many things in one, which the soul.'
[14] E.p.: 'here knows.'
[15] [Ezechiel i, 15–25.]
[16] E.p.: 'which, at the descent of the Holy Spirit, assails the soul in a flame of love.'
[17] [Ezechiel i, 28.]

streams that water the earth,[18] even as the father of Axa gave these to her when she longed for them, for these irrigating waters penetrate both soul and body.[19]

16. Oh, wondrous thing, that all these lamps of the Divine attributes should be one simple being in which alone they are experienced, and yet that the distinction between them should be visible and perceptible,[20] the one being as completely enkindled as the other and the one being substantially the other! Oh, abyss of delights, the more abundant in proportion as thy riches are gathered together in infinite unity and simplicity, so that each one is known and experienced in such a way that the perfect knowledge and absorption of the other may not be impeded thereby, but rather each thing within thee is the light of the other, so that through thy purity, oh, Divine wisdom, many things are seen in thee when one thing is seen,[21] since thou art the store-house of the treasures of the Eternal Father. For in thy splendours are

The deep caverns of sense

17. These caverns are the faculties of the soul—memory, understanding and will—of which the depth is proportionate to their capacity for great blessings, for they can be filled with nothing less than the infinite.[1] By consider-

---

[18] [Judges i, 15. If we follow the Vulgate we shall read 'watery ground' for 'springs,' but the application is less apt.]

[19] E.p.: 'Oh, to what a height is this happy soul now raised! Oh, how is it exalted! How greatly does it wonder at what it sees, even within the limits of faith! Who shall be able to say this, since it is so completely immersed in the waters of these Divine splendours, where with bounteous hand the Eternal Father pours forth the upper and the lower streams that water the earth, for these irrigating waters penetrate both soul and body.'

[20] E.p.: 'one simple being, and yet in it the distinction between them is conceived and understood.'

[21] E.p.: 'is a light which hinders not the other, and through thy purity, oh, Divine wisdom, many things are known in thee in one.'

[1] E.p.: 'for they cannot be filled save with the infinite.'

ing what they suffer when they are empty we can realize in some measure the greatness of their joy and delight when they are filled with their God, for one contrary can give light to another.[2] In the first place, it must be noted that these caverns of the faculties, when they are not empty and purged and cleansed from all creature affection, are not conscious of their great emptiness, which is due to their profound capacity; for in this life any trifle that remains within them suffices to keep them so cumbered and fascinated that they are neither conscious of their loss nor do they miss the immense blessings that might be theirs, nor are they aware of their own capacity. And it is a wondrous thing that, despite their capacity for infinite blessing, the least thing suffices to cumber them, so that they cannot receive these blessings[3] until they are completely empty, as we shall say hereafter. But, when they are empty and clean, the hunger and thirst and yearning of their spiritual sense become intolerable; for, as the capacities[4] of these caverns are deep, their pain is deep likewise; as is also the food that they lack, which, as I say, is God. And this great feeling of pain commonly occurs towards the close of the illumination and purification of the soul, ere it attain to union,[5] wherein it has satisfaction. For, when the spiritual appetite is empty and purged from every creature and from every creature affection, and its natural temper is lost, and it has become attempered to the Divine, and its emptiness is disposed to be filled, and the Divine communication of union with God has not yet reached it, then the suffering caused by this emptiness and thirst is worse than death, especially when the soul is vouchsafed some foresight or glimpse of the Divine ray and this is not communicated to it. It is souls in this condition

[2] [Cf. p. 45, l. 26, above.]
[3] E.p. adds: 'perfectly.'
[4] [Lit., 'the stomachs.']
[5] E.p.: 'to perfect union.'

that suffer with impatient love, so that they cannot remain long without either receiving or dying.[6]

18. With respect to the first cavern which we here describe—namely, the understanding—its emptiness is thirst for God, and this is so great that David compares it to that of the hart, finding no greater thirst wherewith to compare it, for the thirst of the hart is said to be most vehement. Even as the hart[7] (says David) desires the fountains of the waters, even so does my soul desire Thee, O God.[8] This thirst is for the waters of the wisdom of God which is the object of the understanding.

19. The second cavern is the will, and the emptiness thereof is hunger for God, so great that it causes the soul to swoon, even as David says, in these words: 'My soul desires and faints in the tabernacles of the Lord.'[9] And this hunger is for the perfection of love to which the soul aspires.

20. The third cavern is the memory, whereof the emptiness is the melting away and languishing of the soul for the possession of God, as Jeremias notes in these words: *Memoria memor ero et tabescet in me anima mea.*[10] That is: With remembrance I shall remember. *Id est:* I shall remember well and my soul shall melt away within me; turning over these things in my heart, I shall live in hope of God.

21. The capacity of these caverns, then, is deep; for that which they are capable of containing, which is God, is deep and infinite; and thus in a certain sense their capacity will be infinite, and likewise their thirst will be infinite, and their hunger also will be deep and infinite, and their languishing and pain are infinite death. For, although the soul suffers not so intensely as in the next

[6] A omits all the rest of the commentary on this stanza, except §§ 59, 60.
[7] E.p.: 'wherewith to compare it, when he says: Even as the hart, etc.'
[8] Psalm xli, 1 [A.V., xlii, 1].
[9] Psalm lxxxiii, 3 [A.V., lxxxiv, 2].
[10] Lamentations iii, 20–1. E.p. omits the Latin text.

life, it suffers nevertheless a vivid image of that infinite privation, since it is to a certain extent prepared to receive fullness; although this suffering is of another kind, for it dwells in the bosom of the love of the will, and this love does not alleviate the pain;[11] for the greater it is, the greater is the impatience of the soul for the possession of its God, for Whom it hopes continually with intense desire.

22. But, seeing it is certain that, when the soul desires God with entire truth, it already (as Saint Gregory says in writing of Saint John[12]) possesses Him Whom it loves, how comes it, O God, that it yearns for Him Whom it already possesses? For, in the desire which, as Saint Peter says,[13] the angels have to see the Son of God, there is neither pain nor yearning, since they possess Him already; so it seems that, if the soul possesses God more completely according as it desires Him more earnestly, the possession of God should give delight and satisfaction to the soul. Even so the angels have delight when they are fulfilling their desire in possession, and satisfying their spirit continually with desire, yet have none of the weariness that comes from satiety; wherefore, since they have no weariness, they continually desire, and because they have possession they have no pain. Thus, the greater is the desire of the soul in this state, the more satisfaction and desire it should experience, since it has the more of God and has not grief or pain.[14]

[11] E.p.: 'and their languishing and pain are in a way infinite. And thus, when the soul suffers, although it suffers not so intensely as in the next life, yet [its suffering] seems to be a vivid image of that [suffering] yonder, since the soul is to a certain extent prepared to receive fullness, the privation of which is the greatest pain; although this pain is of another kind, for it dwells in the bosom of the love of the will, and here [on earth] love alleviates not pain.'

[12] Hom. XXX in Evang. E.p. omits: 'in writing of St. John.'

[13] [1 St. Peter i, 12.]

[14] E.p. abbreviates: 'and satisfaction to the soul; and the greater is its desire, the more satisfaction and delight it should now feel

23. In this matter, however, it is well to note clearly the difference that exists between the possession of God through grace itself alone and the possession of Him through union; for the one consists in deep mutual love, but in the other there is also communication. There is as great a difference between these states as there is between betrothal and marriage. For in betrothal there is only a consent by agreement, and a unity of will between the two parties, and the jewels and the adornment of the bride-to-be, given her graciously by the bridegroom. But in marriage there is likewise communication between the persons, and union.[15] During the betrothal, although from time to time the bridegroom sees the bride and gives her gifts, as we have said, there is no union between them, for that is the end of betrothal. Even so, when the soul has attained to such purity in itself and in its faculties that the will is well purged of other strange tastes and desires, according to its lower and higher parts, and when it has given its consent to God with respect to all this, and the will of God and of the soul are as one in a consent that is ready and free, then it has attained to the possession of God through grace of will, in so far as can be by means of will and grace; and this signifies that God has given it, through its own consent, His true and entire consent, which comes through His grace.[16]

---

in this desire, since it has the more of God; and thus it ought not to feel grief or pain.'

[15] E.p.: 'In this matter, however, we must note the difference that exists between the possession of God through grace alone and the possession of Him through union; for the one is a question of mutual love and the other argues a very special communication. This difference may be understood after the manner of that which exists between betrothal and marriage. For in betrothal there is an agreement and one will between the two parties, and the few jewels and ornaments of the bride-to-be given her graciously by the bridegroom. But in marriage there is likewise union and communication between the persons.'

[16] E.p. abbreviates: 'to the possession of God through grace, in the betrothal and conformity of its will.'

24. And this is the lofty state of spiritual betrothal of the soul with the Word, wherein the Spouse grants the soul great favours, and visits it most lovingly and frequently, wherein the soul receives great favours and delights. But these have nothing to do with those of marriage, for they are all preparations for the union of marriage; and, though it is true that they come to the soul[17] when it is completely purged from all creature affection (for spiritual betrothal, as we say, cannot take place until this happens), nevertheless[18] the soul has need of other and positive preparations on the part of God, of His visits and gifts whereby He purifies the soul ever more completely and beautifies and refines it so that it may be fitly prepared for such high union. In some souls more time is necessary than in others, for God works here according to the state of the soul.[19] This is prefigured in those maidens who were chosen for King Assuerus; although they had been taken from their own countries and from their fathers' houses, yet, before they were sent to the king's bed, they were kept waiting for a year, albeit within the enclosure of the palace.[20] For one half of the year they were prepared with certain ointments[21] of myrrh and other spices, and for the other half of the year with other and choicer ointments, after which they went to the king's bed.

25. During the time, then, of this betrothal and expectation of marriage in the unctions of the Holy Spirit, when the ointments that prepare the soul for union with God are very choice, the yearnings of the caverns of the soul are wont to be extreme and delicate. For, as those ointments are a most proximate preparation for union with God, because they are nearest to God and for this cause make

---

[17] E.p.: 'But these have nothing to do with those of the spiritual marriage, for, though it is true that they all come to the soul.'
[18] E.p. adds: 'for union and marriage.'
[19] E.p. omits: 'for God . . . the soul.'
[20] [Esther ii, 12.]
[21] C: 'certain odours.'

the soul more desirous of Him and inspire it with a more delicate affection for Him, the desire is more delicate and also deeper; for the desire for God is a preparation for union with God.

26. Oh, how good a place would this be to warn souls whom God is leading to these delicate anointings to take care what they are doing and into whose hands they commit themselves, lest they go backward, were not this beyond the limits of that whereof we are speaking! But such is the compassion and pity that fills my heart when I see souls[22] going backward, and not only failing to submit themselves to the anointing of the spirit so that they may make progress therein, but even losing the effects of that anointing which they have received, that I must not fail to warn them here as to what they should do in order to avoid such loss, even though this should cause us to delay the return to our subject a little. I shall return to it shortly, and indeed all this will help us to understand the properties of these caverns. And since it is very necessary, not only for these souls that prosper on this way but also for all the rest who seek their Beloved, I am anxious to describe it.

27.[23] First, it must be known that, if a soul is seeking God, its Beloved is seeking it much more; and, if it sends after Him its loving desires, which are as fragrant to Him as a pillar of smoke that issues from the aromatic spices of myrrh and incense, He likewise sends after it the fragrance of His ointments, wherewith He draws the soul and causes it to run after Him. These ointments are His Divine inspirations and touches, which, whenever they are His, are ordered and ruled with respect to the perfection of the law of God and of faith, in which perfection the soul must ever draw nearer and nearer to God. And thus the soul must understand that the desire of God in all the favours that He bestows upon it in the unction and fra-

---

[22] E.p.: 'certain souls.'
[23] P begins here and continues as far as § 59, with certain omissions.

grance of His ointments is to prepare it for other choicer and more delicate ointments which are more after the temper of God, until it reaches such a delicate and pure state of preparation that it merits union with God and substantial transformation in all its faculties.

28. When, therefore, the soul reflects that God is the principal agent in this matter, and the guide of its blind self[24] Who will take it by the hand and lead it where it could not of itself go (namely, to the supernatural things which neither its understanding nor its will nor its memory could know as they are), then its chief care will be to see that it sets no obstacle in the way of the guide, who is the Holy Spirit, upon the road by which God is leading it, and which is ordained according to the law of God and faith, as we are saying. And this impediment may come to the soul if it allows itself to be led by another blind guide; and these blind guides that might lead it out of its way are three, namely, the spiritual director, the devil, and its own self.

29. With regard to the first of these, it is of great importance for the soul that desires to profit, and not to fall back, to consider[25] in whose hands it is placing itself; for as is the master, so will be the disciple, and as is the father, so will be the son. There is hardly anyone who in all respects will guide the soul perfectly along the highest stretch of the road, or even along the intermediate stretches, for it is needful that such a guide should be wise and discreet and experienced. The fundamental requirement of a guide in spiritual things is knowledge and discretion; yet, if a guide have no experience of the higher part of the road, he will be unable to direct the soul therein, when God leads it so far. A guide might even do the soul great harm if, not himself understanding the way of the spirit,[26] he

24 [*Lit.*, 'and the blind man's boy.'] E.p. omits this phrase.
25 C adds 'most diligently' and omits 'great' earlier in the sentence.
26 E.p.: 'the roads of the spirit.'

should cause the soul, as often happens, to lose the unction of these delicate ointments, wherewith the Holy Spirit gradually prepares it for Himself, and if instead of this he should guide the soul by other and lower paths of which he has read here and there, and which are suitable only for beginners. Such guides know no more than how to deal with beginners—please God they may know even so much!—and refuse to allow souls to go beyond these rudimentary acts of meditation and imagination, even though God is seeking to lead them farther, so that they may never exceed or depart from their natural capacity,[27] whereby they can achieve very little.

30. And in order that we may understand this the better, we must know that the state of beginners comprises meditation and discursive acts. In this state, it is necessary for the soul to be given material for meditation, and to make interior acts on its own account, and to take advantage of the spiritual heat and fire which come from sense; this is necessary in order to accustom the senses and desires to good things, so that, by being fed with this delight, they may become detached from the world. But, when this has been to some extent effected, God begins to bring the soul into the state of contemplation, which is wont to happen very quickly, especially in religious, because these, having renounced things of the world, quickly attune their senses and desires to God; and then they have nothing to do save to pass from meditation to contemplation, which happens when the discursive acts and the meditation of the soul itself cease, and the first fervours and sweetness of sense cease likewise, so that the soul cannot meditate as before, or find any help in the senses; for the senses remain in a state of aridity, inasmuch as their treasure is transformed into spirit, and no longer falls within the capacity of sense. And, as all the operations which the soul can perform on its own account naturally

[27] E.p. omits: 'so that . . . capacity.'

depend upon sense only, it follows that God is the agent in this state and the soul is the recipient; for the soul behaves only as one that receives and as one in whom these things are being wrought; and God as One that gives and acts and as One that works these things in the soul, giving it spiritual blessings in contemplation,[28] which is Divine love and knowledge in one—that is, a loving knowledge, wherein the soul has not to use its natural acts and meditations, for it can no longer enter into them as before.

31. It follows that at this time the soul must be led in a way entirely contrary to the way wherein it was led at first. If formerly it was given material for meditation, and practised meditation, this material must now be taken from it and it must not meditate; for, as I say, it will be unable to do so even though it would, and it will become distracted. And if formerly it sought sweetness and fervour, and found it, now it must neither seek it nor desire it, for not only will it be unable to find it through its own diligence, but it will rather find aridity, for it turns from the quiet and peaceful blessings which were secretly given to its spirit, to the work that it desires to do with sense; and thus it will lose the one and not obtain the other, since no blessings are now given to it by means of sense as they were formerly. Wherefore in this state the soul must never have meditation imposed upon it, nor must it make any acts, nor strive after sweetness or fervour;[29] for this would be to set an obstacle in the way of the principal agent, who, as I say, is God. For God secretly and quietly infuses into the soul loving knowledge and wisdom without any intervention of specific acts,[30] although sometimes He specifically produces them in the soul for some length of

[28] E.p.: 'that God in this state is in a special way the agent who infuses and teaches, and the soul is one that receives, [to whom He is] giving very spiritual blessings in contemplation.'

[29] E.p.: 'any acts produced by means of reflection, nor strive knowingly after sweetness or fervour.'

[30] E.p.: 'without any great difference, expression or multiplication of acts.'

time. And the soul has then to walk with loving advertence to God, without making specific acts, but conducting itself, as we have said, passively,[31] and making no efforts of its own, but preserving this simple, pure and loving advertence, like one that opens his eyes with the advertence of love.

32. Since God, then, as giver, is communing with the soul by means of loving and simple knowledge, the soul must likewise commune with Him by receiving with a loving and simple knowledge or advertence, so that knowledge may be united with knowledge and love with love. For it is meet that he who receives should behave in conformity with that which he receives, and not otherwise, in order to be able to receive and retain it as it is given to him; for, as the philosophers say, anything that is received is in the recipient according to the manner of acting of the recipient.[32] Wherefore it is clear that if the soul at this time were not to abandon its natural procedure of active meditation, it would not receive this blessing in other than a natural way. It would not, in fact, receive it, but would retain its natural act alone, for the supernatural cannot be received in a natural way, nor can it have aught to do with it.[33] And thus,[34] if the soul at this time desires to work on its own account, and to do aught else than remain, quite passively and tranquilly, in that passive and loving advertence whereof we have spoken, making no natural act, save if God should unite it with Himself in

[31] E.p.: 'without performing any other specific acts than those to which it feels that He is inclining it, but conducting itself, as it were, passively.'

[32] E.p. omits: 'for . . . recipient.' G gives the phrase in Latin.

[33] G: 'for the supernatural cannot be contained in the soul that is occupied in natural operations and acts.'

[34] E.p.: 'were not to abandon its ordinary discursive procedure, it would not receive this blessing save in a scanty and imperfect way, and thus it would not receive it with that perfection wherewith it was bestowed; for, being so superior and infused a blessing, it cannot be contained in so scanty and imperfect a form. And thus, etc.'

some act, it would set a total and effective impediment in the way of the blessings which God is communicating to it supernaturally in loving knowledge.[35] This comes to pass first of all in the exercise of purgation,[36] as we have said above, and afterwards in increased sweetness of love. If, as I say, and as in truth is the case, the soul continues to receive these blessings passively and after the supernatural manner of God, and not after the manner of the natural soul,[37] it follows that, in order to receive them, this soul must be quite disencumbered, at ease, peaceful, serene and adapted to the manner of God; like the air, which receives greater illumination and heat from the sun when it is pure and cleansed and at rest. And thus the soul must be attached to nothing—nay, not even to any kind of meditation or sweetness, whether of sense or of spirit. For the spirit needs to be so free and so completely annihilated that any thought[38] or meditation which the soul in this state might desire, or any pleasure to which it may conceive an attachment, would impede and disturb it and would introduce noise into the deep silence which it is meet that the soul should observe, according both to sense and to spirit, so that it may hear the deep and delicate voice of God which speaks to the heart in this secret place, as He said through Osee,[39] in the utmost peace and tranquillity, so that the soul may listen and hear, as David heard, the words of God, when He speaks this peace in the soul. When this comes to pass, and the soul is conscious of being led into silence,

[35] E.p. omits: 'whereof we have spoken' and continues 'reasoning [i.e. meditating] not as formerly, it would place an impediment in the way of the blessings which God is communicating to it in loving knowledge.'

[36] C: 'in loving knowledge in the exercise of purgation.'

[37] E.p.: 'after the manner of God and not after the manner of the soul.'

[38] E.p.: 'any particular thought.'

[39] Osee ii, 14.

and hearkens, it must forget even that loving advertence of which I have spoken, so that it may remain free for that which is then desired of it; for it must practise that advertence only when it is not conscious of being brought into solitude or rest or forgetfulness or attentiveness of the spirit, which is always accompanied by a certain interior absorption.[40]

33. Wherefore[41] at no time or season, when once the soul has begun to enter into this pure and restful state of contemplation, must it seek to gather to itself meditations, neither must it desire to find help in spiritual sweetness or delight,[42] but it must stand in complete detachment above all this and its spirit must be freed from it, as the prophet Habacuc said that he must needs do, in these words: 'I will stand upon my watch over my senses—that is, leaving them below—and I will fix my step upon the munition of my faculties—that is, not allowing them to advance a step in thought—and I will watch to see that which will be said to me—that is, I will receive that which is communicated to me.'[43] For we have already said that contemplation is receiving, and it is not possible that this loftiest wisdom and lineage of contemplation can be received save in a spirit that is silent and detached from[44] sweetness and knowledge. For this is that which is said by Isaias, in these words: 'Whom shall He teach knowledge and whom shall He

[40] E.p.: 'and hearkens, even the loving awareness of which I have spoken must be most pure, without any anxiety or reflection, so that the soul almost forgets it through being wholly occupied in hearing, in order that it may remain free for that which is then desired of it.'

[41] E.p.: 'This manner and [sic] forgetfulness is always accompanied by a certain interior absorption. Wherefore, etc.'

[42] E.p. adds: 'as is said at length in the tenth chapter of the first book of the *Dark Night*, and previously in the last chapter of the second book, and in the first chapter [*the second in our edition*] of the third book of the *Ascent of Mount Carmel*.'

[43] [Habacuc ii, 1.] E.p. adds: 'passively.'

[44] E.p.: 'from particular.'

make to hear[45] that which is heard?'[46] Them that are weaned from milk—that is, from sweetness and pleasures—and them that are drawn from the breasts—that is, from attachment to particular acts and knowledge. Take away the mist and the mote and the hairs, and cleanse thine eye, and the bright sun shall shine upon thee, and thou shalt see. Set the soul in the liberty of peace, and draw it away from the yoke and slavery of its operation, which is the captivity of Egypt; for all this is little more than gathering straw to make bricks; and lead it to the promised land flowing with milk and honey.

34. Oh, spiritual director, remember that it is to give the soul this freedom and holy rest which belongs to His sons that God calls it into the wilderness. There it journeys clad in festal robes, and with jewels of silver and of gold, having now despoiled Egypt[47] and taken away its riches. And not only so, but the Egyptians are drowned[48] in the sea of contemplation, where the Egyptian of sense finds no support or foothold, and sets free the child of God—that is, the spirit that has gone forth from the narrow limits and bounds of natural operation (which is to say from its lowly understanding, its crude perception, and its miserable liking)—so that God may give it the sweet manna; and, though the sweetness of this contains within itself all these sweetnesses and delights for which thou desirest to make the soul work, nevertheless, being so delicious that it melts in the mouth, the soul shall not taste of it if it desire to taste of any other delight or aught else, for it shall not receive it. Endeavour, then, to detach[49] the soul from all coveting of sweetness, pleasure and meditation, and disturb it not with care and solicitude of any kind for higher

45 E.p.: 'to understand.'
46 Isaias xxviii, 9.
47 Gr, P add: 'which is the sensual part.'
48 [Lit., 'they are drowned.'] E.p.: 'but it drowns its enemies.' C: 'but it drowns the Egyptians.'
49 E.p.: 'to uproot.'

things, still less for lower things, but bring it into the greatest possible degree of solitude and withdrawal. For the more nearly the soul attains all this, and the sooner it reaches this restful tranquillity, the more abundantly does it become infused with the spirit of Divine wisdom, the loving, tranquil, lonely, peaceful, sweet ravisher of the spirit. At times the soul will feel itself to be tenderly and serenely ravished and wounded, knowing not by whom, nor whence, nor how, since the Spirit communicates Himself without any act on the part of the soul.[50]

35. And the smallest part of this that God brings to pass in the soul in holy rest and solitude is an inestimable blessing, greater than either the soul itself, or he that guides it, can imagine; and, if this be not realized at the time, it will in due course become manifest. But now, at least, the soul will be able to attain to a perception of estrangement and withdrawal from all things, sometimes more so than at others, together with a sweet aspiration of love and life in the spirit, and with an inclination to solitude and a sense of weariness with regard to creatures and the world. For, when the soul tastes of the spirit, it conceives a distaste for all that pertains to the flesh.

36. But the interior blessings that this silent contemplation leaves impressed upon the soul without its perception of them are, as I say, inestimable; for they are in fact the most secret and delicate anointings of the Holy Spirit, whereby He secretly fills the soul with riches and gifts and graces, for, after all, being God, He acts as God.[51] These blessings, then, and these great riches, these sublime and delicate anointings and touches of the Holy Spirit, which, on account of their delicate and subtle purity, can be understood neither by the soul nor by him that has to do with it, but only by Him Who infuses them in order to make the soul more pleasing to Himself: these bless-

[50] E.p. adds: 'in the sense aforementioned.'
[51] E.p. adds: 'and works as God.'

ings, with the greatest[52] facility, by even the very slightest of such acts as the soul may desire to make by applying its sense or desire to the attainment of some knowledge or sweetness or pleasure, are disturbed and hindered, which is a grave evil and a great shame and pity.

37. Oh, how grave a matter is this, and what cause it gives for wonder, that, while the harm done is inconspicuous, and the interference almost negligible, the harm should be more serious, and a matter for deeper sorrow and regret, than the disquieting and ruining of many souls of a more ordinary nature[53] which have not attained to this state of such supreme fineness and delicacy. It is as though a portrait of supreme beauty were touched by a clumsy hand, and were daubed with strange, crude colours. This would be a greater and a more crying shame than if many more ordinary portraits were besmeared in this way, and a matter of greater grief and pity. For, when the work of so delicate a hand has been so roughly treated, who will be able to restore its beauty?[54]

38. Although the gravity of this evil cannot be exaggerated, it is so common that there will hardly be found a single spiritual director who does not inflict it upon souls whom God is beginning, in this way, to draw nearer to Himself[55] in contemplation. For, whenever God is anointing the soul with some most delicate unction of loving knowledge—serene, peaceful, lonely and very far removed from sense and from all that has to do with thought—and when the soul cannot meditate or find pleasure in

---

52 C, G: 'the most welcome' [*gratísima* for *grandísima*].

53 E.p.: 'than one which would appear much greater in ordinary souls.'

54 E.p. omits this sentence. G has: 'For who will be able to amend and perfect that which was wrought by that Divine hand and which this [unskilful director] spoils with his lack of comprehension?'

55 [The verb is *recoger*, from which is derived *recogimiento*, 'recollection.']

aught,[56] whether in higher things or in lower, or in any knowledge, since God is keeping it full of that lonely unction and inclined to solitude and rest, there will come some director who has no knowledge save of hammering and pounding like a blacksmith, and, because his only teaching is of that kind, he will say: 'Come now, leave all this, for you are only wasting time and living in idleness. Get to work, meditate and make interior acts, for it is right that you should do these things for yourself and be diligent about them, for these other things are the practices of Illuminists and fools.'

39. And thus, since such persons have no understanding of the degrees of prayer or of the ways of the spirit, they cannot see that those acts which they counsel the soul to perform, and that progress along the path of meditation, have been done already, for such a soul as we have been describing has by this time attained to negation of sense; and, when the goal has been reached, and the road traversed, there is no need to set out on the road again, for to do this would only be to walk away[57] from the goal. And thus, not understanding that such a soul is already upon the way[58] of the spirit, where there is no meditation, that its meditation[59] is now coming to an end, that God is the agent,[60] and that He is secretly speaking to the solitary soul, while the soul keeps silence, such a director applies fresh ointments[61] to the soul, relating to cruder knowledge and sweetness, and, by imposing these things upon it, he takes away its solitude and recollection, and consequently spoils

[56] E.p.: 'and when He is keeping it in such a state that it cannot find pleasure in aught, or meditate upon aught.'

[57] C: 'to descend.'

[58] B, G, e.p.: 'is already in the life.'

[59] C, G, Gr, e.p.: 'its sense.'

[60] E.p. adds: 'in a particular way.'

[61] G: 'such a soul, by making acts or meditating, does naught else than apply to itself fresh ointments.' [The word translated 'ointments,' both here and in the text, is generally rendered 'unctions' above.]

the wondrous work that God was painting in it. In this way the soul neither does one thing nor makes progress in another; it is just as if the director were merely striking an anvil.[62]

40. Let such as these take heed and remember that the Holy Spirit is the principal agent and mover of souls and never loses His care for them; and that they themselves are not agents, but only instruments to lead souls by the rule of faith and the law of God, according to the spirit that God is giving to each one. Let them not, therefore, merely aim at guiding a soul according to their own way and the manner suitable to themselves, but let them see if they know the way by which God is leading the soul, and, if they know it not, let them leave the soul in peace and not disturb it. And, in conformity with this, let them seek to lead the soul into greater solitude and liberty and tranquillity, and to give it a certain freedom so that the bodily and spiritual senses may not be bound to anything when God leads the soul in this way, and let them not worry or grieve, thinking that it is doing nothing. For when it is detached from all knowledge of its own, and from every desire and all affections of its sensual part, and dwells in the pure negation of poverty of spirit, wholly emptied of the mists of sweetness, wholly weaned from the breast and from milk (which is what the soul must be careful to do, as far as in it lies, and the director must aid the soul to deny itself in all these ways), it is impossible[63] that God will not perform His own part. It is more impossible than that the sun should fail to shine in a serene and unclouded sky; for as the sun, when it rises in the morning and shines into your house, will enter if you open the shutter,[64] even so will God, Who keeps Israel and slumbers not, still less

62 P: 'were striking hard earth.' E.p. omits: 'it is . . . anvil.'
63 E.p. adds: 'according to the method of procedure of the Divine goodness and mercy.'
64 C, G: 'the window.' E.p.: 'if you open the door.'

sleeps,[65] enter the soul that is empty and fill it with blessings.

41. God, like the sun, is above our souls and ready to enter them. Let spiritual directors, then, be content with preparing the soul according to evangelical perfection, which consists in the detachment and emptiness of sense and of spirit; and let them not seek to go beyond this in the building up of the soul, for that work belongs only to the Lord, from Whom comes down every perfect gift.[66] For, if the Lord build not the house, in vain does he labour that builds it;[67] and in every soul, in the manner that seems good to Him, He will build a supernatural building. Prepare, then, the nature of the soul by annihilating its operations, for these disturb rather than help. That is your office; and the office of God, as the Wise Man says,[68] is to direct the soul to supernatural blessings by ways and in manners whereof neither you nor the soul can know anything. Say not, again: 'Oh, he is making no progress, for he is doing nothing!' For if the understanding of the soul[69] at that time has no more pleasure in objects of the understanding than it had before, it is making progress in walking towards the supernatural. And say not: 'Oh, but he understands nothing distinctly.' For if the soul were to understand anything distinctly,[70] it would be making no progress, for God is incomprehensible and transcends the understanding; and thus the greater the progress it makes, the farther it must withdraw from itself, walking in faith, believing and not understanding;[71] and thus it approaches God more nearly by not understanding than by understanding. Grieve not, therefore, at this, for if the understanding goes not backward and desires not to occupy itself with distinct knowledge

---

[65] Psalm cxx, 4 [A.V., cxxi, 4].
[66] St. James i, 17.
[67] Psalm cxxvi, 1 [A.V., cxxvii, 1].
[68] [Proverbs xvi, 9.]
[69] E.p. omits: 'the understanding of.'
[70] E.p. adds: 'at that time.'
[71] E.p.: 'and not seeing.'

and other ideas pertaining to this world, it is making progress. For in this case not to go backward is to go forward; it is to progress in faith,[72] for, when the understanding knows not, neither can know, what God is, it is walking toward Him by not understanding; and thus what you are condemning in your penitent is fitting for his good, rather than that he should embarrass himself with distinct kinds of understanding.[73]

42. 'Oh,' you will say, 'but if the understanding understands not distinctly, the will at least will be idle and will not love, for it is impossible to love that which one understands not.' There is truth in this, especially as regards the natural acts and operations of the soul, where the will loves only that of which the understanding has distinct knowledge. But in the contemplation[74] of which we are speaking, wherein God, as we have said, infuses into the soul, there is no necessity for distinct knowledge, nor for the soul to perform any acts, for God, in one act, is communicating[75] to the soul loving knowledge, which at one and the same time is like light giving heat without any distinction being perceptible between the two, and at that time as is understanding, even so is love in the will. As this knowledge is general and dark, and the understanding is unable to understand distinctly that which it understands, the will likewise loves in a general way without the making of any distinction. And, as God in this delicate communication is both light and love, He informs these two faculties equally, though at times He acts on the one more than on the other. At times, therefore, the soul is more conscious of understanding than of love, and at other times it is more conscious of love[76] than of understanding; and at times all is

[72] P, e.p.: 'For to go forward is to progress in faith.'
[73] E.p. adds: 'and not walk in perfect faith.'
[74] E.p.: 'But in the period of contemplation.'
[75] E.p.: 'nor for the soul to engage in much reasoning, for at that time God is communicating.'
[76] E.p. has 'of more intense love,' and omits the rest of the paragraph.

understanding, and there is hardly any love; while at other times all is love and there is no understanding. And thus, as far as the acts are concerned which the soul performs on its own account, there can be no love without understanding; but in the acts which God performs in the soul, it is different, for He can communicate Himself in the one faculty and not in the other. Thus He can enkindle the will by means of a touch of the heat of His love, although the understanding may have no understanding thereof, just as a person can receive heat from a fire without seeing that he is near the fire. And in this way the will may oftentimes feel itself to be enkindled or filled with tenderness and love without knowing or understanding anything more distinctly than before, since God is setting love in order in it, even as the Bride says in the Songs, in these words: 'The King introduced me into the cellar of wine, and set in order charity in me.'[77]

43. There is no reason, therefore, to fear that the will in this state will be idle; for, if it ceases to perform acts concerning particular kinds of knowledge, as far as its own efforts are concerned, God performs them within it, inebriating it in infused love, either by means of the knowledge of contemplation, or without such knowledge, as we have just said; and these acts are as much better than those made by the soul and as much more meritorious[78] and delectable, as the mover and infuser of this love[79]—namely, God—is better than the soul; and God establishes love in the soul because the will is near God and is detached from other pleasures. The soul, therefore, must see to it that

[77] Canticles ii, 4.
[78] E.p.: 'And therefore there is no reason to fear that the soul in this state will be idle for, if it ceases to perform acts governed by particular kinds of knowledge, as far as its own efforts are concerned, He inebriates it, nevertheless, in infused love, by means of the knowledge of contemplation, as we have just said; and these acts which are performed through following infused contemplation are as much better and as much more meritorious.'
[79] E.p.: 'the mover who infuses this love.'

the will is empty and stripped of its affections; for, if it is not going backward by desiring to experience some sweetness or pleasure, it is going forward, even though it have no particular perception of this in God, and it is soaring upward to God above all things, since it takes no pleasure in anything. It is going toward God, although it may be taking no particular and distinct delight in Him, nor may be loving Him with any distinct act, for it is taking greater pleasure in Him secretly, by means of that dark and general infusion of love, than it does in all things that are distinct,[80] for it sees clearly in this state that nothing gives it so much pleasure as that solitary quiet. And it is loving Him above all things that can be loved, since it has flung from itself all other kinds of sweetness and pleasure which have become distasteful to it. And there is thus no reason to be troubled, for, if the will can find no sweetness and pleasure in particular acts, it is going forward; seeing that to refrain from going backward and from embracing anything that belongs to sense is to go forward towards the inaccessible, which is God, and thus there is no wonder that the soul has no perception thereof.[81] Wherefore, in order to journey to God, the will has rather to be continually detaching itself from everything delectable and pleasant than to be conceiving an attachment to it. In this way it completely fulfils the precept of love, which is to love God above all things; and this cannot be unless it have spiritual emptiness and detachment[82] with regard to them all.[83]

44. Neither is there any cause for misgivings when the memory is voided of its forms and figures, for, since God has no form or figure, the memory is safe if it be voided of form or figure, and it is approaching God the more nearly; for, the more it leans upon the imagination, the farther it

80 E.p.: 'than if it were governed by distinct kinds of knowledge.'
81 E.p. omits: 'and thus . . . thereof.'
82 Thus B, C, G, Gr, P. T, e.p.: 'special emptiness.'
83 E.p.: 'and if this is to happen with all perfection, it must happen with this special emptiness and detachment as to them all.'

is going from God, and the greater is the peril wherein it walks, since God is incomprehensible and therefore cannot be apprehended by the imagination.

45. Such directors as we have been describing fail to understand souls that are now walking in this solitary and quiet contemplation,[84] because they themselves have not advanced beyond a very ordinary kind of meditation, or similar act, nor perhaps have arrived even so far; and they think, as I have said, that these souls are idle, because the animal man—that is, one that advances not beyond the animal feelings of the sensual part of the soul—perceives not, as Saint Paul says, the things that are of God.[85] Wherefore they disturb the peace of this quiet and hushed contemplation which God has been giving these souls by His own power, and they make their penitents meditate and reason and perform acts, not without causing them great displeasure, repugnance and distraction, since their souls would fain remain in their quiet and peaceful state of recollection; but their directors persuade them to strive after sweetness and fervour, though they ought rather to advise them the contrary. The penitents, however, are unable to do as they did previously, and can enter into none of these things, for the time for them has now passed and they belong no more to their proper path; and so they are doubly disturbed, and believe that they are going to perdition; and their directors encourage them in this belief, and parch their spirits, and take from them the precious unctions wherewith God was anointing them in solitude and tranquillity. This, as I have said, is a great evil; their directors are plunging them into mire and mourning,[86]

[84] G continues, after 'wherein it walks': 'and the farther it withdraws itself from it [i.e. the imagination], the more surely it journeys. And those [directors] who are not experienced cannot properly understand these souls, nor do they know that the Lord is keeping them in this state of quiet contemplation.'

[85] 1 Corinthians ii, 14.

[86] [i.e. mourning for what they lose and the mire of their present unhappy state from which they strive to get free.]

for they are losing one thing and labouring without profit at the other.

46. Such persons have no knowledge of what spirituality is, and they offer a great insult and great irreverence to God, by laying their coarse hands where God is working. For it has cost Him dearly to bring these souls to this place and He greatly esteems having brought them to this solitude and emptiness of their faculties and operations, that He may speak to their heart, which is what He ever desires. He has Himself taken them by the hand, and He Himself reigns in their souls in abundant peace and quietness, causing the natural acts[87] of their faculties to fail wherewith they toiled all night and wrought nothing. And He has brought peace to their spirits without the operation of sense, for neither sense nor any act thereof is capable of receiving spirit.

47. How precious in His sight is this tranquillity or slumbering or annihilation of sense can be clearly seen in that adjuration, so notable and effective, that He utters in the Songs, where He says: 'I adjure you, daughters of Jerusalem, by the goats and harts of the fields, that ye awaken not my beloved nor cause her to wake until she please.'[88] Herein, by introducing these solitary and retiring animals, He gives us to understand how much He loves that solitary forgetfulness and slumber. But these spiritual directors will not let the soul have repose or quiet, but demand that it shall continually labour and work, that it may leave no room for God to work, and that that which He is working may be undone and wiped out through the operation of the soul. They have become as the little foxes which tear down the flowering vine of the soul;[89] for which reason God complains through Isaias, saying: 'You have devoured[90] My vineyard.'[91]

87 E.p.: 'the discursive acts.'
88 Canticles iii, 5.
89 Canticles ii, 15. E.p.: 'which destroy.'
90 G, e.p.: 'You have destroyed.' C: 'You have eaten.'
91 Isaias iii, 14.

48. But, it may possibly be said, these directors err with good intent, through insufficiency of knowledge. This, however, does not excuse them for the advice which they are rash enough to give without first learning to understand either the way that the soul is taking or its spirit. If they understand not this, they are laying their coarse hands upon things that they understand not, instead of leaving them for those who understand them better; for it is a thing of no small weight, and no slight crime, to cause the soul to lose inestimable blessings by counselling it to go out of its way and to leave it prostrate.[92] And thus one who rashly errs, being under an obligation to give reliable advice—as is every man, whatever his office—shall not go unpunished, by reason of the harm that he has done. For the business of God has to be undertaken with great circumspection, and with eyes wide open, most of all in matters so delicate and sublime as the conduct of these souls, where a man may bring them almost infinite gain if the advice that he gives be good and almost infinite loss if it be mistaken.

49. But if you will still maintain that such a director has some excuse, though for myself I can see none, you will at least be unable to say that there is any excuse for one who, in his treatment of a soul, never allows it to go out of his jurisdiction, for certain vain reasons and intentions which he best knows. Such a person will not go unpunished, for it is certain that, if that soul is to make progress by going forward on the spiritual road, wherein God is ever aiding it, it will have to change the style and method of its prayer, and it will of necessity require instruction of a higher kind and a deeper spirituality than that of such a director. For not all directors have sufficient knowledge to meet all the possibilities and cases which they encounter on the spiritual road, neither is their spirituality so perfect that they know how a soul has to be

[92] [*Lit.*, 'right on the ground.']

guided and directed in every state of the spiritual life; at least no man should think that he knows everything concerning this, or that God will cease leading a given soul farther onward. Not everyone who can hew a block of wood is able to carve an image; nor is everyone who can carve it able to smooth and polish it; nor is he that can polish it able to paint it; nor can everyone that is able to paint it complete it with the final touches. Each one of these, in working upon an image, can do no more than that with which he himself is familiar, and, if he tries to do more, he will only ruin his work.

50. How, then, we may ask, if you are only a hewer of wood, and merely try to make a soul despise the world and mortify its desires; or, if at best you are a carver, which means that you can lead a soul to holy meditations, but can do no more: how, in such a case, will this soul attain to the final perfection of a delicate painting, the art of which consists neither in the hewing of wood, nor in the carving of it, nor even in the outlining of it, but in the work which God Himself must do in it? It is certain, then, that if your instruction is always of one kind, and you cause the soul to be continually bound to you, it will either go backward, or, at the least, will not go forward.[93] For what, I ask you, will the image be like, if you never do any work upon it save hewing and hammering, which in the language of the soul is exercising the faculties? When will this image be finished? When or how will it be left for God to paint it? Is it possible that you yourself can perform all these offices, and consider yourself so consummate a master that this soul shall never need any other?

51. And supposing that you have sufficient experience to direct some one soul, which perchance may have no ability to advance beyond your teaching, it is surely impossible for you to have sufficient experience for the direc-

[93] P omits the remainder of this paragraph, and the three paragraphs following.

tion of all those whom you refuse to allow to go out of your hands; for God leads each soul along different roads and there shall hardly be found a single spirit who can walk even half the way which is suitable for another. Who can be like Saint Paul and have the skill to make himself all things to all men, that he may gain them all?[94] You yourself tyrannize over souls, and take away their liberty, and arrogate to yourself the breadth and liberty of evangelical doctrine, so that you not only strive that they may not leave you, but, what is worse, if any one of them[95] should at some time go and ask the advice of another director, or discuss with him anything that he could not suitably discuss with you, or if God should lead him in order to teach him something which you teach him not, you behave to him (I say it not without shame) like a husband who is jealous of his wife; nor is your jealousy even due to a desire for the honour of God—it is due only to your own pride and presumption.[96] For how can you know that that soul has not the need to go to another? Great is the indignation of God with such directors, whom He promises punishment when He speaks through the prophet Ezechiel and says: 'Ye fed not My flock but clothed yourselves with their wool and drank their milk; I will require My flock at your hand.'[97]

52. Such persons, then, ought to give these souls freedom, for they have an obligation to allow them to go to others and to put a good face upon it, since they know not by what means God desires such souls to make progress, especially when they dislike the instruction that they are receiving, which is a sign that God is leading them on farther by another way and that they need another director. The director

[94] [1 Corinthians ix, 22.]

[95] E.p.: 'if you know that any one of them.'

[96] G: 'you behave harshly to him, which is not due to your zeal (celo) for the honour and glory of God, but to jealousy (celos) coming from your own pride and presumption.'

[97] Ezechiel xxxiv, 2, 3, 10.

himself, in such a case, should advise a change, since any other advice springs from foolish pride and presumption.

53.[98] Let us now leave this question and speak of another pestilential habit of such directors as these, or of others even worse than they. For it may come to pass that God will be anointing certain souls with holy desires and impulses to leave the world, to change their life and condition, to serve Him and despise the world (it is a great thing in His eyes that they should have been brought thus far, for the things of the world are not according to the heart of God), and these directors, using human arguments or putting forward considerations quite contrary to the doctrine of Christ and His way of mortification and despising of all things, advise them to delay their decision, or place obstacles in their path, from motives of their own interest or their own pleasure, for because they fear where no fear is; or, what is still worse, they sometimes labour[99] to remove these desires from their penitents' hearts. Such directors show a wrong spirit, and are undevout, and clad, as it were, in very worldly garb, having little of the tenderness of Christ, since they neither enter themselves, nor allow others to enter. And our Saviour says: 'Woe unto you that have taken away the key of knowledge, and enter not in yourselves nor allow others to enter!'[100] For these persons in truth are placed like barriers and obstacles at the gate of Heaven, remembering not that God has placed them there that they may compel those whom God calls to enter in, as He has commanded;[101] whereas they, on the other hand, are compelling souls not to enter in by the narrow gate that leads to life; in this way such a man is a blind guide who can obstruct the guidance of the Holy

98 G omits this paragraph.
99 E.p.: 'set out.'
100 St. Luke xi, 52.
101 E.p. adds: 'in His Gospel.' C: 'saying through St. Luke: Insist, make them come in, that My house may be filled with guests.'

Spirit in the soul. This comes to pass in many ways, as has here been said; some do it knowingly, others unconsciously; but neither class shall remain unpunished, since, having assumed their office, they are under an obligation to know and consider what they do.

54. The other blind guide of whom we have spoken, who can hinder the soul in this kind of recollection, is the devil, who, being himself blind, desires the soul to be blind also. When the soul is in these lofty and solitary places wherein are infused the delicate unctions of the Holy Spirit (at which he has great grief and envy, for he sees the soul flying beyond him, and can in no wise lay hold on it, though he sees that it is gaining great riches), the devil tries to cover this detachment and withdrawal, as it were, with cataracts of knowledge and mists of sensible sweetness, which are sometimes good, so that he may entice the soul more surely, and thus cause it to have commerce once more with sense, and to look at these things and embrace them, so that it may continue its journey to God in reliance upon this good knowledge and these delights. And herein he distracts it and very easily withdraws it from that solitude and recollection, wherein, as we have said, the Holy Spirit is working these great things secretly. And then the soul, being of itself inclined to sensible enjoyment, especially if these are the things which it is really desiring, is very easily led to cling to such kinds of knowledge and such delights, and withdraws itself from the solitude wherein God works. For (it says), as previously it was doing nothing, this other state seems better, for it is now doing something. It is a great pity that it cannot realize how, for the sake of one mouthful, it is preventing itself from feeding wholly upon God Himself, when He absorbs it in these solitary and spiritual unctions of His mouth.

55. In this way, with hardly any trouble, the devil works the greatest injuries, causing the soul to lose great riches, and dragging it forth like a fish, with the tiniest bait, from

the depths of the pure waters of the spirit, where it had
no support or foothold but was engulfed and immersed in
God. And hereupon he drags it to the bank, giving it help
and support, and showing it something whereon it may
lean, so that it may walk upon its own feet with great labour
instead of floating in the waters of Siloe, that go with
silence,[102] bathed in the unctions of God. And this the
devil does to such an extent[103] that it is a matter for great
marvel; and, since a slight injury is more serious to a soul
in this condition than is a serious injury to many other
souls, as we have said,[104] there is hardly any soul walking
on this road which does not meet with great injuries and
suffer great losses. For the evil one takes his stand, with
great cunning, on the road which leads from sense to
spirit,[105] deceiving and luring the soul by means of sense,
and giving it sensual things, as we have said, so that it may
rest in them and not escape from him; and the soul is
entrapped with the greatest ease,[106] for it knows of nothing better than this, and thinks not that anything is being
lost by it, but rather considers it a great blessing, and receives it readily, thinking that God has come to visit it;
and in this way it fails to enter into the innermost chamber
of the Spouse, but stands at the door to see what is happening. The devil, as Job says, beholdeth every high thing
—that is to say, concerning souls—that he may assault
it.[107] And if perchance any soul enters into recollection,
he labours to bring about its ruin by means of horrors,
fears or pains of the body, or by outward sounds and noises,
causing it to be distracted by sense,[108] in order to bring

102 [Isaias viii, 6.]
103 P: 'And to this the devil attaches such importance.'
104 E.p.: 'and since a slight injury inflicted upon many souls in
this condition is more serious.'
105 C, Gr, P add: 'as is his invariable custom, so that it [the
soul] shall not pass from sense to spirit.'
106 T: 'with the greatest difficulty.'
107 [Job xli, 25: A.V., xli, 34.]
108 E.p.: 'by the sound.'

it out and distract it from the interior spirit, until he can do no more and so leaves it. And with such ease does he corrupt these precious souls, and squander their great riches, that, although he thinks this of greater importance than to bring about the fall of many others, he esteems it not highly because of the facility with which it is done and the little effort that it costs him. In this sense we may understand that which God said to Job concerning the devil, namely: 'He shall drink up a river and shall not marvel, and he trusteth that the Jordan may run into his mouth—by the Jordan being understood the summit of perfection. In his eyes as with a hook shall he take him, and with stakes shall he bore through his nostrils.'[109] That is, with the darts of the knowledge, wherewith he is piercing the soul, he will disperse its spirituality; for the breath which goes out through his nostrils, when they are pierced, is dispersed in many directions. And later he says: 'The beams of the sun shall be under him and they shall scatter gold under him as mire.'[110] For he causes souls that have been enlightened to lose the marvellous rays of Divine knowledge, and from souls that are rich he takes away and scatters the precious gold of Divine adornment.

56. Oh, souls! Since God is showing you such sovereign[111] mercies as to lead you through this state of solitude and recollection, withdrawing you from your labours of sense, return not to sense again. Lay aside your operations, for, though once, when you were beginners, they helped you to deny the world and yourselves, they will now be a great obstacle and hindrance to you, since God is granting you the grace of Himself working within you. If you are careful to set your faculties[112] upon naught soever, withdrawing them from everything and in no way hindering them, which is the proper part for you to play in this state, and if you

---

109 Job xl, 18–19 [A.V., xl, 23–4].
110 Job xli, 21 [A.V., xli, 30].
111 C, Gr: 'noted.' G: 'singular.'
112 E.p.: 'your operations.'

only wait upon God with loving and pure attentiveness, as I said above, in the way which I there described (working no violence to the soul[113] save to detach it from everything and set it free,[114] lest you disturb and spoil its peace or tranquillity), God will feed[115] your soul for you with heavenly food,[116] since you are not hindering Him.[117]

57. The third blind guide of the soul is the soul itself, which, not understanding itself, as we have said, becomes perturbed and does itself harm. For it knows not how to work save by means of sense, and thus, when God is pleased to bring it into that emptiness and solitude where it can neither use its faculties nor make any acts, it sees that it is doing nothing, and strives to do something:[118] in this way it becomes distracted and full of aridity and displeasure, whereas formerly it was rejoicing in the rest of the spiritual silence and peace wherein God was secretly giving it joy. And it may come to pass that God persists in keeping the soul in that silent tranquillity, while the soul persists in crying out with its imagination and walking with its understanding; even as children, whom their mothers carry in their arms so that they may not have to walk, keep crying and striking out with their feet because they are anxious to walk, and thus neither make any progress themselves nor allow their mothers to do so. Or it is as when a painter is painting a portrait and his subject will not allow him to do anything because he keeps moving.

58. The soul in this state must bear in mind that, al-

---

113 [P. Silverio's text has (for 'working no violence to the soul') 'which must be when you have no desire to be attentive, for you must work no violence to the soul.' This seems to be a corruption.] E.p. abbreviates: 'with loving and pure attentiveness, without working violence to the soul.'

114 B, G, e.p.: 'and raise it.'

115 B: 'will cure.'

116 [Lit., 'celestial refection.'] C: 'spiritual perfection.'

117 G: 'God will regale it for you and fill it with spiritual blessings if you hinder Him not by means of operations of sense.'

118 E.p. adds: 'more sensibly and expressly.'

though it is not conscious of making any progress, it is making much more than when it was walking on foot; for it is because God is bearing it in His arms that it is not conscious of such movement. And although it is doing[119] nothing, it is nevertheless accomplishing much more than if it were working, since God is working within it. And it is not remarkable that the soul should be unable to see this, for sense cannot perceive that which God works in the soul. Let the soul leave itself in the hands of God and have confidence in Him and entrust itself neither to the hands nor to the works of others; for, if it remains thus, it will make sure progress, since it is in no danger save when it desires to occupy its faculties in something.[120]

59. Let us now return to the matter of these deep caverns of the faculties wherein we said that the suffering of the soul is wont to be great when God is anointing and preparing it with these subtle[121] unctions in order that He may unite it with Himself. These unctions are sometimes so subtle and sublime that they penetrate the inmost substance of the depth of the soul,[122] preparing it and filling it with sweetness in such a way that its suffering and fainting with desire in the boundless emptiness of these caverns is likewise boundless. Here we must note this: if the unctions that were preparing these caverns for the union of the spiritual marriage are as sublime as we have said, what will the possession be which they afterwards attain? It is certain that, even as was the thirst and hunger and suffering of the caverns, so now will be the satisfaction and fullness and delight thereof; and, as was the delicacy

[119] E.p.: 'it seems to be doing.'
[120] E.p.: 'and have confidence in Him; for, if it do this, it will make sure progress, for it is in no danger save when it desires, on its own account or in its own way, to work with its faculties.' P ends the treatise here and A recommences with the following paragraph.
[121] E.p.: 'subtle and delicate.'
[122] E.p.: 'the inmost part of the ground [i.e. bottom] of the soul.'

of the preparations, even so will be the wonder of the possession and fruition of sense,[123] which is the vigour and virtue that belong to the substance of the soul that it may perceive and have fruition of the objects of the faculties.

60. These faculties the soul here calls caverns, and with great propriety,[124] for, as it perceives[125] that they are able to contain the deep intelligences and splendours of these lamps, the soul is able to see clearly that they have a depth as great as is that of the intelligence and the love; and that they have capacity and depth as great as are the various things[126] which they receive from the intelligences, the sweetnesses and the fruitions; all of which things are established and received in this cavern of the sense of the soul, which is the soul's virtue of capacity for possessing, perceiving and having pleasure in everything, as I say. Even as the common sense of the fancy is a receptacle for all objects of the outward senses, even so this ordinary sense of the soul is enlightened and made rich by a possession that is so lofty and glorious.

Which were dark and blind

61. There are two reasons for which the eye may be unable to see: either it may be in darkness or it may be blind. God is the light and the object[1] of the soul; when this light illumines it not, it is in darkness, even though its power of vision may be most excellent. When it is in sin, or when it employs its desires upon aught else, it is then blind; and even though the light of God then shines upon it,[2] it sees it not, being blind. The darkness of the soul is the ignorance of the soul;[3] before God enlightened it

123 E.p.: 'the fruition and possession of the feeling of the soul.'
124 C: 'and very profoundly.'
125 [Lit., 'they perceive.' Cf. p. 251, below.]
126 E.p.: 'the various causes.'
1 E.p.: 'and the true object.'
2 E.p.: 'even though it may not lack the light of God.'
3 E.p.: 'By the darkness of the soul is [meant] its practical ignorance.'

through this transformation, it was blind and ignorant concerning many good things of God, even as the Wise Man says that he was blind before Wisdom illumined him, using these words: 'He illumined my ignorance.'[4]

62. Speaking spiritually, it is one thing to be in darkness and another to be in thick darkness; for to be in thick darkness is to be blind (that is, as we have said, in sin); but to be in darkness only is something that may happen when one is not in sin. This may be in two ways: in the natural sense, when the soul has no light from certain natural things; and in the supernatural sense, when it has no light from supernatural things; and, with regard to both these things, the soul here says that its understanding[5] was dark before this precious union.[6] For, until the Lord said: *Fiat lux*,[7] thick darkness was upon the face of the abyss of the cavern of sense; and the deeper is this abyss and the more profound are its caverns, when God, Who is light, enlightens it not, the more abysmal and profound is the thick darkness that is upon it. And thus it is impossible for the soul to raise its eyes to the Divine light, or even to think of such light, for it knows not of what manner is this light, since it has never seen it; wherefore it cannot desire it, but will rather desire thick darkness, knowing not what it is like; and it will go from one darkness to another, guided by that darkness, for darkness cannot lead to anything save to fresh darkness. Then, as David says: 'Day unto day uttereth speech, and night unto night showeth its night.'[8] And thus one abyss calls to another abyss; an abyss of thick darkness to another abyss of thick darkness and an abyss of light to another abyss of light; each like calls to its like and infuses it.[9] And thus the light of the grace that God had

---

[4] Ecclesiasticus li, 26.
[5] So Gr, T, e.p., A, B, C, G have: 'its sense.'
[6] E.p.: 'that its understanding was dark, without God.'
[7] Genesis i, 3.
[8] Psalm xviii, 2 [A.V., xix, 2].
[9] E.p. omits: 'and infuses it.'

already given to this soul, wherewith He had opened the eye of its abyss to the Divine light, and so had made it pleasing to Himself, has called to another abyss of grace, which is this Divine transformation of the soul in God, whereby the eye of sense is so greatly enlightened and made pleasing to Him[10] that light and will are both one, the natural light is united to the supernatural and the supernatural light alone shines; even as the light created by God was united with that of the sun and the light of the sun alone now shines without the other failing.

63. And the soul was also blind inasmuch as it took pleasure in other things than God; for the blindness of the higher and rational sense is that desire which, like a cataract and a cloud, overlays and covers the eye of reason,[11] so that the soul shall not see the things that are in front of it. And thus, for as long as the soul took any pleasure in sense, it was blind and could not see the great riches and Divine beauties that were behind. For just as, if a man sets anything before his eyes, however small, this suffices to obstruct his sight so that he cannot see other things that may be in front of him, however large they be, just so any small desire or idle act in the soul suffices to obstruct its vision of all these great and Divine things, which come after the pleasures and desires for which the soul longs.

64. Oh, that one might describe here how impossible it is for the soul that has other desires to judge of the things of God as they are! For, in order to judge the things of God aright, the soul must cast out wholly from itself its own desire and pleasure and must not judge them together with Him; else it will infallibly[12] come to consider the things of God as though they were not of God and those that are not of God as though they were of God. For, when

[10] E.p. reads 'very greatly enlightened and made pleasing to Him' and omits the rest of the paragraph.

[11] E.p.: 'of the heart' [*corazón* for *razón*].

[12] E.p. omits this word.

that cataract and cloud covers the eye of judgment, the soul sees nothing but the cataract[13]—sometimes of one colour, sometimes of another, just as it may happen to be; and the soul thinks that the cataract is God, for, as we have said, it can see nothing beyond the cataract, which covers the senses, and God cannot be apprehended by sense. And thus desire and the pleasures of the soul hinder it from a knowledge of lofty things, as the Wise Man says, in these words: 'The union of vanity obscureth good things, and the inconstancy of desire overturneth the sense, though there be no malice.'[14]

65. Wherefore those persons who are not spiritual enough to be purged of their desires and pleasures, and still to some extent follow their animal nature with respect to these, may think much of the base and vile things of the spirit, which are those that come nearest to the sensual condition wherein they still live, and they will consider them to be of great importance; while those things that are lofty and spiritual, which are those that are farthest withdrawn from sense, they will count of small importance and will not esteem them, and will even consider them to be folly, as Saint Paul says, in these words: 'The animal man perceiveth not the things of God; they are to him as foolishness and he cannot understand them.'[15] The animal man is he that still lives according to the desires and pleasures of his nature. For, although these may be derived from spirit and be born there, yet, if one desires to cling to them with his natural desire, they then become natural desires; for it is of small importance that the object of this desire should be supernatural if the desire proceeds from itself and has its root and strength in nature, for it has the same substance and nature as if it related to matter and a natural object.[16]

---

[13] Here and below, e.p. reads 'cloud' for 'cataract.'
[14] Wisdom iv, 12.
[15] 1 Corinthians ii, 14.
[16] E.p. abbreviates: 'and not esteem them. He is an animal man who still lives according to the desires of his nature, for although

66. You will say to me: 'But when God is desired, is not this supernatural?' I reply that it is not always so, but only when God infuses this desire, and Himself gives it its strength,[17] and then it is a very different thing. When you, of your own accord, desire to possess Him, this is no more than natural;[18] nor will it ever be otherwise unless it be informed by God. And thus when you, of your own accord, desire to cling to spiritual pleasures, and exercise your own natural desire, you are spreading a cataract over the eye of the soul and you are an animal being and cannot therefore understand or judge that which is spiritual, which is higher than any natural desire and sense. And if you are still doubtful, I know not what to say to you save to bid you read these words again, and then perhaps you will cease to doubt, for what I have said is the substance of the truth, and I cannot possibly enlarge upon it here any further. This sense, then, which before was dark, without this Divine light of God, and was blind, because of its desires, is now in such a condition that its deep caverns, by means of this Divine union:

With strange brightness Give heat and light together to their Beloved!

67. For, now that these caverns of the faculties are so wonderfully and marvellously infused[1] with the wondrous splendours of those lamps, as we have said, which are burning within them, they are sending back to God in God, over and above the surrender which they are making to God, since they are illumined and enkindled in God, those same splendours which the soul has received with

---

occasionally these may be connected with spiritual things, yet, if a man desires to cling to them with his natural desire, they then become natural desires; for it is of small importance that the object of this desire should be spiritual, etc.'

[17] E.p.: 'but only when the motive is supernatural and God gives such a desire its strength.'

[18] E.p. adds: 'in its manner,' and omits the rest of the sentence.

[1] E.p.: 'placed.' T: 'so greatly mortified and so marvellously infused.'

loving glory;[2] they turn to God in God, and become themselves lamps enkindled in the splendours of the Divine lamps, giving to the Beloved some of the same light and heat of love that the soul receives; for in this state, after the same manner as they receive, they are giving to the Giver with the very brightness that He gives to them; even as does glass when the sun strikes it; although the former is after a nobler manner, because the exercise of the will intervenes.

68. 'With strange brightness' signifies that the brightness is strange in a way that is far remote from all common thought and all description and every way and manner.[3] For the brightness with which God visits the soul is like to the brightness wherewith the understanding receives Divine wisdom and is made one with the understanding of God; for one cannot give save in the way wherein is given to him. And like to the brightness[4] wherewith the will is united with goodness[5] is the brightness wherewith the soul gives to God in God the same goodness; for the soul receives it only to give it again. In the same way, according to the brightness wherewith the soul has knowledge of the greatness of God, being united therein, it shines and gives heat of love. According to the brightness of the other Divine attributes which are here communicated to the soul— fortitude, beauty, justice, etc.—are the manners of brightness wherewith the sense, having fruition, is giving to its Beloved, in its Beloved, that same light and heat that it is receiving from its Beloved; for, since in this state it has been made one and the same thing with Him, it is after a certain manner God by participation; for, although this

---

[2] E.p. alters the order of the clauses in this sentence, but makes no other change save the addition of 'of themselves' after 'the surrender.'

[3] E.p. ends the sentence at 'description.'

[4] E.p. abbreviates: 'wherewith the understanding received Divine wisdom. And like to the brightness.'

[5] T: 'with the will.' E.p.: 'with the Divine will.'

is not so as perfectly as in the next life, the soul is, as we have said, as it were a shadow of God. And in this way, since the soul, by means of this substantial[6] transformation, is the shadow of God, it does in God and through God that which He does through Himself in the soul, in the same way as He does it.[7] For the will of these two is one;[8] and, even as God is giving Himself to the soul with free and gracious will, even so likewise the soul, having a will that is the freer and the more generous in proportion as it has a greater degree of union with God, is giving God in God to God Himself, and thus the gift of the soul to God is true and entire.[9] For in this state the soul truly sees that God belongs to it, and that it possesses Him with hereditary possession, as an adopted child of God,[10] by rightful ownership, through the grace that God gave to it of Himself, and it sees that, since He belongs to it, it may give and communicate Him to whomsoever it desires; and thus it gives Him to its Beloved,[11] Who is the very God that gave Himself to it. And herein the soul pays all that it owes; for, of its own will, it gives as much as it has received with inestimable delight and joy, giving to the Holy Spirit that which is His in a voluntary surrender, that He may be loved as He deserves.

69. And herein is the inestimable delight of the soul: to see that it is giving to God that which is His own and which becomes Him according to His infinite Being. For, although it is true that the soul cannot give God Himself to Himself

6 E.p. omits 'substantial.'

7 E.p. omits: 'in . . . does it.'

8 C, G, Gr add: 'and the operation of the soul and of God is one.'

9 E.p.: 'a greater degree of union with God in God, is as it were giving to God God Himself, through that loving complacency which it has for the Divine Being and perfections, and this is a mystical and affective gift of the soul to God.'

10 E.p. omits 'with hereditary possession.'

11 E.p. abbreviates: 'gave to it of Himself. It gives Him, then, to its Beloved.'

anew, since He in Himself is ever Himself, yet, in so far as
the soul is itself concerned, it gives perfectly and truly,[12]
giving all that He had given to it, to pay the debt of love.
And this is to give as has been given to it, and God is repaid
by that gift of the soul—yet with less than this He cannot
be paid. And this He takes with gratitude, as something
belonging to the soul that it gives to Him anew,[13] and
because of this He loves the soul and surrenders Himself
to it anew, wherein the soul loves Him.[14] And so at this
time there is a reciprocal love between God and the soul,
in the agreement of the union and surrender of marriage,
wherein the possessions of both, which are the Divine
Being, are possessed by each one freely, and[15] are possessed likewise by both together in the voluntary surrender
of each to the other, wherein each says to the other that
which the Son of God said to the Father in Saint John,
namely: *Omnia mea tua sunt, et tua mea sunt et clarificatus
sum in eis.*[16] That is: All My things are Thine, and Thine
are Mine, and I am glorified in them. In the next life this
happens without any intermission in the fruition thereof.
And in this state of union, when the communication between the soul and God takes place in the act and exercise
of love, that gift can evidently be made by the soul,[17]
although it is greater than its capacity and its being; for
it is evident that one who possesses many kingdoms and
peoples as his own, although they be much greater in importance than himself, can perfectly well give them to whom
he desires.

70. This is the great satisfaction and contentment of the
soul, to see that it is giving to God more than it is itself

[12] E.p.: 'and wisely.'
[13] E.p. has 'in the aforementioned sense' for 'anew.'
[14] [*Lit.,* 'He loves the soul'; probably a slip (*al* for *el*).]
[15] E.p. omits: 'are possessed by each one freely, and.'
[16] St. John xvii, 10.
[17] [P. Silverio's text has 'to' for 'by'; this is probably a slip
(*al* for *el*) similar to that noted in n. 14, above.]

worth, since it is giving to God Himself with such great liberality, as that which is its own, with that Divine light and that warmth of love which are given to it; in the next life this comes to pass through the light of glory,[18] and, in this life, through most enlightened faith.[19] And in this way, the deep caverns of sense, with strange brightness, give heat and light together to their Beloved. 'Together,' because the communication of the Father and of the Son and of the Holy Spirit in the soul are made together, and are the light and fire of love.

71. But here we must make a brief observation on the brightness wherewith the soul makes this surrender. Concerning this it must be noted that, in the act of this union, as the soul enjoys a certain image of fruition which is caused by the union of the understanding and the affection in God, being delighted thereby and constrained, it makes the surrender of God to God, and of itself in God, in wondrous manners. For, with respect to love, the soul presents itself to God with strange brightness; and equally so with respect to this shadow of fruition; and likewise with respect to praise, and, in the same way, with respect to gratitude.

72. With regard to the first of these, which is love, the soul has three principal kinds of love which may be called brightnesses. The first is that the soul now loves God, not through itself, but through God Himself; which is a wondrous brightness, since it loves through the Holy Spirit,[20] even as the Father loves the Son, as Saint John says: 'May the love wherewith Thou hast loved Me,' says the Son to the Father, 'be in them and I in them.'[21] The second kind of brightness is to love God in God; for in this vehement union the soul is absorbed in the love of God

---

[18] E.p. adds: 'and of love.'

[19] E.p. adds: 'and most enkindled love.'

[20] E.p.: 'since it loves enkindled by the Holy Spirit, and having in itself the Holy Spirit.'

[21] St. John xvii, 26.

and God surrenders Himself to the soul with great vehemence. The third kind of love which is brightness is that the soul here loves Him for Who He is; it loves Him not only because He is bountiful, good, glorious,[22] and so forth, with respect to itself, but much more earnestly because He is all this in Himself essentially.

73. And with regard to this image of fruition there are also three other principal kinds of brightness, no less wonderful. The first is that the soul in this state has fruition of God through God Himself, for as the soul in this state unites understanding with wisdom and goodness and so forth,[23] albeit not so clearly as it will do in the next life, it delights greatly in all these things, understood distinctly, as we have said above. The second principal brightness belonging to this love is that the soul delights itself duly in God alone, without any intermingling of creatures. The third delight is that it enjoys Him for Who He is alone, without any other intermingling of its own pleasure.[24]

74. And with respect to the praise which the soul offers to God in this union, there are three kinds of brightness here also. First, the soul praises God as a duty, for it sees that He created it to offer Him praise, as He says through Isaias: 'I have formed this people for Myself; it shall sing My praises.'[25] The second kind of brightness of this praise comes from the blessings which the soul receives and the delight that it has in offering praise.[26] The third is that it praises God for that which He is in Himself; even if to do so caused the soul no delight at all, it would still praise Him for Who He is.

75. With respect to gratitude, again, there are three

[22] E.p.: 'bountiful, good, liberal.' T: 'bountiful, good [used substantivally], glory.'

[23] E.p. adds: 'which it knows with such enlightenment.' A, B, C, G, Gr read: 'in omnipotence, wisdom and goodness, and so forth.'

[24] E.p. adds: 'or of anything created.'

[25] Isaias xliii, 21.

[26] E.p.: 'in praising this great Lord.'

principal kinds of brightness. First, there is gratitude for the natural and spiritual blessings and the benefits which the soul has received. Secondly, there is the great delight which the soul has in praising God, because it is absorbed with great vehemence in this praise. Thirdly, the soul praises God only for that which He is, and this praise is much more profound and delectable.

STANZA IV

How gently and lovingly thou awakenest in my bosom,
 Where thou dwellest secretly and alone!
And in thy sweet breathing, full of blessing and glory,
 How delicately thou inspirest my love!

EXPOSITION

HERE the soul turns to its Spouse with great love, extolling Him and giving Him thanks for two wondrous effects which He sometimes produces within it by means of this union, noting likewise in what way He produces each and also the effect upon itself which in each case is the result thereof.

2. The first effect is the awakening of God in the soul, and the means whereby this is produced are those of gentleness and love. The second effect is the breathing of God in the soul and the means thereof are in the blessing and glory that are communicated to the soul in this breathing. And that which is produced thereby in the soul is a delicate and tender inspiration of love.

3. The stanza, then, has this meaning: Thine awakening, O Word and Spouse, in the centre and depth of my soul, which is its pure and inmost substance,[1] wherein alone, secretly and in silence, Thou dwellest as its Lord, not only as in Thine own house, nor even as in Thine own bed, but

---

[1] E.p. omits: 'which . . . substance.'

intimately and closely united as in mine own bosom—how gentle and how loving is this! That is, it is exceedingly gentle and loving; and in this delectable breathing which in this Thine awakening Thou makest delectable for me, filled as it is with blessing and glory, with what delicacy dost Thou inspire me with love and affection for Thyself! Herein the soul uses a similitude of the breathing of one that awakens from his sleep; for in truth, the soul in this condition feels it to be so. There follows the line:

How gently and lovingly thou awakenest in my bosom,

4. There are many ways in which God awakens in the soul: so many that, if we had to enumerate them, we should never end. But this awakening of the Son of God which the soul here desires to describe, is, as I believe, one of the loftiest and one which brings the most good to the soul. For this awakening is a movement of the Word in the substance[1] of the soul, of such greatness and dominion and glory, and of such intimate sweetness, that it seems to the soul that all the balms and perfumed spices and flowers in the world are mingled and shaken and revolved together to give that sweetness; and that all the kingdoms and dominions of the world and all the powers and virtues of Heaven are moved.[2] And not only so, but all the virtues and substances and perfections and graces of all created things shine forth and make the same movement together and in unison. For, as Saint John says, all things in Him are life,[3] and in Him they live and are and move, as the Apostle says likewise.[4] Hence it comes to pass that, when this great Emperor moves in the soul, Whose kingdom, as Isaias says, is borne upon His shoulders[5] (namely, the three

---

[1] E.p.: 'in the depth.'
[2] A, B, T: 'move it.'
[3] St. John i, 3.
[4] Acts xvii, 28.
[5] Isaias ix, 6. E.p.: 'Hence it comes to pass that, when this great Emperor is pleased to reveal Himself to the soul, moving

spheres, the celestial, the terrestrial and the infernal, and the things that are in them; and He sustains them all, as Saint Paul says, in the Word of His power),[6] then all the spheres seem to move together. Just as, when the earth moves, all material things that are upon it move likewise, as if they were nothing, even so,[7] when this Prince moves, He carries His court with Him, and the court carries not Him.

5. Yet this comparison is highly unsuitable, for in this latter case not only do all seem to be moving, but they also reveal the beauties of their being, virtue, loveliness and graces, and the root of their duration and life. For there the soul is able to see how all creatures, above and below,[8] have their life and duration in Him, and it sees clearly that which the Book of Wisdom expresses in these words: 'By Me kings reign, by Me princes rule and the powerful exercise justice and understand it.'[9] And although it is true that the soul is now able to see that these things are distinct from God, inasmuch as they have a created being, and it sees them in Him, with their force, root and strength, it knows equally that God, in His own Being, is all these things, in an infinite and pre-eminent way, to such a point that it understands them better in His Being[10] than in themselves. And this is the great delight of this awakening:[11] to know the creatures through God and not God through the creatures; to know the effects through their cause and not the cause through the effects; for the latter knowledge is secondary and this other is essential.[12]

---

by means of this manner of enlightenment and yet not moving in the soul, Who bears His kingdom, as Isaias says, upon His shoulder.'

[6] Hebrews i, 3.

[7] E.p.: 'Just as, if the earth were to move, all natural things that are upon it would move likewise, even so.'

[8] E.p.: 'inferior and superior.'

[9] The quotation is from Proverbs viii, 15.

[10] E.p.: 'in this its beginning.'

[11] E.p. adds here: 'to know the effects through their cause' and omits the remainder of the paragraph.

[12] C omits this and the preceding clause.

6. And the manner of this knowledge[13] in the soul, since God is immovable, is a wondrous thing, for, although in reality God moves not,[14] it seems to the soul that He is indeed moving; for, as the soul is renewed and moved by God that it may behold this supernatural sight, and there is revealed to it in this great renewal that Divine life and the being and harmony of every creature in it which has its movements in God, it seems to the soul that it is God that is moving, and thus the cause takes the name of the effect which it produces, according to which effect it may be said that God is moving, even as the Wise Man says: 'Wisdom is more movable than all movable things.'[15] And this is not because it moves itself, but because it is the beginning and root of all movement; remaining in itself stable, as the passage goes on to say, it renews all things. And thus what is here meant is that wisdom is more active than all active things. And thus we should say here that it is the soul that is moved in this motion, and is awakened from the sleep of its natural vision to a supernatural vision,[16] for which reason it is very properly given the name of an awakening.

7. But God, as the soul has been enabled to see, is always moving, ruling and giving being and virtue and grace and gifts to all creatures, containing them all in Himself, virtually, presentially and substantially;[17] so that in one single glance[18] the soul sees that which God is in Himself and that which He is in the creatures. Even so, when a palace is thrown open, a man may see at one and the same time the eminence of the person who is within the palace

[13] E.p.: 'of this movement.'
[14] E.p. omits 'in reality' and continues: 'the soul is renewed and moved by Him, and there is revealed to it in a wondrous renewal that Divine life and the being and harmony of every creature, so that the cause takes the name,' etc.
[15] Wisdom vii, 24.
[16] E.p. omits: 'from the sleep . . . supernatural vision.'
[17] E.p.: 'and most eminently.'
[18] E.p. omits: 'in one single glance.'

and also what he is doing. And it is this, as I understand, that happens upon this awakening and glance of the soul. Though the soul is substantially in God, as is every creature,[19] He draws back from before it some of the veils and curtains which are in front of it, so that it may see of what nature He is,[20] and then there is revealed to it, and it is able to see (though somewhat darkly, since not all the veils are drawn back)[21] that face of His[22] that is full of graces. And, since it is moving all things by its power, there appears together with it that which it is doing, and it appears to move in them, and they in it, with continual movement; and for this reason the soul believes that God has moved and awakened, whereas in reality that which has moved and awakened is itself.

8. For such is the lowly nature of this kind of life which we live that we believe others to be as we are ourselves; and we judge others as we are ourselves, so that our judgment begins with[23] ourselves and not outside ourselves. In this way the thief believes that others steal likewise; and he that lusts, that others are lustful like himself; and he that bears malice, that others bear malice, his judgment proceeding from his own malice; and the good man thinks well of others, his judgment proceeding from the goodness of his own thoughts; and so likewise he that is negligent and slothful[24] thinks that others are the same. And hence, when we are negligent and slothful in the sight of God, we think that it is God Who is slothful and negligent with us, as we read in the forty-third Psalm, where David says to God: 'Arise, Lord, why sleepest Thou?'[25] He attributes to God qualities that are in man; for though it is they that have fallen and are asleep, yet it is God Whom he bids arise

19 E.p. omits: 'Though the soul . . . creature.'
20 E.p.: 'may see what He is.'
21 E.p. adds: 'for there remains that of faith.'
22 E.p.: 'that Divine face.'
23 So T. A, B, C, G, Gr: 'proceeds from and begins with.'
24 [Lit., 'asleep'; and so also below.]
25 Psalm xliii, 23 [A.V., xliv, 23].

and awaken, though He that keepeth Israel never sleeps.

9. But in truth, though every blessing that comes to man is from God,[26] and man, of his own power, can do naught that is good, it is true to say that our awakening is an awakening of God, and our uprising is an uprising of God. And thus it is as though David had said: Raise us up and raise us up again[27] and awaken us, for we are asleep and we have fallen in two ways. Wherefore, since the soul had fallen into a sleep, whence of itself it could never awaken, and it is God alone that has been able to open its eyes and cause this awakening, it very properly describes it as an awakening of God, in these words: 'Thou awakenest in my bosom.' Do Thou awaken us, then, and enlighten us, my Lord, that we may know and love the blessings that Thou hast ever set before us, and we shall know that Thou hast been moved to grant us favours, and that Thou hast been mindful of us.

10. That which the soul knows and feels in this awakening concerning the excellence of God is wholly indescribable,[28] for, since there is a communication of the excellence of God in the substance of the soul, which is that breast of the soul whereof the lines here speak, there is heard in the soul the immense power of the voice of a multitude of excellences, of thousands upon thousands of virtues.[29] In these the soul is entrenched and remains terribly and firmly arrayed among them like ranks of armies and made sweet and gracious in all the sweetnesses and graces of the creatures.[30]

---

[26] E.p. abbreviates, from the end of § 7, thus: 'there appears together with it that which it is doing. And this is the awakening of the soul, although furthermore, in truth, though every blessing that comes to man is from God.'

[27] [Lit., 'Raise us up twice.']

[28] A, Bz, T, e.p.: 'invisible.'

[29] G, Gr, add: 'of God, which can never be numbered.'

[30] E.p.: 'concerning the excellence of God in the depth of the soul is wholly indescribable. This is the sleep of the soul whereof the lines here speak. There resounds in the soul an im-

11. But this question will be raised: How can the soul bear so violent[31] a communication while in the flesh, when indeed there is no means and strength in it to suffer so greatly and not faint away, since the mere sight of King Assuerus on his throne, in royal apparel and adorned with gold and precious stones,[32] caused Queen Esther such great fear when she saw how terrible he was to behold that she fainted away, as she confesses in that place where she says she fainted away by reason of the fear caused by his great glory, since he seemed to her like an angel and his face was full of graces.[33] For glory oppresses him that looks upon it if it glorifies not. And how much more should the soul faint here, since it is no angel that it sees, but God, Whose face is full of graces[34] of all the creatures and of terrible power and glory and Whose voice is the multitude of His excellences? Concerning this Job enquires, when we have such difficulty in hearing a drop,[35] who shall be able to abide the greatness of His thunder.[36] And elsewhere he says: 'I will not that He contend and treat with me with much strength, lest perchance He oppress me with the weight of His greatness.'[37]

12. But the reason why the soul faints not away and fears not in this awakening which is so powerful and glorious is twofold. First, being, as it now is, in the state of

_____

mense power, in the voice of a multitude of excellences, of thousands upon thousands of virtues. In these the soul halts and stops, and remains terribly and firmly arrayed like hosts of armies, and made sweet and gracious in that which comprises all the sweetnesses and graces of the creatures.'

[31] [*Lit.*, 'so strong.']

[32] Gr, T: 'precious pearls.'

[33] Esther xv, 16.

[34] E.p.: 'since it is no angel that it knows, but God Himself, the Lord of the angels, Whose face is full of graces.'

[35] Several MSS. have 'particle' [cf. A.V., 'portion']. A reads: 'spark.' E.p. has: 'if we can scarcely hear a whisper thereof, how shall one be able,' etc.

[36] Job xxvi, 14.

[37] Job xxiii, 6.

perfection, wherein its lower part is throughly purged and
conformed with the spirit, it has not the suffering and pain
that are wont to be experienced in spiritual communications
of spirit and sense when these are not purged and prepared
to receive them; although this suffices not to prevent the
soul from suffering when it is faced with such greatness
and glory; since, although its nature be very pure, yet it
will be corrupted because it exceeds nature, even as a
physical faculty is corrupted by any sensible thing which
exceeds its power,[38] in which sense must be taken that
which we quoted from Job. The second reason is the more
relevant: it is that which the soul gave in the first line—
namely, that God shows Himself gentle and loving. For,
just as God shows the soul this greatness and glory in
order to comfort and magnify it, just so does He grant it
grace so that it receives no suffering, and protect its nature,
showing the spirit His greatness, with tenderness and love,
without the natural senses perceiving this, so that the soul
knows not if it is in the body or out of the body.[39] This may
easily be done by that God Who protected Moses with His
right hand that he might see His glory.[40] And thus the
soul feels the gentleness and lovingness of God proportionately to His power and dominion and greatness, since in
God all these things are one and the same. And thus the
delight of the soul is strong, and the protection given to it
is strong in gentleness and love, so that it may be able to
endure the strength of this delight; and thus the soul, far

[38] [This reading is obtained by substituting in the Spanish
text *excedente* for *excelente*, a change suggested by P. Gurdon.
No other reading seems to make sense of the passage.]

[39] E.p. abbreviates: 'and prepared to receive them. The second
and more important reason is that which is given in the first line
—namely, that God shows Himself gentle and loving. For, just
as He shows the soul this greatness and glory in order to comfort
and magnify it, just so does He grant it grace and strength, and
protect its nature, showing His greatness to the spirit with tenderness and love.'

[40] Exodus xxxiii, 22.

from fainting away, becomes strong and powerful. For, when Esther swooned, this was because the King showed himself to her at first unfavourably; for, as we read in that place, he showed her his burning[41] eyes and the fury of his breast. But when he looked favourably upon her, stretching out his sceptre and touching her with it and embracing her, she returned to herself, for he had said to her that he was her brother and she was not to fear.

13. And thus, when the King of Heaven has shown Himself as a friend to the soul, as its equal[42] and its brother, the soul is no longer afraid. For when, in gentleness and not in wrath, He shows to it the strength of His power and the love of His goodness, He communicates to it the strength and love of His breast, and comes out to it from the throne (which is the soul[43]), even as a spouse from his bridal chamber where he was hidden. He inclines to the soul, touches it with the sceptre of His majesty and embraces it as a brother. The soul beholds the royal apparel and perceives its fragrance—namely, the wondrous virtues of God; it observes the splendour of gold, which is charity; it sees the glittering of the precious stones, which are knowledge of created substances, both higher and lower;[44] it looks upon the face of the Word, which is full of graces that strike this queen (which is the soul) and likewise clothe her, so that she is transformed in these virtues of the King of Heaven and sees herself a queen indeed, and says of herself truly that which David says in the forty-fourth Psalm, namely: 'The queen stood at Thy right hand in apparel of gold and surrounded with variety.'[45] And, since all this comes to pass in the inmost substance of the soul, it adds next:

Where thou dwellest secretly and alone!

41 E.p.: 'burning and enkindled.'
42 E.p.: 'as its Spouse.'
43 E.p. omits: 'which is the soul.'
44 E.p.: 'which are supernatural knowledge.'
45 Psalm xliv, 10 [A.V., xlv, 9].

14. The soul says that He dwells secretly in its breast, because, as we have said, this sweet embrace is made in the depth of the substance of the soul.[1] That is to say that God dwells secretly in all souls[2] and is hidden in their substance; for, were this not so, they would be unable to exist. But there is a difference between these two manners of dwelling, and a great one. For in some He dwells alone, and in others He dwells not alone; in some He dwells contented[3] and in others He dwells displeased; in some He dwells as in His house, ordering it and ruling everything, while in others He dwells as a stranger in the house of another, where He is not allowed to do anything or to give any commands. Where He dwells with the greatest content and most completely alone is in the soul wherein dwell fewest desires and pleasures of its own; here He is in His own house and rules and governs it. And the more completely alone does He dwell in the soul, the more secretly He dwells; and thus in this soul wherein dwells no desire neither any other image or form of aught that is created, He dwells most secretly, with the more intimate, more interior and closer embrace, according as the soul, as we say, is the more purely and completely withdrawn from all save God. And thus He dwells secretly, since the devil cannot attain to this place and to this embrace, neither can any understanding attain[4] to a knowledge of the manner thereof. But He dwells not secretly with respect to the soul which is in this state of perfection, for it ever perceives that He is within it. Only when the Beloved causes these awakenings to take place does it seem to the soul that He Who aforetime was asleep in its bosom is awakening; and, although it felt and enjoyed His presence, it was as if the Beloved were asleep in its

---

[1] E.p. adds: 'and its faculties.'

[2] C adds: 'as absolute lord of them.'

[3] E.p. abbreviates: 'But there is a difference between these two manners of dwelling; for in some He dwells contented.'

[4] E.p.: 'well attain.'

bosom;[5] and the understanding and love of two persons cannot be mutually communicated until both have awakened.[6]

15. Oh, how happy is this soul that is ever conscious of God reposing and resting within its breast! Oh, how well is it that it should withdraw from all things, flee from business and live in boundless tranquillity, lest anything, however small,[7] should disturb or move the bosom[8] of the Beloved within it. He is there, habitually, as it were, asleep in this embrace with the substance of the soul;[9] and of this the soul is quite conscious, and habitually has full fruition,[10] for, if He were forever awake within it, what would this state be like? Knowledge and love would be forever communicated to the soul, and it would be living in glory. For, if one single awakening of God within the soul, and one glance from His eye, set it in such bliss, as we have said, what would its condition be if He were habitually awake[11] within it?

16. In other souls, that have not attained to this union, He dwells secretly likewise; and He is not displeased, because they are not yet perfectly prepared for union. Such souls are not as a rule conscious of His presence save when He effects certain delectable awakenings within them, but these are not of the same kind as that other awakening, nor have they aught to do with it. This awakening is not so secret from the devil, or from the understanding, as that other, for something can always be understood concerning it by means of the movements of sense, inasmuch as sense is not completely annihilated until the soul attains to union, but still preserves certain actions pertaining to the

[5] E.p. ends the paragraph here.
[6] C: 'for when one of two persons is asleep, the understanding of both cannot be mutually communicated until both are awake.'
[7] [Lit., 'lest a speck.']
[8] A: 'or renew the sleep' [renueve el sueño for remueva el seno].
[9] E.p.: 'with the soul.'
[10] C adds: 'of His awakenings, though not always.'
[11] A, T: 'habitually disposed.'

147

spiritual element,[12] for it is not yet wholly spiritualized. But in this awakening which the Spouse effects in this perfect soul, everything is perfect; for it is He that is its sole cause.[13] Thus, in that inspiration and awakening, which is as if a man awakened and breathed, the soul is conscious of the breathing of God, wherefore it says:

And in thy sweet breathing, full of blessing and glory, How delicately thou inspirest my love!

17. Of that breathing of God I should not wish to speak, neither do I desire now to speak; for I see clearly that I cannot say aught concerning it, and that, were I to speak of it, it would seem less[1] than it is. For it is a breathing of God Himself,[2] wherein, in that awakening of lofty knowledge of the Deity, the Holy Spirit breathes into the soul in proportion to the knowledge[3] wherein He most profoundly absorbs it in the Holy Spirit, inspiring it with most delicate love for Himself according to that which it has seen; for, the soul being[4] full of blessing and glory, the Holy Spirit has filled it with goodness and glory, wherein He has inspired it with a love for Himself which transcends all description and all sense, in the deep things of God. And for that reason I leave speaking of it here.[5]

[12] E.p. omits: 'pertaining to the spiritual element.' C has 'sensual' for 'spiritual.'
[13] E.p. adds: 'in the sense mentioned above.'
[1] C: 'much less.'
[2] E.p. adds: 'to the soul.'
[3] C: 'to the intelligence and knowledge.'
[4] Bz, C, Gr, e.p.: 'for, His breathing being.'
[5] E.p.: 'wherein He inspires it with a love for Himself which transcends all glory and all sense, and for that reason I leave speaking of it.'

Exposition of the stanzas which treat of the most intimate and perfected union and transformation of the soul in God, written by P. Fray John of the Cross, Discalced Carmelite, at the request of Doña Ana de Peñalosa and composed in prayer by their author in the year 1584.[1]

PROLOGUE

I HAVE felt some unwillingness, most noble and devout lady, to expound these four stanzas which you have requested me to explain, for they relate to things so interior and spiritual that words commonly fail to describe them, since spirit transcends sense and it is with difficulty that anything can be said of the substance of the spirit[2] if one have not deep spirituality. Wherefore, having little thereof myself, I have delayed writing until now, when it appears that the Lord has opened knowledge somewhat to me and given me some fervour (which must arise from your devout desire, for perhaps, as these words have been written for you,[3] His Majesty desires them to be expounded for you). So I have taken courage, knowing for certain that out of my own resources I can say naught that is of any value, especially in things of such sublimity and substance. Wherefore my part herein will be limited to the defects and errors that this book may contain, for which reason I submit it all to the better judgment and understanding of

[1] So S, with which are practically identical Bg and P. C omits the title, beginning with the word 'Prologue.' Bz begins: 'Stanzas made by the soul in the final union with God, made and commented by Father Fray John of the Cross.'

[2] Bg, P omit: 'of the spirit.' Bz, C read as in the first redaction.

[3] S: 'for your devotion.'

149

our holy[4] Mother the Roman Catholic Church, with whose guidance no man goes astray. And, with this preamble, relying upon Divine Scripture, and making clear that all which is said herein is as far removed from all that there is to say as is a picture from a living person, I shall make bold to say that which I know.

2. And there is no reason for marvelling that God should grant such high[5] and rare favours[6] to those souls on whom He bestows consolations. For if we consider that He is God, and that He bestows them as God, with infinite love and goodness, it will not seem to us unreasonable. For God said that the Father and the Son and the Holy Spirit would come to him that loved Him and make their abode in him,[7] and this would come to pass by His making him live and dwell in the Father and the Son and the Holy Spirit, in the life of God, as the soul explains in these stanzas.

3. For although in the stanzas which we expounded above we spoke of the most perfect degree of perfection[8] to which a man may attain in this life, which is transformation in God, nevertheless these stanzas treat of a love which is even more completed and perfected within this same state of transformation. For, although it is true that both those stanzas and these speak of a state of transformation beyond which, as such, a soul cannot pass, yet none the less, with time and practice, as I say, the soul may become more completely perfected and grounded in love. Even so, when a log of wood has been set upon the fire, it is transformed into fire and united with it;[9] yet, as the fire grows hotter and the wood remains upon it for a longer time, it glows much more and becomes more completely enkindled, until it gives out sparks of fire and flame.

[4] Bz, S omit: 'holy.'
[5] Bg, P: 'such high and sublime.'
[6] Bz: 'such high and rare marvels and favours.'
[7] St. John xiv, 23.
[8] C: 'of prayer and perfection.'
[9] Bg, P: 'and consumed in it.'

4. And it is of this degree of enkindled love that the soul must be understood as speaking when it is at last so far transformed and perfected interiorly in the fire of love[10] that not only is it united with this fire but it has now become one living flame within it. Such the soul feels itself to be, and as such it speaks in these stanzas, with an intimate and delicate sweetness of love, burning in the flame thereof, and extolling in these stanzas certain effects thereof which are wrought in itself. These I shall expound in the same order as with the other stanzas, setting them down first all together, then setting down each stanza and expounding it briefly, and finally setting down each line and expounding it by itself alone.[11]

[10] C: 'of Divine love.'
[11] C: 'and finally expounding each verse by itself alone.' S adds: 'Fray John of the Cross, Discalced Carmelite.' C adds: 'Fray John of the ✠. Soli Deo honor et gloria. Amen.'

END OF THE PROLOGUE

STANZAS MADE BY THE SOUL
IN THE INTIMATE UNION OF GOD[1]

1. Oh, living flame of love   That tenderly woundest my
   soul in its deepest centre,[2]
   Since thou art no longer oppressive, perfect me now if it
   be thy will,   Break the web of this sweet encounter.

2. Oh, sweet burn![3]   Oh, delectable wound!   Oh, soft
   hand!   Oh, delicate touch
   That savours of eternal life and pays every debt!   In
   slaying, thou hast changed death into life.

3. Oh, lamps of fire,   In whose splendours the deep caverns of sense which were dark and blind
   With strange brightness   Give heat and light together to
   their Beloved!

4. How gently and lovingly thou awakenest in my bosom,
   Where thou dwellest secretly and alone!
   And in thy sweet breathing, full of blessing and glory,
   How delicately thou inspirest my love![4]

[1] S adds: 'its Beloved Spouse.'
[2] Bz, P: 'That tenderly woundest the deepest centre of my soul.'
[3] Bz: 'Oh, sweet captivity!' [*cautiverio* for *cauterio*].
[4] The MSS. here add the note which will be found above as
note 2 on pp. 30–31.

STANZA THE FIRST

Oh, living flame of love   That tenderly woundest my soul
in its deepest centre,[1]
Since thou art no longer oppressive, perfect me now if it be
thy will,   Break the web of this sweet encounter.

EXPOSITION

THE SOUL feels itself to be at last wholly enkindled in
Divine union, and its palate to be wholly bathed in glory
and love, and from the very inmost part[2] of its substance to
be flowing veritable rivers of glory, abounding in delights,
for it perceives that from its belly are flowing the rivers of
living water which the Son of God said would flow from
such souls.[3] It seems to this soul that, since it is transformed in God with such vehemence and is in so lofty a
way possessed of Him, and is adorned with such a marvell-
lous wealth of gifts and virtues, it is very near to bliss, from
which it is divided only by a slender web. And, seeing that
that delicate flame of love that burns within it is, as it
were, glorifying it with a glory both gentle and powerful
whensoever it assails it, to such a degree that, whensoever
it is absorbed and assailed, it believes that it is about to
enter upon eternal life[4] and that this web of mortal life
will be broken, and that there remains but a very short
space of time, yet during this space it cannot be perfectly
glorified in its essence, the soul addresses this flame, which
is the Holy Spirit, with great yearning, begging Him now
to break this its mortal life in that sweet encounter, so
that of a truth He may communicate to it perfectly that

[1] P: 'That tenderly woundest the deepest centre of my soul'
[2] Bg, C, P: 'from the very last part.'
[3] St. John vii, 38.
[4] Bg, P: 'eternal life and glory.'

153

which it believes Him to be about to give to it whensoever He meets it—namely, complete and perfect glory. And thus the soul says:

Oh, living flame of love

2. In order to extol the fervour and delight wherewith it speaks in these four stanzas, the soul begins each of them with the word 'Oh' or 'How,' which words signify affectionate exultation. Each time that they are used they show that something is passing within the soul beyond that which can be expressed by the tongue. And the word 'Oh' serves also to express a deep yearning and earnest supplication with the aim of persuasion; for both these reasons the soul uses that word in this stanza, intimating and extolling its great desire, and endeavouring to persuade love to set it free.[1]

3. This flame of love is the Spirit of its Spouse—that is, the Holy Spirit. And this flame the soul feels within it, not only as a fire that has consumed and transformed it in sweet love, but also as a fire which burns within it and sends out flame, as I have said, and that flame, each time that it breaks forth, bathes the soul in glory and refreshes it with the temper of Divine life. And this is the operation of the Holy Spirit in the soul that is transformed in love, that the acts that He performs within it cause it to send out flames, which are the enkindling of love, wherein the will of the soul is united, and it loves most deeply, being made one with that flame in love. And thus these acts of love of the soul are most precious,[2] and even one of them is of greater merit and worth than all that the soul has done in its life apart from this transformation, however much this may be. Like to the difference that exists between a habit and an act is that which exists between transformation in love and the flame of love; it is the same difference as

[1] Bz: 'to desire it.' Bg, P read as in the text, but add: 'from mortal flesh.'
[2] Bg, P: 'most pure.'

that between the log of wood that is enkindled and the flame which it sends forth, for the flame is the effect of the fire that burns there.

4. Wherefore it may be said that the soul that is in this state of transformation of love is in its ordinary habit, and that it is like to the log of wood that is continually assailed by the fire; and the acts of this soul are the flame that arises from the fire of love: the more intense is the fire of union, the more vehemently does its flame issue forth. In this flame the acts of the will are united and rise upward, being carried away and absorbed in the flame of the Holy Spirit, even as the angel rose upward to God in the flame of the sacrifice of Manue.[3] In this state, therefore, the soul can perform no acts, but it is the Holy Spirit that performs them and moves it to perform them; wherefore all its acts are Divine, since it is impelled and moved to them by God. Hence it seems to the soul that whensoever this flame breaks forth, causing it to love with the Divine temper and sweetness, it is granting it eternal life, since it raises it to the operation of God in God.

5. This is the language used by God when He speaks to souls that are purified and clean: words wholly enkindled,[4] even as David said: 'Thy word is vehemently enkindled.'[5] And the Prophet asked: 'Are not my words as a fire?'[6] These words, as God Himself says, through Saint John, are spirit and life,[7] and are felt to be such by souls that have ears to hear them, who, as I say, are souls that are pure and enkindled with love. But those that have not a healthy palate,[8] and desire other things, cannot relish the spirit and life that these words contain, but rather find insipidity in them. For this reason, the loftier were the words spoken

---

[3] Judges xiii, 20.
[4] Bg, P: 'these words are wholly enkindled.'
[5] Psalm cxviii, 140. [*Ignitum eloquium tuum vehementer.*]
[6] Jeremias xxiii, 29.
[7] St. John vi, 64.
[8] Bg, P: 'that keep not their palate clean.'

by the Son of God, the more they displeased certain persons because of these persons' impurity, as when the Lord preached that sweet[9] and loving doctrine of the Holy Eucharist, and many of His hearers turned back.[10]

6. Because such persons are not attracted by this language of God, which He speaks inwardly, they must not think that others will not be attracted by it. On the occasion here mentioned it greatly attracted Saint Peter, so that he said to Christ: 'Lord, whither shall we go, for Thou hast the words of eternal life?'[11] And the Samaritan woman forgot her water and her pitcher, because of the sweetness of the words of God. And thus, when this soul is so near to God that it is transformed in the flame of love, wherein the Father and the Son and the Holy Spirit communicate Themselves to it, how is it a thing incredible that it should be said to enjoy a foretaste of eternal life, though this cannot be perfectly so, since that is not permitted by the conditions of this life? But the delight caused in the soul by that flaming of the Holy Spirit is so sublime that it teaches the soul what is the savour of eternal life. For that reason it speaks of the flame as living; not that it is not always living, but because its effect is to make the soul live spiritually in God, and experience[12] the life of God, even as David says: 'My heart and my flesh have rejoiced in the living God.'[13] There was no necessity for him to use the word 'living,'[14] since God is ever living; he uses it to show that spirit and sense had a living experience of God, being wrought in God[15]—which is to have experience[16] of the living God, that is to say, the life of God and life eternal. David spoke in that passage of the living God because he

[9] S: 'that sovereign.'
[10] [St. John vi, 67.]
[11] St. John vi, 69.
[12] Bg, P: 'and live.'
[13] Psalm lxxxiii, 3 [A.V., lxxxiv, 2].
[14] Bg, P: 'to use the words "living God." '
[15] Bg, P: 'being made living in God.'
[16] [Cf. p. 36, n. 22, above.]

had had experience of Him in a living manner, albeit not perfectly, but he had had, as it were, a foretaste of eternal life. And thus in this flame the soul has so living[17] a perception of God and experiences Him with such great sweetness and delight that it says: 'Oh, living flame of love!'

That tenderly woundest

7. That is, that touchest me tenderly with Thy heat. For, inasmuch as this flame is a flame of Divine life, it wounds the soul with the tenderness of the life of God; and so deeply and profoundly does it wound it and fill it with tenderness that it causes it to melt in love, so that there may be fulfilled in it that which came to pass to the Bride in the Song of Songs. She conceived such great tenderness that she melted away, wherefore she says in that place: 'When the Spouse spake, my soul melted.'[1] For this is the effect that the speaking of God causes in the soul.

8. But how can we say that this flame wounds the soul, when there is nothing in the soul to be wounded, since it is wholly consumed[2] by the fire of love? It is a marvellous thing: for, as love is never idle, but is continually in movement, it is ever throwing out sparks, like a flame, in every direction; and, as the office of love is to wound, that it may enkindle with love and cause delight, so, when it is, as it were, a living flame within the soul, it is ever sending forth its arrow-wounds, like most tender sparks of delicate love, joyfully and happily exercising the arts and playings of love. Even so, in his palace,[3] at his marriage, did Assuerus show forth his graces to Esther his bride,[4] revealing to her there his riches and the glory of his greatness.[5] Thus that which the Wise Man said in the Proverbs is now ful-

---

17 Bz: 'has so certain.'
1 Canticles v, 6.
2 Bg, P: 'wholly captivated and consumed.'
3 Bg, P: 'in the palace of his love.'
4 C: 'his fairest bride.'
5 [Esther ii, 17–18.]

filled in this soul, namely: 'I was delighted every day as I played[6] before him at all times, playing over all lands, and my delight is to be with the children of men, namely, by giving myself to them.'[7] Wherefore these wounds, which are the playings[8] of God, are the sparks of these tender touches of flame which touch the soul intermittently and proceed from the fire of love, which is not idle, but whose flames, says the stanza, strike and wound

My soul in its deepest centre,

9. For this feast of the Holy Spirit takes place in the substance of the soul, where neither the devil nor the world nor sense can enter;[1] and therefore the more interior[2] it is, the more is it secure, substantial and delectable; for the more interior it is, the purer is it, and the more of purity there is in it, the more abundantly and frequently and widely does God communicate Himself. And thus the delight and rejoicing of the soul and the spirit is the greater herein because it is God that works all this and the soul of its own power does naught therein; for the soul can do naught of itself, save through the bodily senses and by their help, from which in this case the soul is very free and very far removed, its only business being the reception of God, Who alone can work in the depth[3] of the soul, without the aid of the senses, and can move the soul therein. And thus all the movements of such a soul are Divine; and, although they come from Him, they belong to the soul likewise, for God works them in the soul, with its own aid, since it gives its will and consent thereto. And, since to say that He wounds the soul in its deepest centre is to imply that the soul has other centres which are less

---

[6] Bz: 'We were delighted every day as we played.'

[7] Proverbs viii, 30–1.

[8] Bg, P: 'the fires' [*fuegos* for *juegos*].

[1] Bg, P: 'where neither sense enters nor can the devil attain.'

[2] Bg, P: 'the more delectable and interior.'

[3] Bg, P: 'in the depth and inmost part.'

rofound,[4] it is necessary to explain in what way this is so.

10. In the first place, it must be known that the soul, nasmuch as it is spirit, has neither height nor depth, neither reater nor lesser degrees of profundity in its own being, s have bodies that can be measured. For, since there are o parts in the soul, there is no difference between its inward and its outward being; it is all the same, and it has no lepths of greater or lesser profundity of a kind that can be measured; for it cannot be more enlightened in one part han in another, as is the case with physical bodies, but the vhole of it is enlightened in one manner, either to a greater or to a lesser degree, in the same way as the air is enlightened or unenlightened,[5] to a greater or a lesser degree.

11. We term the deepest centre of a thing the farthest point to which its being and virtue and the force of its operation and movement can attain, and beyond which they cannot pass. Thus fire and a stone have natural movement and power, and strength to reach the centre of their sphere, and cannot pass beyond it, neither can help reaching it and remaining in it, save by reason of some contrary and violent impediment. Accordingly, we shall say that a stone, when in some way it is within the earth, is in some way in its centre, and this although it be not in the deepest part of the earth, because it is within the sphere of its centre and activity and movement; but we shall not say that it is in its deepest centre, which is the middle of the earth, and therefore it still has power and force and inclination to descend and to attain to this farthest and deepest centre if that which impedes it be taken away; and when it attains to its centre and there remains to it no more power and inclination of its own to move farther, we shall say that it is in its deepest centre.

12. The centre of the soul is God; and, when the soul has attained to Him according to the whole capacity[6] of

[4] Bz, C, S: 'other and profounder centres.'
[5] Bz omits: 'or unenlightened.'
[6] P: 'according to the quality.'

its being, and according to the force of its operation and inclination, it will have reached its last and deepest centre in God, which will be when with all its powers it understands and loves and enjoys God; and, so long as it has not attained as far as this, as is the case in this mortal life, wherein the soul cannot attain to God with all its powers,[7] then, although it be in this its centre, which is God, by grace and by His own communication which He has with it, still, inasmuch as it has the power of movement and strength to go farther, and is not satisfied, then, although it may be in the centre,[8] it is nevertheless not in the deepest centre, since it is capable of going to the deepest centre of God.[9]

13. It is to be observed, then, that love is the inclination of the soul and the strength and power which it has to go to God, for, by means of love, the soul is united with God; and thus, the more degrees of love the soul has, the more profoundly does it enter into God and the more is it centred in Him. Therefore we can say that, as are the degrees of the love of God of which the soul is capable, so are the centres of which it is capable in God, each one being more interior than another; for the strongest love is the most unitive love,[10] and in this sense we may understand the many mansions which, said the Son of God, were in His Father's house.[11] So that, for the soul to be in its centre, which is God, as we have said, it suffices for it to have one degree of love, since with one degree alone it may be united with Him through grace. If it have two degrees of love, it will be united and have entered into another and a more interior centre[12] with God; and, if it attain to three, it will have entered into the third; and, if it attain to the last degree, the love of God will succeed in wounding the soul

[7] Bz omits: 'with all its powers.'
[8] C: 'although it is satisfied.'
[9] S: 'the deepest centre in God.'
[10] C: 'the most vital love.'
[11] St. John xiv, 2.
[12] C: 'degree.'

even in its remotest and deepest centre—that is, in transforming and enlightening it as regards all its being and
power and virtue, such as it is capable of receiving, until it
be brought into such a state that it appears to be God. In
this state it is as when the crystal that is clear and pure is
assailed by the light; the more degrees of light it receives, the
greater concentration of light there is in it, and the greater
is its enlightenment. And the copiousness of light may
reach such a point that it comes to appear to be wholly
light, and cannot be distinguished from the light; being
enlightened to the greatest possible extent, it appears to be
light itself.[13]

14. And thus, when the soul says here that the flame of
love wounds it in its deepest centre, it means that the Holy
Spirit wounds and assails it in the farthest point attained
by its own substance, virtue and power. This it says, not
because it desires to indicate here that this flame wounds
it as substantially and completely as it will do in the beatific
vision of God in the life to come, for, although in this
mortal life the soul may reach as high a state of perfection
as that whereof we are speaking, it reaches not the perfect
state of glory, nor can it do so, although peradventure it
may happen that God will grant it such a favour fleetingly.
But it says this to indicate the copiousness and abundance
of delight and glory of which it is conscious in this kind of
communication in the Holy Spirit. This delight is the
greater and the more tender when the soul is the more
fervently and substantially transformed and centred in
God; and this, being the maximum to which the soul can
attain in this life (though, as we say, not as perfectly as
in the life to come), is called the deepest centre. It is true
that the habit of charity in the soul may be as perfect in
this life as in the next, but neither its operation nor its
fruit can be so, although the fruit and the operation of love

13 C abbreviates: 'to appear to be wholly light, and there is
no kind of distinction between it and the light, but all appears
to be light.'

grow in this state to such an extent that they become very much like those of the life to come; so much so that to the soul it appears that they are so and it ventures to use those words which one ventures to use only of the next life, namely: 'in the deepest centre of my soul.'

15. And since rare occurrences, of which few have had experience,[14] are the more marvellous and the less credible, as is that which we are describing as happening to the soul in this state, I do not doubt that certain persons, who understand it not through their learning neither know it by experience,[15] will either disbelieve it or will consider it to be exaggerated, or will think that it is not in itself as great a thing as it is. But to all these I reply that the Father of lights, Whose hand is not shortened and Who, like the sun's ray, sheds His blessings abundantly without respect of persons, wheresoever there is cause, showing Himself likewise joyfully to men as they walk in the roads and paths, hesitates not, neither disdains, to have His delights in common[16] with the sons of men all over the round earth. And it must not be held incredible that in a faithful soul which has already been tried and proved and purged in the fire of tribulations and trials and various temptations, and found faithful in love, there should be fulfilled that which was promised by the Son of God—namely that, if any man loved Him, the Holy Spirit would come within him and would abide and dwell in him.[17] And this comes to pass when the understanding is divinely illumined in the wisdom of the Son, and the will is made glad in the Holy Spirit, and the Father, with His power and strength, absorbs the soul in the embrace and abyss of His sweetness.[18]

16. And if, as is truly the case, this habitually comes to

[14] C: 'have had knowledge.'
[15] S omits 'not' and has 'and' for 'neither.'
[16] Bz omits 'in common.'
[17] St. John xiv, 23.
[18] So C, S. Bz: 'in the delectable embrace of His sweetness.' Bg, P: 'in the embrace of His sweetness.'

pass in certain souls, it is credible that such a soul as that whereof we are speaking will not be backward in receiving these favours from God. For that which we are describing as coming to pass in it, through the operation of the Holy Spirit which He brings about in it, is much greater than that which comes to pass in the communication and transformation of love. For the one is like a burning coal; but the other, as we have said, is like a coal heated with such fervency[19] that it not only burns, but gives forth living flame. And thus these two kinds of union—that is, of union alone, and of love and union with enkindling of love—are in a certain way comparable respectively to the fire of God which, says Isaias, is in Sion, and to the furnace of God which is in Jerusalem.[20] The one signifies the Church Militant, wherein the fire of charity is enkindled to no extreme degree; and the other signifies the vision of peace, which is the Church Triumphant, where this fire is as in a furnace enkindled in perfection of love. Although, as we said, this soul has not attained to such perfection as this, yet, in comparison with the other and common union, it is like a furnace enkindled, and its vision is as much more peaceful and glorious and tender as the flame is brighter and more resplendent than that of a burning coal.

17. Therefore, when the soul feels that this living flame of love is communicating all blessings to it after a living manner, because this Divine love brings everything with it, it says: 'Oh, living flame of love, that tenderly woundest.' This is as though it were to say: Oh, love enkindled, that with thy loving movements art delectably glorifying me according to the capacity and power of my soul—that is to say, art giving me Divine intelligence according to the ability and capacity of my understanding, and communicating love to me according to the utmost power of my will, and delighting me in the substance of the soul with the torrent of thy delight, in thy Divine contact and substantial

[19] Bz: 'a coal which will absorb so much fire.'
[20] Isaias xxxi, 9.

union, according to the greater purity of my substance and the capacity and freedom of my memory. This comes to pass, and in a greater degree than it is possible for the soul to describe, at the time when this flame of love uprises in it. Inasmuch as the soul has been well purged[21] with respect to its substance and to its faculties—memory, understanding and will—the Divine Substance,[22] which, as the Wise Man says, toucheth all things by reason of its purity,[23] absorbs it in a profound and subtle and sublime manner; and in that absorption of the soul in wisdom, the Holy Spirit brings to pass the glorious vibrations of His flame;[24] and, since it is so sweet, the soul then says:

Since thou art no longer oppressive,[1]

18. That is to say, since thou dost no longer afflict or oppress or weary as thou didst aforetime. For it must be known that this flame, which is God,[2] when the soul was in the state of spiritual purgation—that is, when it was entering upon contemplation—was not as friendly and sweet to it as it now is in this state of union. And we must tarry here for some time in order to explain how this comes to pass.

19. Here it must be known that, before this Divine fire of love is introduced into the substance of the soul, and is united with it, by means of a purity and purgation which is perfect and complete, this flame, which is the Holy Spirit, is wounding the soul, and destroying and consuming in it the imperfections of its evil habits; and this is the operation of the Holy Spirit, wherein He prepares it for Divine union[3] and the transformation of love in God. For it must

21 Bg, P add: 'and made pure.'
22 Bg, P: 'the Divine Wisdom.'
23 Wisdom vii, 24.
24 C: 'of His soul' [*alma* for *llama*].
1 [Cf. p. 42, n. 1, above.]
2 Cf. p. 19, above.
3 S: 'for due union.'

be known that the same fire of love which afterwards is
united with the soul and glorifies it is that which aforetime
assailed it in order to purge it; even as the fire that penetrates
the log of wood is the same that first of all attacked and
wounded it with its flame, cleansing and stripping it of its
accidents of ugliness,[4] until, by means of its heat, it had
prepared it to such a degree that it could enter it and transform it into itself, which is what spiritual persons call the
Purgative Way. In this operation the soul endures great
suffering and experiences grievous afflictions in its spirit,
which habitually overflow into the senses, at which times
this flame is very oppressive. For in this preparatory state
of purgation the flame is not bright to it, but dark, and if it
gives it any light at all, it is only that it may see and feel
its own faults and miseries. Neither is it sweet to it, but
grievous; for, although at times it kindles within it the heat
of love, this is accompanied by torment and affliction. And
it is not delectable to it, but arid; for, although at times,
through its benignity, it gives the soul a certain amount of
comfort which will strengthen and encourage it, yet, both
before and after this happens, it compensates and recom-
penses it with further trials. Nor does it bring it either
refreshment or peace, but consumes and proves it, making it
to faint and grieve at its own self-knowledge. And thus it is
not glorious to it; rather it makes it miserable and bitter, by
means of the spiritual light of self-knowledge which it sheds
upon it;[5] for God sends fire, as Jeremias says, into its bones,
and instructs it, and, as David says likewise, tries it by fire.

20. And thus at this time the soul suffers great darkness
with respect to the understanding, great aridities and afflictions with respect to the will, and grievous knowledge of
its miseries in the memory, inasmuch as its spiritual eye is
very bright with respect to self-knowledge. And in its sub-

---

[4] [*Lit.*, 'its ugly accidents.'] C: 'its cold accidents' [*fríos* for
feos].
[5] Bz omits: 'by means . . . sheds upon it.'

stance the soul suffers from abandonment and the greatest[6] poverty. Dry and cold, and at times hot, it finds relief in naught, nor is there any thought[7] that can console it, nor can it even raise its heart to God, since this flame has become so oppressive to it. Even so, says Job, did God treat him in this operation, where he says: 'Thou art changed to be cruel to me.'[8] For, when the soul suffers all these things together, it seems to it in truth that God has become cruel to it and bitter.[9]

21. The sufferings of the soul at this time are indescribable: they are, indeed, very little less than those of purgatory.[10] I can think now of no way to describe this state of oppression, to explain how great it is and to show what an extreme is reached by that which the soul feels and suffers in it, save by using these words of Jeremias which refer to it: 'I am the man that see my poverty by the rod of His indignation; He hath threatened me and brought me into darkness and not into light; so greatly is He turned against me and turneth His hand. My skin and my flesh He hath made old: He hath broken my bones. He hath surrounded me round about and hath compassed me with gall and labour. He hath set me in dark places as those that are dead for ever. He hath builded against me round about, that I may not get out. He hath made my imprisonment heavy; yea, and when I have lifted up my voice and cried, He hath shut out my prayer. He hath obstructed my ways with square stones and hath turned my steps and my paths upside down.'[11] All this says Jeremias; and he continues at much greater length. Now, inasmuch as in this way God is remedying and curing the soul in its many infirmities that He may bring it health, the soul must needs suffer

[6] Bg, P: 'the profoundest.'
[7] Bz, C: 'a thought.'
[8] Job xxx, 21.
[9] [*Lit.*, 'and tasteless.']
[10] So Bz, C. The other authorities have 'of a purgatory.' Bg, P read: 'sometimes' for 'indeed.'
[11] Lamentations iii, 1–9.

in this purgation and remedy according to the nature of its sickness. For here, as it were, Tobias lays its heart upon the coals,[12] so that every kind of evil spirit is set free and driven away from it; and thus all its infirmities are here continually brought to light, and, being set before its eyes, are felt by it and cured.

22. And the weaknesses and miseries which the soul had aforetime hidden and set deep within it (which aforetime it neither saw nor felt) are now seen and felt by it, by means of the light and heat of the Divine fire, just as the humidity which was in the wood was not realized until the fire attacked it, and made it sweat and smoke and steam, as the imperfect soul does when it is brought near to this flame. For at this season—oh, wondrous thing!—there arise within the soul contraries against contraries, the things of the soul against the things of God, which assail the soul; and some of these, as the philosophers say, become visible in reacting to others, and they make war in the soul, striving to expel each other in order that they may reign within it. That is to say, the virtues and properties of God, which are perfect in the extreme, war against the habits and properties of the soul, which are imperfect in the extreme, so that the soul has to suffer the existence of two contraries within it. For, as this flame is of brightest light, and assails the soul, its light shines in the darkness of the soul, which is as dark as the light is bright; and then the soul is conscious of its vicious, natural darkness, which sets[13] itself against the supernatural light, and it is not conscious of the supernatural light, because it has it not within itself, as it has its own darkness, and the darkness comprehends not the light. And thus it will be conscious of this its darkness for so long as the light beats upon it, for souls can have no perception of their darkness save when the Divine light beats upon them and only when the Divine light drives out the darkness is the soul illumined and transformed and

12 Tobias vi, 16.
13 Bg, P: 'opposes.'

able to see the Divine light,[14] its spiritual eye having been cleansed and strengthened by the Divine light. For infinite light will produce total darkness in sight that is impure and weak and the faculty will be subdued by excess of sense. And thus this flame was oppressive to the soul in the sight of its understanding.

23. And since this flame is of itself extremely loving, it assails the will in a loving and a tender manner; and since the will is of itself extremely arid and hard, the hardness of the one is felt by comparison with the tenderness of the other, and the aridity of the one by comparison with the love of the other, and the will becomes conscious of its natural hardness and aridity with respect to God, when this flame beats lovingly and tenderly upon it. And it is not conscious of the love and tenderness of the flame (being prevented by its hardness and aridity, wherein these other contraries, tenderness and love, can find no place) until one group of the contraries is driven out by the other and the love and tenderness of God reign in the will. And in this way this flame has been oppressive to the will—in making it to feel and suffer its hardness and aridity. And in the same way, since this flame is most extensive and vast, and the will is restricted and narrow, the will is conscious of its narrowness and restraint while the flame is beating upon it, until the flame acts upon it and dilates and enlarges it and makes it able to receive it. And likewise, since this flame is sweet and delectable, and the spiritual palate of the will was distempered by the humours of inordinate[15] affections, it was insipid and bitter to it, and it was unable to taste the sweet food of the love of God. And so, when the will is brought near to this most extensive and most delectable flame, it is conscious also of its constraint and insipidity, and is not conscious of the savour of the flame because it

[14] Bg, P: 'beats upon it, and the soul will be enlightened and transformed and will be able to see the Divine light.'
[15] Bg, P: 'distempered.'

feels[16] none within itself, but feels only that which it has in itself—namely, its own misery. And finally, since this flame is of vast wealth and goodness and delight, and the soul of itself has great poverty and has no good thing of its own, nor can give any satisfaction, it realizes and is clearly conscious of its miseries and poverty and wickedness by contrast with this wealth and goodness and delight, and realizes not the wealth and goodness and delight of the flame (for wickedness comprehends not goodness, nor poverty, riches, and so forth) until this flame succeeds in purifying the soul, and together with transformation gives it riches, glories and delights. In this way the flame was at first oppressive to the soul beyond all description, by reason of the battle which was being waged within it by the contrary forces. God, Who is all perfection, wars against all the imperfect habits of the soul, so that He may transform it in Himself and make it sweet, bright and peaceful, as does the fire when it has entered the wood.

24. This severe purgation comes to pass in few souls—in those alone whom the Lord desires to raise to a higher degree of union; for He prepares each one with a purgation of greater or less severity, according to the degree to which He desires to raise it, and also according to its impurity and imperfection. And so this pain is like that of purgatory; for, just as in purgatory spirits are purged in order that they may be able to see God through clear vision in the life to come, so, after their own manner, souls are purged in this state in order that they may be able to be transformed in Him through love in this life.[17]

25. As to the intensity of this purgation—when it is greater and when less, and when it is according to the understanding and when according to the will and how according to the memory, and when and how it comes according to the substance of the soul, and likewise when it purges the entire soul and when its sensual part only, and

16 Bg, P: 'it has.'
17 Bz: 'in this union.'

how it may be known when it is of one kind and when of another, and at what time and point and season of the spiritual way it begins—we have treated this in the *Dark Night of the Ascent of Mount Carmel* and it affects not our purpose here, wherefore I speak not of it. It suffices here to know that God Himself, Who desires to enter the soul by union and transformation of love, is He that aforetime has been assailing it and purging it with the light and heat of His Divine flame, even as the fire that enters the wood is the same fire that has prepared it,[18] as we have said. And thus that very flame that has played inwardly upon the soul and is now sweet to it was aforetime oppressive to it, when it was playing upon it without.[19]

26. And it is this that the soul desires to convey when it says in this line: 'Since thou art no longer oppressive.' This, briefly, is as though the soul were to say: Since not only art thou not dark to me as thou wert aforetime, but art the Divine light of my understanding, wherewith I can now look upon thee, and dost not only not cause my weakness to faint, but art rather the strength of my will wherewith I can love thee and enjoy thee, now that it is wholly converted into Divine love, and since thou art not pain and affliction to the substance of my soul, but art rather its glory and delight and boundless freedom, therefore may there be said of me that which is sung in the Divine Songs, in these words: 'Who is this that cometh up from the desert, abounding in delights, leaning upon her Beloved and scattering love on every side?'[20] Thus, then, it is.

Perfect me now if it be thy will,

27. That is to say: Perfect and consummate the spiritual marriage in me with the beatific vision of Thyself—for it is

---

[18] Bg, P add: 'before entering it.'

[19] S reads: 'Thus that very flame that aforetime was oppressive to it is now sweet to it.' Bz: 'And thus, having played upon it, it was aforetime oppressive to it, in playing upon it.'

[20] Canticles viii, 5. [The quotation ends at the word 'Beloved.']

this that the soul beseeches. For, although it is true that in this state that is so lofty, the more completely transformed in love is the soul the more conformed is it, and that it knows nothing of itself, neither is able to ask anything for itself, but all is for its Beloved; since charity, as Saint Paul says, seeks nothing for itself, but only for the Beloved;[1] nevertheless, since it lives in hope, and thus cannot fail to be conscious of something that is lacking, it sighs deeply, though with sweetness and joy, in proportion as it still lacks complete possession of the adoption of the sons of God, wherein, when its glory is consummated, its desire will be at rest.[2] This desire, although here below the soul may have closer union with God, will never be satisfied or at rest until its glory shall appear, especially if it has already tasted the sweetness and delight thereof, which it has in this state. This sweetness is such that, had God not granted a favour to its flesh, and covered its natural being with His right hand (as He did to Moses in the rock, that he might see His glory and not die[3]) it would have died at each touch of this flame, and its natural being would have been destroyed, since its lower part would have no means of enduring so great and sublime a fire of glory.

28. Wherefore this desire and the soul's entreaty for it are not accompanied by pain, for the soul in this state is no longer capable of suffering pain, but its entreaty is made with delectable and sweet desire, and the soul entreats conformity between its spirit and its senses. It is for this reason that it says in this line: 'Perfect me now, if it be Thy will.' For the will and desire are to such an extent united with God that the soul regards it as its glory that it should fulfil the will of God in it. Such are the glimpses of glory and love that in these touches filter through the crevices of the door of the soul, in order to enter, though they cannot do so because of the smallness of our earthly house, that

---

[1] 1 Corinthians xiii, 5.
[2] Bz, C: 'will be removed.' S: 'will be ended.'
[3] Exodus xxxiii, 22.

the soul would have little love if it entreated not to be allowed to enter into that perfection and consummation of love. Furthermore, the soul now sees that in that delectable power and communication with the Spouse, the Holy Spirit is impelling and inviting it, by means of that boundless glory which He is setting before its eyes, in wondrous ways and with sweet affections, saying to it in its spirit that which is said to the Bride in the Songs, which she relates in these words: 'See that which my Spouse is saying to me: "Arise and make haste, my love, my dove, my fair one, and come; for winter is now past and the rain is ended and gone far away, and the flowers have appeared in our land. And the time of pruning has come and the voice of the turtle is heard in our land; the fig tree has produced her fruits, the vines in flower have yielded their fragrance. Arise, my love, my fair one, and come, my dove, into the holes of the rock, into the cavern of the wall; show me thy sweet face, let thy voice sound in my ears, for thy voice is sweet, and thy countenance is comely." '[4] All these things the soul perceives, and she most clearly understands, in the sublime sense of glory, that the Holy Spirit is showing them to her in that tender and sweet flame,[5] desiring to bring her in to that glory. Wherefore the soul, being thus impelled, here makes answer: 'Perfect me now if it be Thy will.' Herein she makes the Spouse those two petitions which He taught us in the Gospel, namely: *Adveniat regnum tuum. Fiat voluntas tua.*[6] And thus it is as though she were to say: Give me this kingdom perfectly, if it be Thy will—that is, according to Thy will. And that this may come to pass:

Break the web of this sweet encounter.

29. It is this web which hinders so important a business as this, since it is easy to reach God once the obstacles which

---

[4] Canticles ii, 10–14.
[5] [*Lit.*, 'flaming.']
[6] St. Matthew vi, 10.

separate the soul from union with God are taken away and the webs are broken. The webs which can hinder this union and which must be broken if the soul is to approach God and possess Him perfectly may be said to be three, namely: the temporal, which comprises all creatures; the natural, which comprises the operations and inclinations that are purely natural; and the third, the sensual, which comprises only[1] union of the soul with the body, which is sensual and animal life, whereof Saint Paul says: 'We know that if this our earthly house be dissolved we have a dwelling-place of God in the heavens.'[2] The first two webs must of necessity be broken in order that we may attain to this possession of the union of God, wherein all things of the world shall be put aside and renounced, and all the natural affections and appetites be mortified, and the operations of the soul, from being natural, become Divine. All this was broken and effected in the soul by the oppressive encounters of this flame when it was oppressive to it; for, through spiritual purgation, as we have said above, the soul succeeds in breaking these two webs and thence in becoming united with God, as it now is, and there remains to be broken only the third web of this life of sense. For this reason the soul here speaks of a web and not of webs; for there is now no other web to be broken than this, which, being already so delicate and fine and so greatly spiritualized by this union with God, is not attacked by the flame severely, as were the two others, but sweetly and delectably. For this reason the soul speaks here and calls the encounter 'sweet,' for it is the sweeter and the more delectable inasmuch as the soul believes it to be about to break the web of life.

30. Therefore it must be known, with regard to the natural dying[3] of souls that reach this state, that, though the manner of their death, from the natural standpoint, is similar to that of others, yet in the cause and mode of their

---

[1] Bg, P omit: 'only.'
[2] 2 Corinthians v, 1.
[3] Several manuscripts read 'love' for 'dying.'

death there is a great difference. For while the deaths of others may be caused by infirmities or length of days, when these souls die, although it may be from some infirmity, or from old age, their spirits are wrested away by nothing less than some loving impulse and encounter far loftier and of greater power and strength than any in the past, for it has succeeded in breaking the web and bearing away a jewel, which is the spirit. And thus the death of such souls is very sweet and gentle, more so than was their spiritual life all their life long, for they die amid the delectable encounters and sublimest impulses of love, being like to the swan, which sings most gently[4] when it is at the point of death. For this reason David said that the death of saints in the fear of God was precious,[5] for at such a time all the riches of the soul come to unite together, and the rivers of love of the soul are about to enter the sea, and these are so broad and dense and motionless[6] that they seem to be seas already. From the beginning to the end, their treasures unite together to accompany the just man as he departs and goes forth to his kingdom, and praises are heard from the ends of the earth,[7] which, as Isaias says, are the glories of the just man.

31. When, therefore, at the time of these glorious encounters, the soul feels itself very near to going forth[8] to possess its kingdom completely and perfectly, in the abundance wherewith it sees itself enriched (for it knows itself now to be pure and rich and full of virtues and prepared for this, since in this state God permits it to see His beauty[9] and entrusts it with the gifts and virtues that He has given it, and all this turns into love and praise, without a trace of presumption or vanity, since there is no leaven of

4 Bg, P: 'most sweetly.'
5 Psalm cxv, 15 [A.V., cxvi, 15].
6 [Cf. p. 52, n. 11, above.]
7 C: 'praises of the blessings of the earth are heard.'
8 Bg, P: 'very near to ascending.'
9 [Or, 'its (own) beauty.']

imperfection to corrupt the mass), and when it sees that it has only now to break this frail web of natural life wherein it feels itself to be enmeshed and imprisoned, and its liberty to be impeded, together with its desire to behold itself loosed[10] and to see itself with Christ (for it grieves that a life which is so strong and high should be obstructed by another that is so weak and low), it begs that this web may be broken, saying: 'Break the web of this sweet encounter.'

32. This life is called a web for three reasons: first, because of the bond that exists between spirit and flesh; second, because it makes a division between God and the soul; third, because even as a web is not so thick[11] and dense but that the light can shine through it, even so in this state this bond appears to it to be a very fine web, since it is greatly spiritualized and enlightened and refined so that the Divinity cannot but shine through it. And when the soul becomes conscious of the power of the life to come, it feels keenly the weakness of this other life, which appears to it as a very fine web—even as a spider's web, which is the name that David gives to it, saying: 'Our years shall be considered as a spider.'[12] And it is much less still in the eyes of a soul that is so greatly enlarged; for, since this soul has entered into the consciousness of God, it is conscious of things in the way that God is; and in the sight of God, as David also says, a thousand years are as yesterday when it is past.[13] And according to Isaias all nations are as if they were not.[14] And they have the same importance to the soul, namely, all things are to it as nothing, and to its own eyes it is itself nothing: to it its God alone is all.

33. But here one point should be noticed. Why does the soul here beg that the web may be broken, rather than cut or allowed to wear itself out, since all these things would

---

10 Bg, P: 'to be loosed.'
11 Bg, C: 'so opaque.'
12 Psalm lxxxix, 9 [A.V., xc, 9].
13 Psalm lxxxix, 4 [A.V., xc, 4].
14 Isaias xl, 17. Bg, P add: 'before Him.'

seem to have the same result? We may say that this is for
four reasons. First, in order to use language of greater propriety, for in an encounter it is more proper to say that a
thing is broken than that it is cut or wears away. Second,
because love delights in the force of love and in forceful
and impetuous contacts, and these are produced by breaking rather than by cutting or wearing away. Third, because
love desires that the act should be very brief, so that it
may then be the more quickly concluded; the quicker[15]
and more spiritual is it, the greater is its power and worth.
For virtue in union is stronger than virtue that is scattered;
and love is introduced as form is introduced into matter,
namely, in an instant, and until then there has been no act
but only dispositions for an act; and thus spiritual acts are
performed in the soul as in an instant, since they are infused by God, but the other acts, which are performed by
the soul of its own accord, may more properly be called
dispositions of successive affections and desires which never
succeed in becoming perfect acts of love or contemplation,
save occasionally when, as I say, God forms and perfects
them with great rapidity in the spirit.[16] For this cause the
Wise Man said that the end of a prayer is better than the
beginning, and, as is commonly said, the short prayer
penetrates the Heavens. Wherefore the soul that is already
prepared can perform more acts and acts of greater intensity[17] in a short time than the soul that is not prepared
can perform in a long time; and merely because of its
thorough preparation, it is wont to remain for a long time[18]
in the act of love or contemplation. And the soul that is
not prepared wastes its strength in the preparation of the
spirit, and even when this is done the fire has not yet penetrated the wood, whether because of its great humidity, or
because of the scant heat generated in the preparation, or

15 Bg, C, P: 'the briefer.'
16 S: 'God forms them in the spirit.'
17 Bg, P: 'more acts and more interior acts.'
18 Bz, C: 'for a sufficient time.'

for both these causes. But into the soul that is prepared the act of love enters continuously, for the spark seizes upon the dry fuel at each contact; and thus the soul that is kindled in love prefers the short act of breaking the web to the duration of the act of cutting it or of its wearing away. The fourth reason is that the web of life[19] may be more quickly destroyed, for cutting a thing and allowing it to wear away are acts performed after greater deliberation, as it is necessary to wait until the thing is riper, or worn, or for some other condition, whereas breaking apparently needs not to wait for maturity or for anything else.

34. And this is the desire of the enamoured soul, which brooks not the delay of waiting until its life come naturally to an end or until at such a time it be cut, because the force of love and the propensities which it feels make it desire and entreat that its life may be at once broken by some encounter and supernatural assault of love. The soul in this state knows very well that it is the habit of God to take away before their time the souls that He greatly loves, perfecting in them in a short time, by means of that love, that which in any event[20] they might have gained gradually in their ordinary progress. It is this that is said by the Wise Man:[21] 'He that is pleasing to God is made beloved, and living among sinners he was translated and taken away, lest wickedness should alter[22] his understanding or deceit beguile his soul. Being made perfect in a short space, he fulfilled a long time. For his soul was pleasing to God, therefore hastened He to take him out of the midst,' etc.[23] Thus far we quote the words of the Wise Man, wherein it will be seen with what propriety and reason the soul uses that word 'break'; for in these words the Holy Spirit uses the

[19] Bg, P: 'that life.'
[20] Bg, P: 'in a long time.'
[21] Bz abbreviates: 'perfecting them in a short time, for it is this that is said by the Wise Man.'
[22] C: 'should take away.'
[23] Wisdom iv, 10–11, 13–14.

two terms 'take away'[24] and 'haste,' which are far removed from the idea of any delay.[25] In speaking of 'haste,' God indicates the speed wherewith He has caused the love of the just man to be perfected in a short time; and by the words 'take away' He indicates that He has borne him off before his natural time. For this reason it is a great thing for the soul to practise the acts of love in this life, so that, when a soul is perfected in a short time, it may not stay long, either in this world or the next, without seeing God.

35. But let us also now see why the soul calls this interior assault of the Holy Spirit an encounter rather than by any other name. The reason is because, as we have said, the soul in God is conscious of an infinite desire that its life may come to an end, yet, because the time of its perfecting is not yet come, this is not accomplished; and it sees that, to the end that it may be the more completely perfected and raised up[26] above the flesh, God makes these assaults upon it that are glorious and Divine and after the manner of encounters, which, as they have the object of purifying it and bringing it out of the flesh, are indeed encounters, wherewith He penetrates the soul continually, deifying its substance and making it Divine, wherein the Being of God absorbs the soul above all being. The reason for this is that God has encountered the soul and pierced it to the quick in the Holy Spirit, Whose communications are impetuous when they are full of fervour,[27] as is this encounter, which the soul, since it has a lively taste of God, calls sweet; not that many other touches and encounters which it receives in this state are not also sweet, but rather that this is eminently so above all the rest; for God effects it, as we have said,[28] in order to loose the soul and glorify it

[24] [The word translated 'take away' has in the original Spanish the meaning of 'take away violently,' 'snatch away.']

[25] S adds: 'in that which is done by God.'

[26] Bg, Bz, P: 'and carried away.'

[27] Bz: 'are favoured.'

[28] Bg, P have 'shines upon it' for 'effects it.' Bz omits: 'for God . . . said.'

quickly. Wherefore the soul takes courage to say: 'Break the web of this sweet encounter.'

36. To sum up this whole stanza, then, it is as though the soul were to say: Oh, flame of the Holy Spirit, that so intimately and tenderly dost pierce the substance of my soul and cauterize it with Thy glorious heat! Since Thou art now so loving as to show Thyself with the desire of giving Thyself to me in eternal life; if before now my petitions did not reach Thine ears, when with yearnings and fatigues of love my sense and spirit suffered by reason of my great weakness and impurity and the little fortitude of love that I had, I entreated Thee to loose me, and to bear me away with Thee, for with desire did my soul desire Thee since my impatient love would not suffer me to be conformed with the condition of this life that Thou desiredst me still to live,[29] and the past assaults of love sufficed not, because they were not of sufficient quality for me to attain my desire; now that I am so greatly strengthened in love that not alone do my sense and spirit not fail before Thee, but rather my heart and my flesh are strengthened in Thy sight, they rejoice in the living God with a great conformity between their various parts. Therefore do I entreat that which Thou desirest me to entreat, and that which Thou desirest not, that desire I not, nor can I desire it,[30] nor does it pass through my mind to desire it; and, since my petitions are now more effective and more greatly esteemed in Thine eyes (for they go forth from Thee and Thou movest me to make them, and I pray to Thee with delight[31] and rejoicing in the Holy Spirit, and my judgment comes forth from Thy countenance, which comes to pass when Thou esteemest and hearest my prayers), do Thou break the slender web of this life, and let it not come to pass that age and years cut it after a natural manner, so that I may be able

[29] C: 'that Thou wouldst desire should come to me.'
[30] S omits: 'nor can I desire it.'
[31] Bz: 'with fervour.'

to love Thee with the fullness and satisfaction which my
soul desires without end, for ever.

STANZA II

**Oh, sweet burn!   Oh, delectable wound![1]   Oh, soft hand!
Oh, delicate touch
That savours of eternal life and pays every debt!   In slay-
ing, thou hast changed death into life.**

EXPOSITION

IN THIS stanza the soul explains how the three Persons of
the Most Holy Trinity, Father, Son and Holy Spirit, are
They that[2] effect within it this Divine work of union. Thus
the 'hand,' the 'burn' and the 'touch' are in substance one
and the same thing; and the soul gives them these names,
inasmuch as they describe the effect which is caused by each.
The 'burn' is the Holy Spirit, the 'hand' is the Father
and the 'touch,' the Son. And thus the soul here magnifies
the Father and the Son and the Holy Spirit, dwelling upon[3]
three great favours[4] and blessings which They work within
it, since They have changed its death into life, transforming it in Themselves. The first is the delectable wound,
which the soul attributes to the Holy Spirit, wherefore it
is called a sweet[5] burn. The second is the desire for eternal
life, which it attributes to the Son, and therefore calls a
delicate touch. The third is His having transformed the soul
in Himself, which is a gift[6] wherewith it is well pleased;
this is attributed to the Father, and therefore the soul calls

---

[1] S has 'flame' [*llama* for *llaga*].
[2] Bg, P omit: 'are They that.'
[3] Bg omits: 'dwelling upon.'
[4] P has 'walls' for 'favours.'
[5] Only Bg, P have 'sweet.'
[6] So Bg, P. The other authorities have 'a debt.'

it a soft hand. And although the soul here names the three things, because of the properties of their effects, it addresses only one of them, saying: 'Thou hast changed death into life.' For they all work in one, and thus the soul attributes the whole of their work to one, and the whole of it to all of them. There follows the line:

Oh, sweet burn!

2. This burn, as we said, here signifies the Holy Spirit, for, as Moses says in Deuteronomy, our Lord God is a consuming fire[1]—that is, a fire of love. This fire, as it is of infinite power, is able, to an extent which cannot be measured, to consume and transform into itself the soul that it touches. But it burns and absorbs everything according to the preparation thereof; one thing more and another less; and this according to its own pleasure, and after the manner and at the time which it pleases. And since God is an infinite fire of love, when therefore He is pleased to touch the soul with some severity, the heat of the soul rises to such a degree of love that the soul believes that it is being burned with a heat greater than any other in the world. For this reason, in this union it speaks of the Holy Spirit as of a burn; for, just as in a burn the fire is most intense and vehement, and its effect is greater than that of other fires, so the soul describes the act of this union as a burn with respect to other acts, since it is, more properly than any other, an enkindled fire of love. And inasmuch as this Divine fire, in this case, has transformed the soul into itself, not only is the soul conscious of the burn, but it has itself become one burn of vehement fire.

3. And it is a wondrous thing, worthy to be related, that, though this fire of God is so vehement and so consuming that it would consume a thousand worlds more easily than fire here on earth consumes a straw of flax, it consumes not the soul wherein it burns in this way, neither

[1] Deuteronomy iv, 24.

destroys it, still less causes it any affliction, but rather, in proportion to the strength of love, it brings it delight and deifies it, glowing and burning in it sweetly. And this is due to the purity and perfection of the spirit wherein it burns in the Holy Spirit.[2] Thus did it come to pass, as we read in the Acts of the Apostles, when this fire descended with great vehemence and enkindled the disciples;[3] and, as Saint Gregory says,[4] they burned inwardly and sweetly in love. And this is that which is intended by the Church, when she says to this same purpose: There came fire from Heaven, burning not but giving splendour; consuming not but enlightening.[5] For, in these communications, since the object of God is to magnify the soul, this fire wearies it not and afflicts it not but rather enlarges it and delights it; nor does it blacken it and cover it with ashes, as fire does to coal, but it makes it glorious and rich, for which cause the soul calls it a sweet burn.

4. And thus the happy soul that by great good fortune attains to this burning knows everything, tastes everything, does all that it desires, and prospers, and none prevails against it and nothing touches it. For it is of this soul that the Apostle says: 'The spiritual man judgeth all things, and he himself is judged of no man.'[6] Et iterum:[7] 'The spiritual man searcheth all things, yea, the depth of God.'[8] For this is the property of love, to seek out all the good things of the Beloved.

5. Oh, the great glory of you souls that are worthy to attain to this supreme fire,[9] for, while it has infinite power to consume and annihilate you, it is certain that it consumes you not, but grants you a boundless consummation in

2 So S. The other authorities omit: 'in the Holy Spirit.'
3 Acts ii, 3.
4 Hom. XXX, in Evang.
5 [In officio feriæ 2æ Pent.]
6 1 Corinthians ii, 15.
7 Bz: 'And again.'
8 1 Corinthians ii, 10.
9 Bg, P: 'to this state of supreme fire.'

glory![10] Marvel not that God should bring certain souls to so high a state; for the sun is conspicuous for certain marvellous effects which it causes; as the Holy Spirit says, it burns the mountains of the saints after three manners.[11] Since, then, this burn is so sweet, as we have here explained, how delectable, may we believe, will it not be in one that is touched by it? Of this the soul would fain speak, yet speaks not, but keeps this esteem in its heart, and in its mouth the wonder implied in this word 'Oh,' saying: 'Oh, sweet burn!'

Oh, delectable wound![1]

6. Having addressed the burn, the soul now addresses the wound caused by the burn; and, as the burn was sweet, as has been said, the wound, according to reason, must be like to the burn. And thus the wound caused by a sweet burn will be a delectable wound, for, since the burn is one of sweet love, the wound will be one of sweet love and thus will be sweetly delectable.

7. And for an explanation to be made of the nature of the wound here addressed by the soul, it must be known that a burn caused by material fire always leaves a wound on the part subjected to it. And fire has this property that, if it be applied to a wound that was not caused by fire, it is turned into a wound inflicted by fire. And this burn of love has the property that, when it touches a soul, whether this soul be wounded by other wounds, such as miseries and sins, or whether it be whole, it at once leaves it wounded with love. Thus wounds due to another cause have now become wounds of love.[2] But there is this difference between this loving burn and a burn caused by material fire, that the wound made by the latter can only be healed by

10 [See p. 60, n. 15, above.]
11 [Ecclesiasticus xliii, 4.]
1 S has 'flame' [*llama* for *llaga*].
2 Bz abbreviates: 'wounded by other wounds, they have now become wounds of love.'

the application of other medicines, whereas the wound made by the burn of love can be cured by no other medicine, but only by the same burn that has caused the wound. And the same burn that cures the wound inflicts a wound as it cures it; for each time that the burn of love touches the wound of love, it inflicts a greater wound of love, and thus it cures and heals the more inasmuch as it wounds the more; for when the lover is most wounded he is most whole and the cure wrought by love is the infliction of a hurt and a wound over and above the wound already inflicted, until the wound is so severe that the soul comes to be wholly dissolved in the wound of love. And in this way, when it is now completely cauterized and turned into a wound of love, it regains its perfect health in love, because it is transformed in love. In this way must be understood the wound of which the soul here speaks: it is altogether wounded and altogether healthy. Yet, though the soul is altogether wounded and altogether healthy, the burning of love still performs its office, which is to touch and to wound with love; and, inasmuch as this love is wholly delectable and wholly healthy, the effect which it produces is a relieving[3] of the wound, after the manner of a good physician. Wherefore the soul well says in this place: 'Oh, delectable wound!' Oh, then, wound the more delectable according as the fire of love that causes it is the loftier and the more sublime! For, as the Holy Spirit inflicted the wound only in order to relieve it, and as He has a great desire and will to relieve the soul, the wound will be great, for greatly will it be relieved.[4]

8. Oh, happy wound, inflicted by One Who cannot but heal! Oh, fortunate and most happy wound, for thou

[3] [The past participle of this verb (*regalar*) has also the meaning 'delectable.' It is so translated in the verse-line above and elsewhere in this passage, and where the words 'relief,' 'relieve' occur, the play on the noun (or verb) and the adjective is to be understood.]

[4] Bg, P omit: 'for greatly will it be relieved.'

wert inflicted only for relief, and the quality of thy pain is the relief and delight of the wounded soul! Great art thou, oh, delectable wound, since great is He that has inflicted thee; and great is thy relief, because the fire of love is infinite and it relieves thee according to thy capacity and greatness. Oh, then, thou delectable wound! So much the more sublimely delectable[5] art thou in proportion as the burn has touched the infinite centre[6] of the substance of the soul, burning all that was capable of being burned, that it might relieve all that was capable of being relieved. We may represent this burn and this wound as being the highest degree to which the soul can attain in this state. There are many other ways wherein God cauterizes the soul which attain not so far as this, nor are they like this; for this is purely a touch of the Divinity in the soul, without any form or figure, whether intellectual or imaginary.

9. But there is another and a most sublime way wherein the soul may be cauterized, by means of an intellectual figure, which is after this manner. It will come to pass that, when the soul is enkindled in the love of God, although not to the high degree of which we have spoken (though it is most meet that it should be so for that which I am about to describe), the soul will be conscious of an assault upon it made by a seraph with an arrow or a dart[7] completely enkindled in fire of love, which will pierce the soul, now enkindled like a coal, or, to speak more truly, like a flame, and will cauterize it in a sublime manner; and when it has pierced and cauterized it thus with that arrow, the flame (that is, the soul) will rush forth and will rise suddenly and vehemently, even as comes to pass in a red-hot furnace or forge, when they stir or poke the fire,[8] and make the flame

[5] Bg, P [intensify the play upon words by reading]: 'so much the more sublimely and delectably relieved' [regaladamente regalada].

[6] Bg, P: 'the last centre.'

[7] [Cf. p. 63, n. 12, above. The word 'arrow' (flecha) is not found in the first redaction.]

[8] Bz, C add: 'and the fire revives.'

hotter. Then, upon being struck by this enkindled dart,
the soul is conscious of the wound with a sovereign delight;[9]
for, not only is it moved through and through in great
sweetness,[10] by the stirring and the impetuous motion
caused by that seraph, wherein it feels the great heat and
melting of love, but the keen wound and the healing herb
wherewith the effect of the dart was being greatly assuaged[11]
are felt by it like a keen point in the substance of the spirit,
even as in the heart of him whose soul has been thus
pierced.

10. Who can speak fittingly of this intimate point of
the wound which seems to strike the very centre of the
heart of the spirit, which is the point wherein is felt the
refinement of its delight?[12] For the soul feels, as it were, a
grain of mustard seed, most minute, highly enkindled and
wondrous keen, which sends out from itself to its circumference[13] a keen and enkindled fire of love; which fire,
arising from the substance and virtue of that keen point,
wherein lies the substance and the virtue of the herb, is felt
by the soul to be subtly diffused through all its spiritual
and substantial veins, according to its potentiality and
strength. Herein it feels its heat to be increasing and to be
growing in strength and its love to be becoming so refined
in this heat that it seems to have within it seas of loving
fire which reach to the farthest heights and depths of the
spheres, filling it wholly with love. Herein it seems to the
soul that the whole universe is a sea of love wherein it is
engulfed, and it can descry no term or goal at which this
love can come to an end, but feels within itself, as we have
said, the keen point and centre of love.

11. And that whereof the soul now has fruition cannot

[9] C, S: 'with a surpassing sovereign delight.'
[10] Bg: 'in great solitude.'
[11] [Cf. p. 63, n. 16, above.]
[12] C omits this last clause.
[13] C: 'which sows in the circumference.' Bz has 'disseminates'
for 'sows.'

be further described, save by saying that the soul is now conscious of the aptness of the comparison made in the Gospel between the Kingdom of Heaven and the grain of mustard seed; which grain, because of its great heat, although small, grows into a great tree.[14] For the soul sees that it has become like a vast fire of love which arises from that enkindled point in the heart of the spirit.

12. Few souls attain to a state as high as this, but some have done so, especially those whose virtue and spirituality was to be transmitted to the succession of their children. For God bestows spiritual wealth and strength upon the head of a house, together with the first-fruits of the Spirit, according to the greater or lesser number of the descendants who are to inherit his doctrine and spirituality.

13. Let us return, then, to the work done by that seraph, which in truth is to strike and to wound the spirit interiorly. If God should sometimes permit the effect of the wound to pass outward to the bodily senses, to an extent corresponding to the interior wound, the effect of the impact and the wound will be felt without, as came to pass when the seraph wounded[15] the soul of Saint Francis with love, inflicting upon him five wounds, and in that way the effect of these wounds became visible in his body, and he was actually wounded, and received the imprint of the wounds in his body as he had also received them in his soul. For, as a rule, God bestows no favours upon the body without bestowing them first and principally upon the soul. And then, the greater is the delight and strength of love which causes the wound within the soul, the more of it is manifested outwardly in the bodily wound, and if the one grows, the other grows likewise. This comes to pass because, when these souls have been purified and made strong[16] in God, that which to their corruptible flesh causes pain and torture

14 St. Matthew xiii, 31–2.

15 Bg, P: 'struck.'

16 So Bg. The other authorities [and P. Silverio] read 'and set upon God.'

is sweet and delectable to their strong and healthy spirits; wherefore it is a wondrous thing to feel the pain growing in the pleasure. This wonder Job perceived in his wounds, when he said to God: 'Turning to me, Thou tormentest me wonderfully.'[17] For it is a great marvel, and a thing worthy of the abundance of the sweetness and delight which God has laid up for them that fear Him,[18] that, the greater is the pain and torment of which the soul is conscious, the greater is the pleasure and delight[19] which He causes it to enjoy. But when the wound is within the soul only, and is not communicated without, the delight can be far more intense and sublime; for, as the flesh has the spirit in check, so, when the blessings of the spirit are communicated to it, the flesh draws in the rein and bridles this fleet steed, which is the spirit, and restrains its great energy; for, if it makes use of its strength, the rein will break. But until it break, its freedom will be continually oppressed. For, as the Wise Man says: 'The corruptible body presseth down the soul and the earthly tabernacle weigheth down the spiritual sense which of itself museth upon many things.'[20]

14. This I say that it may be understood that he who will ever cling to natural reasoning and ability in his journey to God will not become a very spiritual person. For there are some who think that they can attain to the powers and the height of supernatural spirituality by means of the power and operation of sense alone, though this of itself is low and no more than natural. They cannot attain thereto save by setting aside and renouncing bodily sense and its operation. But it is quite different when a spiritual effect overflows from spirit into sense, for, when this is the case, great spirituality may accrue,[21] as is clear from

[17] Job x, 16.
[18] Psalm xxx, 20 [A.V., xxxi, 19].
[19] S: 'and sweetness.'
[20] Wisdom ix, 15.
[21] Bg, P: 'is apt to accrue.'

what we have said of the wounds, the outward manifestation of which corresponds to an inward power. This came to pass in Saint Paul, when the intensity of his soul's realization of the sufferings of Christ was so great that it overflowed into his body, as he writes to the Galatians, saying: 'I bear in my body the marks[22] of my Lord Jesus.'[23]

15. No more need be said about the burn and the wound, but if they are as we have here depicted them, what, do we believe, will be the hand that inflicts this burn, and what will be the touch? This the soul describes in the line following, lauding it rather than expounding it, and saying:

Oh, soft hand! Oh, delicate touch

16. This hand, as we have said, is the merciful and omnipotent Father. Since it is as generous and liberal as it is powerful and rich, we must understand that it will give rich and powerful gifts to the soul when it is opened to grant it favours, and thus the soul calls it a 'soft' hand. This is as though the soul were to say: Oh, hand, the softer to this my soul as softly touching it and softly laid upon it, since if thou wert to lean hardly upon it the whole world would perish; for at Thy glance alone the earth shakes,[1] the nations faint and the mountains crumble to pieces. Once more, then, I say: Oh, soft hand! For whereas thou wert harsh and severe to Job, since thou didst touch him somewhat heavily,[2] to me thou art as loving[3] and gentle as thou wert hard to him, and art laid upon my soul very firmly, but very lovingly and graciously and softly. For Thou givest death and Thou givest life and there is none that can escape from Thy hand. But Thou, oh, Life Divine, never slayest save to give life, even as Thou never woundest save to heal. When Thou chastisest, Thou touchest lightly,[4]

22 Bz: 'the pains.'
23 Galatians vi, 17.
1 Psalm ciii, 32 [A.V., civ, 32].
2 So S. Bz: 'so heavily.' Bg, C, P: 'so very heavily.'
3 Bz: 'as pleasant.'
4 S: 'sweetly.'

yet Thy touch suffices to consume the world; but, when Thou bringest joy, Thou art laid firmly upon the soul and thus the joys of Thy sweetness are without number. Thou hast wounded me, oh, hand Divine, in order to heal me, and thou hast slain in me that which would have slain me but for the life of God wherein now I see that I live. And this Thou didst with the liberality[5] of Thy generous[6] grace, which Thou showedst me in the touch wherewith Thou didst touch me—namely, the splendour of Thy glory and the image of Thy substance, which is Thy only begotten Son;[7] in Whom, since He is Thy wisdom, Thou reachest from one end to another mightily.[8] And this Thy only begotten Son, oh, merciful hand of the Father, is the delicate touch wherewith in the power of Thy burn Thou didst touch me and wound me.

17. Oh, then, thou delicate touch, Thou Word, Son of God, Who, through the delicateness of Thy Divine Being, dost subtly penetrate the substance of my soul, and, touching it wholly and delicately, dost absorb it wholly in Thyself in Divine ways of delight and sweetness which have never been heard of in the land of Chanaan, nor seen in Theman![9] Oh, delicate touch of the Word, delicate, yea, wondrously delicate to me, which, having overthrown the mountains and broken the stones in Mount Horeb with the shadow of Thy power and strength that went before Thee, didst reveal Thyself more sweetly and powerfully to the Prophet with the whisper of gentle air.[10] Oh, gentle touch, that art so delicate and gentle! Say, Word, Son of God, how dost Thou touch the soul so gently and delicately when Thou art so terrible and powerful? Oh blessed, thrice blessed,[11] the soul whom Thou dost touch so delicately and

[5] C, S: 'liberty.'
[6] Bg, Bz, P: 'gracious.'
[7] Hebrews i, 3.
[8] Wisdom viii, 1.
[9] Baruch iii, 22.
[10] [3 Kings xix, 11–12.]
[11] S omits: 'thrice blessed.'

gently though Thou art so terrible and powerful![12] Tell this out to the world. Nay, tell it not to the world, for the world knows naught of air so gentle, and will not feel Thee, because it can neither receive Thee[13] nor see Thee.[14] Only they who withdraw from the world and whom Thou refinest shall know Thee,[15] my God and my life, and behold Thee when Thou touchest them delicately, since purity corresponds with purity,[16] and thus they shall feel Thee and rejoice in Thee. Thou dost touch them the more delicately because the substance of their souls has been beautified and purified and made delicate, and has been withdrawn from every creature and from every trace and touch of creature, and Thou art dwelling secretly and surely within them. And thou hidest them in the hiding-place of Thy presence (which is the Word) from the disturbance of men.[17]

18. Once again, then, oh, delicate touch, and again most delicate, the stronger and more powerful for being more delicate, that with the strength of Thy delicacy dost melt and remove the soul from all other touches of created things and makest it Thine own alone and unitest it with Thyself. So gracious[18] an effect and impression dost Thou leave in the soul that every other touch, of everything else, whether high or low, seems to it rude and gross,[19] and even the sight of other things will offend it, and to have to do with them[20] and touch them will cause it trouble and grievous torment.

19. And it must be known that, the more delicate in itself is a thing, the broader and more capacious it

12 Bz omits this sentence.
13 S: 'will not receive Thee.'
14 St. John xiv, 17.
15 [Cf. p. 68, n. 15, above.]
16 [*Lit.*, 'delicacy . . . delicacy.']
17 Psalm xxx, 21 [A.V., xxxi, 21].
18 [*Delgado.*] Bg, P: 'delicate' [*delicado*].
19 Bg adds: 'if it touches the soul.'
20 Bg, P: 'to tolerate them.'

is; and the more subtle and delicate it is, the more it becomes diffused[21] and communicative. The Word—that is, the touch which touches the soul—is infinitely subtle and delicate; and the soul is a vessel broad and capacious enough for the great purification and delicacy which belongs to it in this state. Oh, then, thou delicate touch, that dost infuse Thyself the more copiously and abundantly into my soul by reason of Thy greater subtlety[22] and of the greater purity of my soul!

20. And it must also be known that, the more subtle and delicate is the touch, the greater is the delight and pleasure that it communicates where it touches; and the less so it is, the less weight and bulk has the touch.[23] This Divine touch has neither bulk nor weight, for the Word, Who effects it, is far removed from any kind of mode and manner, and free from any kind of weight, of form, figure or accident, such as is wont to restrict and limit substance. And thus this touch of which the soul speaks here, being substantial (that is, of the Divine Substance), is ineffable. Oh, then, at last, thou ineffably delicate touch, that art the Word, that touchest not the soul save with Thy most pure and simple Being,[24] which, being infinite, is infinitely delicate, and therefore touches most subtly, lovingly, eminently and delicately!

That savours of eternal life

21. Although this is not so in a perfect degree, there is indeed a certain savour herein of life eternal, as has been said above, which the soul tastes in this touch of God. And it is not incredible that this should be so if we believe, as we must believe, that this touch is substantial, that is to

[21] Bg: 'diffusive.'

[22] Bz, C, S: 'substance.'

[23] [I suspect a corrupt reading here; the passage as it stands is a literal rendering of the original.]

[24] Bg, P: 'with Thy most simple and sincere Being.' S: 'with Thy purest Substance and Thy most simple Being.'

say, is a touch of the Substance of God in the substance of the soul; and to this many holy men have attained in this life. Wherefore the delicacy of the delight which is felt in this touch is impossible of description; nor would I willingly speak thereof, lest it should be supposed that it is no more than that which I say; for there are no words to expound[1] such sublime things of God as come to pass in these souls; whereof the proper way to speak is for one that knows them to understand them inwardly and to feel them inwardly and enjoy them and be silent concerning them. For the soul in this state sees that these things are in some measure like the white stone which Saint John says will be given to him that conquers, and on the stone a name shall be written, which no man knoweth saving he that receiveth it.[2] This alone can be said of it with truth, that it savours of eternal life. For, although in this life we may not have perfect fruition of it, as in glory, yet nevertheless this touch, being of God, savours of eternal life. And in this way the soul in such a state tastes of the things of God, and there are communicated to it fortitude, wisdom, love, beauty, grace and goodness, and so forth. For, as God is all these things, the soul tastes them in one single touch of God, and thus the soul has fruition of Him according to its faculties and its substance.

22. And in this good which comes to the soul the unction of the Holy Spirit sometimes overflows into the body, and this is enjoyed by all the substance of sense and all the members of the body and the very marrow and bones, not as feebly as is usually the case, but with a feeling of great delight and glory, which is felt even in the remotest joints of the feet and hands. And the body feels such glory in the glory of the soul that it magnifies God after its own manner, perceiving that He is in its very bones, even as David said: 'All my bones shall say, "God, who is like unto

1 Bg, P add: 'and enumerate.'
2 Apocalypse ii, 17.

Thee?" [3] And since all that can be said concerning this matter is less than the truth, it suffices to say of the bodily experience, as of the spiritual, that it savours of eternal life.

And pays every debt!

23. This the soul says because, in the savour of eternal life which it here experiences, it feels that it is being recompensed for the trials through which it has passed in order to come to this state. Herein it feels itself not only duly paid and satisfied, but excessively rewarded, so that it well understands the truth of the promise of the Spouse in the Gospel that He will reward the soul an hundredfold.[1] Thus there has been no tribulation, or temptation, or penance, or any other trial through which the soul has passed on this road[2] to which there does not correspond an hundredfold of consolation and delight in this life, so that the soul may very well now say: 'And pays every debt.'

24. And, in order that we may know what debts are these which the soul now recognizes as paid, it must be known that in the ordinary way no soul can attain to this lofty state and kingdom of the betrothal without first having passed through many tribulations and trials, since, as is said in the Acts of the Apostles, it behoves us to enter through many tribulations into the kingdom of the heavens;[3] which things have in this state passed, for henceforth the soul, being purified, has no more suffering.

25. The trials which are suffered by those that are to come to this state are of three kinds, namely: trials and discomforts, fears and temptations which come from the world, and that in many ways; temptations and aridities and afflictions relating to sense; tribulations, darknesses, perils,[4] abandonments, temptations and other trials relating to

[3] Psalm xxxiv, 10 [A.V., xxxv, 10].
[1] St. Matthew xix, 23.
[2] S omits: 'on this road.'
[3] Acts xiv, 21 [A.V., xiv, 22].
[4] C: 'appetites.'

the spirit, so that in this way the soul may be purged according both to its spiritual and to its sensual part, in the way that we described in the exposition of the fourth line of the first stanza. And the reason why these trials are necessary for the soul that is to reach this state is that, just as a liquor of great excellence is placed only in a strong vessel, which has been made ready and purified, so this most lofty union[5] cannot belong to a soul that has not been fortified by trials and temptations, and purified with tribulations, darknesses and perils, one of which classes, purifies and fortifies sense and the other refines and purifies and disposes the spirit.[6] For even as impure spirits, in order to be united with God in glory, pass through the pains of fire in the life to come, even so, in order to reach the union of perfection in this life, they must pass through the fire of these said pains, a fire which burns more violently in some and less so in others, and for longer in some than in others, according to the degree of union to which God is pleased to raise them and comformably with the degree of purgation which they have to undergo.

26. By means of these trials whereinto God leads the soul and the senses, the soul gradually acquires virtues, strength and perfection, together with bitterness, for virtue is made perfect in weakness,[7] and is wrought by the experience of sufferings. For iron cannot adapt itself and be subservient to the intelligence of the artificer, unless he use fire and a hammer, like the fire which Jeremias says that God put into his understanding, saying: 'He sent fire into my bones and taught me.'[8] And Jeremias likewise says of the hammer: 'Thou hast chastised me, Lord, and I was instructed.'[9] Even so says the Preacher: 'He that is not

---

[5] Bg, P: 'unction.'
[6] Bg, P: 'refines and purges the spirit.'
[7] 2 Corinthians xii, 9.
[8] Lamentations i, 13.
[9] Jeremias xxxi, 18.

tried, what can he know? And he that hath no experience knoweth little.'[10]

27. And here it behoves us to note the reason why there are so few that attain to this lofty state of the perfection of union with God. It must be known that it is not because God is pleased that there should be few[11] raised to this high spiritual state, for it would rather please Him that all souls should be perfect, but it is rather that He finds few vessels which can bear so high and lofty a work. For, when He proves them in small things and finds them weak and sees that they at once flee from labour, and desire not to submit to the least discomfort or mortification,[12] He finds that they are not strong and faithful in the little things wherein He has granted them the favour of beginning to purge and fashion them, and sees that they will be much less so in great things; so He goes no farther with their purification, neither lifts them up from the dust of the earth, through the labour of mortification, since for this they would need greater constancy and fortitude than they exhibit. And thus there are many who desire to make progress and constantly entreat God to bring them and let them pass to this state of perfection, and when it pleases God to begin to bring them through[13] the first trials and mortifications, as is necessary, they are unwilling to pass through them, and flee away, to escape from the narrow road of life and seek the broad road of their own consolation, which is that of their perdition, and thus they give God no opportunity, refusing to receive what they have asked when He begins to give it to them. And so they are like useless vessels: they would fain arrive at the state of perfection but are unwilling to be led thither by the road of trials which leads to it, nor will they hardly set foot upon that road by submitting to the smallest trials which are those that souls are wont to suffer.

[10] Ecclesiasticus xxxiv, 9–10 [cf. p. 72, n. 8, above].
[11] Bg, P: 'is not pleased that there should be many.'
[12] Bg adds: 'or to work with solid patience.'
[13] Bz: 'to fashion them with.'

To these may be made the reply which we find in Jeremias, in these words: 'If thou hast run with those who went on foot, and hast laboured, how canst thou contend with horses? And as thou hast had quietness in the land of peace, how wilt thou do in the pride of Jordan?'[14] This is as though he were to say: If in the trials which commonly and ordinarily afflict all those who live this human life thou countedst all as labour, and thoughtest thyself to be running, because thy pace was so slow, how wilt thou be able to keep pace with the step of a horse—that is to say, with trials that are more than ordinary and common, for which is required more than human strength and swiftness? And if thou hast been loth to break away from the peace and pleasure[15] of this land of thine, which is thy sensual nature, and hast not desired to make war against it or to oppose it in any way, I know not how thou wilt desire to enter the impetuous waters of spiritual tribulation and trial, which are more interior.

28. Oh, souls that seek to walk in security and comfort in spiritual things! If ye did but know how necessary it is to suffer and endure in order to reach this security and consolation, and how without this[16] ye cannot attain to that which the soul desires, but will rather go backward, ye would in no way seek consolation, either from God or from the creatures, but would rather bear the cross, and, having embraced it, would desire to drink pure vinegar and gall, and would count this a great happiness, for, being thus dead to the world and to your own selves, ye would live to God in the delights of the spirit; and, bearing a few outward things with patience and faithfulness, ye would become worthy for God to set His eyes upon you, to purge and cleanse you more inwardly by means of more interior spiritual trials, and to give you more interior blessings. For they to whom God is to grant so notable a favour as to tempt them more

14 Jeremias xii, 5.
15 Bg, P omit: 'and pleasure.'
16 Bg, P: 'and if ye did but understand that.'

interiorly, and thus to advance them in gifts and deservings, must have rendered Him many services, and have had much patience and constancy for His sake, and have been very acceptable in His sight in their lives and works. This was true of the holy man Tobias, to whom Saint Raphael said that, because he had been acceptable to God, He had granted him this favour of sending him a temptation that should prove him the more in order that he might exalt him the more.[17] And all that remained to him of life after that temptation caused him joy, as says the Divine Scripture. In the same way we read of holy Job that, when God accepted him as His servant, as He did in the presence of the good and the evil spirits, He then granted him the favour of sending him those great[18] trials, that he might afterwards exalt him, as indeed He did, by multiplying blessings to him, both spiritual and temporal.[19]

29. In the same way does God act to those whom He desires to exalt with the most important exaltation; He makes and causes them to be tempted in order that He may raise them as far as is possible—that is, that He may bring them to union with Divine wisdom, which, as David says, is silver tried by the fire and proved in the earth[20] (that is, that of our flesh) and purged seven times, which is the greatest purgation possible. And there is no reason to tarry here any longer in order to describe these seven purgations and to show how each of them leads us to this wisdom, and how there correspond to them seven degrees of love in this wisdom,[21] which in this life is to the soul like that silver spoken of by David, but in the life to come will be to it like gold.

30. It greatly behoves the soul, then, to have much

17 Tobias xii, 13.
18 Bg, Bz, C, P: 'heavy.'
19 [Job i, 8; xlii, 12.]
20 Psalm xi, 7 [A.V., xii, 6].
21 Bz omits this clause.

198

patience and constancy in all the tribulations and trials[22]
which God sends it, whether they come from without or
from within, and are spiritual or corporeal, greater or lesser.
It must take them all as from His hand for its healing and its
good, and not flee from them, since they are health[23] to it,
but follow the counsel of the Wise Man, who says: 'If
the spirit of him that has the power descend upon thee,
abandon not thy place'[24] (that is, the place and abode of
thy probation, by which is meant that trial that He sends
thee); for the healing, he says, will cause great[25] sins to
cease. That is, it will cut the roots of thy sins and imperfections, which are evil habits; for battling with trials, perils
and temptations quenches the evil and imperfect habits of
the soul and purifies and strengthens it. Wherefore the soul
must count it a great favour when God sends it interior
and exterior trials,[26] realizing that there are very few who
deserve to be perfected by suffering, and to suffer that they
may come to this lofty state.

31. We return to our exposition. The soul is now aware
that all has turned out very well for it, since now *sicut tenebræ ejus, ita et lumen ejus;*[27] and, as the soul aforetime
shared in tribulations, it now shares in consolations and in
the kingdom; and as all its trials, within and without, have
been amply rewarded by Divine blessings of soul and body,
there is none of its trials that has not a correspondingly great
reward. And thus the soul confesses that it is now well
satisfied, when it says: 'And pays every debt.' In this line
it gives thanks to God, even as David gave Him thanks for
having delivered him from trials, in that verse where he
says: 'Many and grievous are the tribulations that Thou
hast shown me, and Thou didst deliver me from them all,

22 Bz abbreviates: 'which in this life consists in the soul's great
constancy and patience in all the tribulations and trials.'

23 Bz: 'sanctity' [*santidad* for *sanidad*].

24 Ecclesiastes x, 4.

25 Bg, P: 'very great.'

26 Bg, P: 'sends it trials and temptations.'

27 Psalm cxxxviii, 12 [A.V., cxxxix, 12].

and from the depths of the earth hast Thou brought me
out again; Thou hast multiplied Thy magnificence, and,
turning to me, hast comforted me.'[28] And thus this soul
that before reaching this state was without, at the gates
of the palace (like Mardochai, sitting weeping in the streets
of Susan, because his life was in peril, and clothed in
sackcloth, refusing to receive the garments from Queen
Esther, and having received no reward for services rendered
the King, and his faithfulness in defending his honour
and life[29]), is recompensed, like Mardochai, in a single
day for all its trials and services, for not only is it made to
enter the palace and stand before the King, clad in regal
vesture, but likewise it is crowned, and given a sceptre, and
a royal seat, and possession of the royal ring, so that it may
do all that it desires, and need do naught that it desires not
to do in the kingdom of its Spouse; for those that are in
this state receive all that they desire. Herein not only is it
recompensed, but the Jews, its enemies, are now dead—
namely, the imperfect desires that were taking away its
spiritual life, wherein it now lives according to its faculties
and desires. For this cause the soul next says:

In slaying, thou hast changed death into life.

32. For death is naught else than privation of life: when
life comes, there remains no trace of death. With respect to
the spirit, there are two kinds of life; one is beatific, which
consists in seeing God, and this will be attained by means of
the natural death of the body, as Saint Paul says in these
words: 'We know that if this our house of clay be dissolved,
we have a dwelling of God in the heavens.'[1] The other
is perfect spiritual life, which is the possession of God
through the union of love, and this is attained through the
complete mortification of all vices and desires[2] and of the

28 Psalm lxx, 20 [A.V., lxxi, 20–1].
29 Esther iv, 1–4.
1 2 Corinthians v, 1.
2 Bz: 'of all its members and desires.'

oul's entire nature. And until this be done, the soul cannot attain to the perfection of this spiritual life of union
with God, even as the Apostle says likewise in these words:
'If you live according to the flesh, you shall die; but if by
the spirit you mortify the deeds of the flesh, you shall live.'[3]

33. It must be known, then, that that which the soul
here calls death is all that is meant by the 'old man':
namely, the employment of the faculties—memory, understanding and will—and the use and occupation of them in
things of the world, and in the desires and pleasures taken
in created things. All this is the exercise of the old life,
which is the death of the new, or spiritual, life. Herein the
soul will be unable to live perfectly if the old man die not
perfectly likewise, as the Apostle warns us when he says
that we should put off the old man, and put on the new
man, who according to the omnipotent God is created in
justice and holiness.[4] In this new life, which begins when
the soul has reached this perfection of union with God,
as we are saying here, all the desires of the soul and its
faculties according to its inclinations and operations, which
of themselves were the operation of death and the privation
of spiritual life, are changed into Divine operations.

34. And as each living creature lives by its operation, as
the philosophers say, the soul, having its operations in God,
through the union that it has with God, lives the life of
God, and thus its death has been changed into life—which
is to say that animal[5] life has been changed into spiritual
life. For the understanding, which before this union understood in a natural way with the strength and vigour of its
natural light, by means of[6] the bodily senses, is now moved
and informed by another and a higher principle, that of
the supernatural light of God, and, the senses having been

[3] Romans viii, 13.
[4] Ephesians iv, 22–4.
[5] Bg: 'natural.'
[6] Bg, P: 'through the life of.'

set aside, it has thus[7] been changed into the Divine, fo:
through union its understanding and that of God are now
both one. And the will, which aforetime loved after a
low manner, that of death,[8] and with its natural affection,
has now been changed into the life of Divine love; for it
loves after a lofty manner with Divine affection and is
moved by the power and strength of the Holy Spirit in
Whom it now lives the life of love,[9] since, through this
union, its will and His will are now only one. And the
memory, which of itself perceived only figures and phan-
tasms of created things, has become changed through this
union, so that it has in its mind the eternal years spoken of
by David.[10] And the natural desire, which had only capacity
and strength to enjoy creature pleasure that works death, is
now changed so that it tastes and enjoys that which is
Divine, being now moved and satisfied by another and a
more living principle, which is the delight of God; for it is
united with Him and thus it is now only the desire of God.
And finally, all the movements and operations and inclinations which the soul had aforetime, and which belonged to
the principle and strength of its natural life, are now in this
union changed into Divine movements, dead to their own
operation and inclination and alive in God. For the soul,
like the true daughter of God that it now is, is moved
wholly by the Spirit of God, even as Saint Paul teaches,
saying: 'That they that are moved by the Spirit of God are
sons of God Himself.'[11] So, as has been said, the understanding of this soul is now the understanding of God; and
its will is the will of God; and its memory is the memory
of God; and its delight is the delight of God; and the substance of this soul, although it is not the Substance of God,
for into this it cannot be substantially changed, is neverthe-

---

[7] Bg, P: 'it thus understands divinely and has thus.'
[8] Bg, P omit: 'that of death.'
[9] Bg: 'the life of God.'
[10] Psalm lxxvi, 6 [A.V., lxxvii, 5].
[11] Romans viii, 14.

less united in Him and absorbed in Him, and is thus God[12] by participation in God, which comes to pass in this perfect state of the spiritual life, although not so perfectly as in the next life. And in this way the soul is dead to all that was in itself, for this was death to it, and alive to that which God is in Himself; wherefore, speaking of itself, the soul well says in this line: 'In slaying, thou hast changed death into life.' Wherefore the soul may here very well say with Saint Paul: 'I live, now not I, but Christ liveth in me.'[13] In this way the death of this soul is changed into the life of God, and there may also be applied to it the saying of the Apostle: *Absorpta est mors in victoria.*[14] And likewise the words of Osee, the prophet, who, in his own person,[15] says as from God: 'O death, I will be thy death.'[16] This is as though he were to say: I am life, being the death of death, and death shall be absorbed in life.

35. In this wise the soul is absorbed in Divine life, being withdrawn from all that is secular and temporal and from natural desire, and brought into the cellars of the King,[17] where it rejoices and is glad in its beloved, and remembers His breasts more than wine, saying: 'Although I am black, I am beautiful, daughters of Jerusalem; for my natural blackness is changed into the beauty of the heavenly King.'[18]

36. In this state of life, perfect as it is, the soul is, as it were, interiorly and exteriorly keeping festival, and has in its mouth,[19] which is its spirit, a great song of joy to God, as it were a song new and ever new, turned into joy and love, having knowledge of its happy state. At times it has rejoicing and fruition, saying within its spirit those words of

12 S: 'and, thus absorbed, has become God.'
13 Galatians ii, 20.
14 1 Corinthians xv, 54.
15 Bz: 'in his own presence.'
16 Osee xiii, 14.
17 Bz: 'into the halls of the King.' C: 'into the cellar of the King.' Bg, P: 'into the secret mansion (*morada*) of the King.'
18 Canticles i, 4.
19 [*Lit.,* 'palate.']

Job, namely: 'My glory shall be always renewed and as a palm tree shall I multiply my days.'[20] Which is as much as to say: God Who, remaining within Himself unchangeably, makes all things new, as the Wise Man says, being united for ever in my glory,[21] will make my glory ever new—that is to say, He will not suffer it to grow old as it was before; and I shall multiply my days like the palm tree—that is, my merits unto Heaven, even as the palm tree sends out its branches to Heaven. For the merits of the soul that is in this state are ordinarily great in number and quality, and it is accustomed to sing to God in its spirit of all that David says in the Psalm which begins *Exaltabo te, Domine, quoniam suscepisti me*, particularly those last two verses, which say: *Convertisti planctum meum in gaudium mihi, etc., conscidisti saccum meum, et circumdedisti me laetitia.*[22] That my glory may sing to Thee, and I may not be ashamed.[23] O Lord my God, I will praise Thee for ever. And it is no marvel that the soul should experience with such frequency these joys,[24] this jubilation and this fruition, and should make these praises to God, for, apart from the knowledge which it has of the favours that it has received,[25] it now feels God to be so solicitous in granting it favours, and addressing it in such precious and delicate[26] and endearing words, and magnifying it with favour upon favour, that it believes that He has no other soul in the world to favour thus, nor aught else wherewith to occupy Himself, but that He is wholly for itself alone. And, when it feels this, it confesses its feeling like the Bride in the words of the Songs: *Dilectus meus mihi et ego illi.*[27]

---

[20] Job xxix, 18, 20.
[21] Bz: 'being now thus prevented in my glory.'
[22] Psalm xxix, 12 [A.V., xxx, 11].
[23] C gives these words in Latin only.
[24] Bg, P: 'that with such great faith the soul should be enkindled in these joys.'
[25] S: 'that it has known and received.'
[26] Bz: 'and delectable.'
[27] Canticles ii, 16.

STANZA III

Oh, lamps of fire,   In whose splendours the deep caverns
   of sense which were dark and blind
With strange brightness   Give heat and light together to
   their Beloved!

Exposition

MAY God be pleased to grant me His favour here, for in
truth it is very[1] needful if I am to explain the profound
meaning of this stanza: and he that reads it will need to give
it his attention, for, if he have no experience of this, it
will perhaps be somewhat obscure and prolix to him,
though, if he should have such experience, it will perchance
be clear and pleasing. In this stanza, the soul magnifies
its Spouse and gives Him thanks for the great favours which
it receives from the union that it has with Him, by means
whereof it says here that it receives abundant and great
knowledge of Himself, all full of love, wherewith the
faculties and senses, which, before this union, were dark
and blind, have been enlightened and enkindled with love,
and can now be illumined, as indeed they are, and through
the heat of love can give light and love to Him Who illumined and enamoured[2] them. For the true lover is content only when all that he is in himself, and all that he is
worth, and all that he has and receives, are employed in
the Beloved; and the more of this there is, the greater is the
pleasure that he receives in giving it. In this the soul here
rejoices, because with the splendours and the love that it
receives it will be able to shine resplendently before its
Beloved and to love Him. There follows the line:

Oh, lamps of fire,

[1] Bg, P omit 'very.'
[2] Bg, P omit: 'and enamoured.'

2. In the first place it must be known that lamps have two properties, which are to give light and heat. In order to understand the nature of these lamps whereof the soul here speaks, and how they give light and burn within it and give it heat, it must be known that God, in His one and simple Being, is all the virtues and grandeurs of His attributes; for He is omnipotent, wise, good, merciful, just, strong and loving,[1] and so forth, and has other infinite attributes and virtues[2] whereof we have no knowledge; and, as He is all these things in His simple Being, when He is united with the soul, at the time when He is pleased to reveal knowledge to it, it is able to see in Him all these virtues and grandeurs distinctly[3]—namely, omnipotence, wisdom and goodness, mercy, and so forth. And, as each of these things is the very Being of God in one sole reality, which is the Father or the Son or the Holy Spirit, each attribute being God Himself and God being infinite light and infinite Divine fire, as we have said above, it follows from this that, in each of these innumerable attributes, He gives light and heat as God,[4] and thus each of these attributes is a lamp which gives the soul light and gives it also the heat of love.

3. And inasmuch as in a single act of this union the soul receives the knowledge of these attributes, God Himself is[5] to the soul as many lamps all together, each of which, in a distinct way, gives light to it in wisdom and gives it heat, for from each lamp the soul has distinct knowledge and by each is enkindled in love. And thus with respect to all these lamps individually the soul loves and is enkindled[6]

[1] Bg, P omit: 'and loving.'

[2] S omits: 'and virtues.'

[3] Bz omits: 'distinctly.'

[4] Bg: 'in each of these attributes, which, as we said, are innumerable, and are His virtues, He gives light and heat as God.'

[5] Bg, P: 'He is.'

[6] So C, S. Bz: 'the soul is enkindled.' Bg, P: 'And thus with respect to all these lamps the soul understands and loves and is enkindled.'

by each, as also by all of them together, for, as we have said, all these attributes are one being; and thus all these lamps are one lamp, which, according to its virtues and attributes, gives light and heat as many lamps. Wherefore the soul, in a single act of knowledge of these lamps, loves through each one, and herein loves through all of them together, and in that act bears the quality of love through each one, and of each one, and of all together, and through all together. For the splendour given it by this lamp of the Being of God, inasmuch as He is omnipotent, gives it the light and heat of the love of God inasmuch as He is omnipotent. And therefore God is now to the soul a lamp of omnipotence, giving it light and all knowledge[7] according to this attribute. And the splendour given it by this lamp according to the Being of God, inasmuch as He is knowledge, sheds on it the light and heat of the love of God inasmuch as He is wise; and therefore God is now to it a lamp of wisdom. And the splendour given it by this lamp of God inasmuch as He is goodness[8] sheds upon the soul the light and heat of the love of God inasmuch as He is good; and accordingly God is now to it a lamp of goodness. And, in the same way, He is to it a lamp of justice, and of fortitude, and of mercy, and of all the other attributes that in this state are represented to the soul together in God. And the light that the soul receives from them all together is communicated to it by the heat of the love of God wherewith the soul loves God because He is all these things; and thus in this communication and manifestation of Himself that God makes to the soul (which, as I think, is the greatest that He can make to it in this life), He is to it as innumerable lamps which give it knowledge and love of Him.

4. These lamps were seen by Moses on Mount Sinai, where, when God passed by,[9] he fell prostrate on the ground, and began to cry out and to proclaim some of these at-

[7] Bg, P: 'light, love and all knowledge.'
[8] Bz: 'truth.'
[9] Bg: 'when God passed quickly before him.'

tributes, saying: 'Emperor, Lord, God that art merciful, clement, patient, of much compassion, true, that keepest mercy for thousands, that takest away sins[10] and evil deeds and faults, so that there is no man who of himself is innocent before Thee.'[11] Herein it is clear that the majority of the attributes and virtues of God which Moses then learned in God were those of God's omnipotence, dominion, deity, mercy, justice, truth and uprightness; which was a most profound knowledge of God; and since, according to that knowledge,[12] love was likewise communicated to him, the delight of love and the fruition that he experienced therein were most sublime.

5. From this it follows that the delight which the soul receives in the rapture of love communicated by the fire of the light of these lamps is wondrous, and boundless, being as vast as that of many lamps, each of which burns in love, the warmth of one being added to the warmth of another, and the flame of one to the flame of another, as also the light of one to the light of another, so that any attribute is known by any other; and thus all of them become one light and one fire, and each of them becomes one light and one fire. The soul, then, is here completely absorbed in these delicate flames, and wounded subtly by love in each of them, and in all of them together more wounded and deeply alive in the love of the life of God, so that it can see quite clearly that that love belongs to life eternal, which is the union of all blessings. So that the soul in that state in some wise perceives and knows well the truth of those words of the Spouse in the Songs, where He said that the lamps of love were lamps of fire and flames. 'Beauteous art thou in thy footsteps and thy shoes, oh, prince's daughter.'[13] Who can recount the magnificence and rarity of thy delight and majesty in the wondrous splendour and the love of thy lamps?

[10] Bg, P: 'the sins of the world.'
[11] Exodus xxxiv, 6–7.
[12] Bg, P add: 'of God.'
[13] Canticles vii, 1.

6. Divine Scripture relates that of old one of these lamps passed before Abraham and caused him the greatest darksome horror, because the lamp was that of the rigorous justice which He was about to work in the sight of the Chanaanites.[14] Then, oh soul so greatly enriched, shall not all these lamps of the knowledge of God which give thee a pleasant and loving light cause thee more light and joy of love than that single lamp caused horror and darkness in Abraham? And how great and how excellent and how manifold shall be thy joy, since in it all and from it all thou receivest fruition and love, and God communicates Himself to thy faculties according to His attributes and virtues? For, when a man loves another and does him good, he does him good and loves him according to his own attributes and properties. And thus thy Spouse, being as Who He is within thee, grants thee favours; for, since He is omnipotent, He does good to thee and loves thee with omnipotence; and since He is wise, thou perceivest that He does thee good and loves thee with wisdom; and, since He is infinitely good, thou perceivest that He loves thee with goodness; since He is holy, thou perceivest that He loves thee and grants thee favours with holiness; since He is just, thou perceivest that He loves thee and grants thee favours justly; since He is merciful, compassionate and clement, thou perceivest His mercy, compassion and clemency; and, since His Being is strong and sublime and delicate, thou perceivest that He loves thee with strength, sublimity and delicacy; and, since He is clean and pure, thou perceivest that He loves thee with cleanness and purity; and, since He is true, thou perceivest that He loves thee truly; and, since He is liberal, thou knowest that He loves thee and grants thee favours with liberality, without self-interest,[15] solely that He may do thee good; as He is the virtue of the greatest humility, He loves thee with the greatest humility, and with the greatest esteem, making

14 Genesis xv, 12–17.
15 C: 'with liberality, feeling no impediment or self-interest.'

thee His equal, joyfully revealing Himself to thee,[16] in these ways, which are His knowledge, by means of this His countenance full of graces, and saying to thee, in this His union, not without great rejoicing on thy part; I am thine and for thee, and I delight to be such as I am that I may be thine to give Myself to thee.

7. Who, then, can describe that which thou perceivest, oh, blessed soul, when thou knowest thyself to be thus loved and to be exalted with such esteem? Thy belly, which is thy will, is like that of the Bride, and as the heap of wheat which is covered and set about with lilies.[17] For in these grains of the wheat of the bread of life[18] which thou art tasting all together, the lilies of the virtues that surround thee are giving thee delight. For these are the King's daughters, of whom David says that they have delighted thee[19] with myrrh and ambar and other aromatic spices, for the communications of knowledge given thee by the Beloved concerning His graces and virtues are His daughters; and thou art so wholly engulfed and absorbed in them that thou art also the well of living waters that run with vehemence from Mount Libanus, which is God,[20] in the which stream thou art become marvellously glad with all the harmony of thy soul and even of thy body, which has become a Paradise watered by springs Divine.[21] Thus may the words of the Psalm be accomplished in thee, namely: 'The vehemence of the river makes glad the city of God.'[22]

8. Oh, wondrous thing! At this time the soul is overflowing with Divine waters, which flow from it as from an abundant source whose Divine waters gush in all directions. For, although it is true that this communication of which we are speaking is light and fire from these lamps of God,

[16] Bz adds: 'in this union.'
[17] Canticles vii, 2.
[18] [Lit., 'grains of bread of life.']
[19] Bg, P: 'that they delight thee in thy love.'
[20] Canticles iv, 15.
[21] Bz: 'a paradise of Divine rejoicing.'
[22] Psalm xlv, 5 [A.V., xlvi, 4].

yet this fire, as we have said, is here so sweet that, vast as
it is, it is like the waters of life which quench the thirst
of the spirit with the vehemence that it desires. So these
lamps of fire are living waters of the spirit, like those that
came upon the Apostles,[23] which, though they were lamps
of fire, were also pure and clear water, as the prophet Ezechiel called them when he prophesied that coming of the
Holy Spirit, saying: 'I will pour out upon you, saith God,
clean water, and will put My spirit in the midst of you.'[24]
And thus this fire is likewise water, for this fire is pre-figured
in the sacrificial fire that Jeremias hid in the cistern, which
was water when it was hidden and fire when they brought
it out for the sacrifice.[25] And thus this spirit of God, while
hidden in the veins of the soul, is like sweet and delectable
water quenching the thirst of the spirit; and, when the soul
offers the sacrifice of love to God, it becomes living flames
of fire, which are the lamps[26] of the act of love and of the
flames to which we referred above as being described by
the Spouse in the Songs. For this reason the soul here calls
them flames. For not only does it taste them as waters
within itself, but it likewise offers them as an act of love
to God like flames. And, inasmuch as in the spiritual communication of these lamps the soul is enkindled and set
in the exercise of love, in an act of love it calls them lamps
rather than flames, saying: 'Oh, lamps of fire.' All that can
be said in this stanza[27] is less than what there is to be said,
for the transformation of the soul in God is indescribable.
It can all be expressed in this word—namely, that the soul
has become God of God by participation in Him and in
His attributes, which are those that are here called lamps
of fire.

In whose splendours

23 Acts ii, 3.
24 Ezechiel xxxvi, 25.
25 2 Machabees i, 20–22. [Cf. p. 88, n. 28, above.]
26 Bz: 'flames.'
27 Bg, P: 'in this matter.'

9. In order to explain the nature of these splendours of the lamps whereof the soul here speaks and the way wherein the soul shines forth in splendour, we must first make it clear that these splendours are the communications of loving knowledge which the lamps of the attributes of God give forth to the soul, wherein the soul, united according to its faculties, also shines forth like them, being transformed into loving splendours. This brilliance of splendour wherein the soul shines forth with the heat of love is not like that produced by material lamps, which burst into flame and thus illumine the things around them, but is like that of the brilliance within the flames. For the soul is within these splendours, wherefore it says: 'In whose splendours': that is to say, it is 'within' them; and not only so, but, as we have said, it is transformed and turned into splendours. And so we shall say that it is like the air which is within the flame and is enkindled and transformed into flame, for flame is naught else but enkindled air, and the movements made and the splendours produced by this flame are not simply of air, nor simply of the fire, whereof it is composed, but of air and fire together, and the fire causes this union with the air that is enkindled within it.

10. And in this way we shall understand that the soul with its faculties is enlightened within the splendours of God. And the movements of this Divine flame, which are the vibrations and the bursts of flame which we have described above, are not made only by the soul that is transformed in the flames of the Holy Spirit, neither are they made by Him alone; but by the Spirit and the soul together, the Spirit moving the soul, even as the fire moves the air that is enkindled. And thus these movements of God and the soul together are not only splendours, but are also glorifications in the soul. For these movements and bursts of flame are the playing of the fire[1] and the joyful festivals which we said, in the second line of the first stanza, the

---

[1] Bz: 'are the fires and the playing [of the fires].'

Holy Spirit causes within the soul, wherein it seems that He is ever about to grant it eternal life and remove it to His perfect glory, and make it at last to enter truly within Himself. For all the blessings, both the early and the late, the great and the small, that God grants the soul He grants to it always with the motive of bringing it to eternal life,[2] just as all the movements made and the bursts of flame produced by the enkindled air have the purpose of bringing it to the centre of its sphere; and all these movements that it makes are attempts to bring it there. But, because the air is in the sphere proper to it, it cannot bring it; just so, although these movements[3] of the Holy Spirit are most effective in absorbing the soul into great glory, yet this is not perfectly accomplished until the time comes for the soul to leave the sphere of air—which is this life of the flesh —and to enter into the centre of its spirit, which is perfect life in Christ.

11. But it must be understood that these movements[4] are movements of the soul rather than of God; for God moves not. And so these glimpses of glory that are given to the soul are stable, perfect and continuous, with firm serenity[5] in God, as they will also be in the soul hereafter, without any change between greater and lesser, and without any intervening movements; and then the soul will see clearly how, although here below it appeared that God was moving in it, God moves not in Himself, even as the fire moves not in its sphere; and how, since it was not perfect in glory, it had those movements and bursts of flame in a foretaste of glory.[6]

12. From what has been said, and from what we shall now say, it will be more clearly understood how great is

2 Bz: 'to eternal glory.'
3 P, S: 'these motives.'
4 Bg adds: 'of the flame.' P adds: 'of the soul.'
5 Bg, P have 'sweetness' for 'serenity.' [The first redaction (p. 90, above) has 'not' before 'stable.']
6 Bg, P add: 'even as the stars twinkle from afar.'

the excellence of the splendours of these lamps which we are describing, for these splendours by another name are called overshadowings. To understand this it must be understood that 'overshadowing' signifies 'casting of a shadow,' and for a man to cast his shadow over another signifies that he protects him, befriends him and grants him favours. When the shadow covers the person, this is a sign that he who overshadows him is now near to befriend and protect him. For this reason that great favour which God granted to the Virgin Mary—namely, her conception of the Son of God—was called by the angel Saint Gabriel an overshadowing of the Holy Spirit. 'The Holy Spirit,' he said, 'shall come upon thee and the power of the Most High shall overshadow thee.'[7]

13. For the better understanding of the nature of this casting of a shadow by God, or (which is the same thing) these overshadowings of great splendours, it must be understood that everything has and makes a shadow in conformity with its nature and size. If the thing is opaque and dark[8] it makes a dark shadow,[9] and if it is light and fine[10] it makes a light and fine shadow: and thus the shadow of an object which is dark[11] will be a dark shadow of the size of that dark object, and the shadow of a light object[12] will be a light shadow of the size of that light object.

14. Now, inasmuch as these virtues and attributes of God are enkindled and resplendent lamps, and are near to the soul, as we have said, they will not fail to touch the soul with their shadows, which will be enkindled and resplendent likewise, even as are the lamps by which they are cast, and thus these shadows will be splendours. In this way the shadow cast upon the soul by the lamp of the

[7] St. Luke i, 35.
[8] Bz: 'small and dark.'
[9] Bz: 'a small and dark shadow.'
[10] Bg, P: 'clear and light.' Bz, C: 'clear, light and fine.'
[11] [Lit., 'of a darkness.']
[12] [Lit., 'of a light.']

beauty of God will be other beauty, of the nature and proportions of that beauty of God; and the shadow cast by
strength will be other strength of the proportions of the
strength of God; and the shadow cast by the wisdom of
God will be other wisdom[13] of God, of the proportions of
that wisdom of God. And so with the remaining lamps;
or, more correctly, it will be the same wisdom and the
same beauty and the same strength of God, in shadow, for
here on earth the soul cannot perfectly comprehend it,[14]
and since this shadow is in such conformity with the nature
and proportions of God—that is, with God Himself[15]—
the soul has, in shadow, an effective realization of God's
excellence.

15. What, then, will be the shadows that the Holy Spirit
will cast upon this soul—namely, the shadows of the grandeurs of His virtues and attributes? For He is so near to
the soul that He not only touches it in shadows, but is
united with it in shadows and splendours, and it understands and experiences God in each of them according to
His nature and proportions in each of them? For it understands and experiences Divine power[16] in the shadow of
omnipotence; and it understands and experiences Divine
wisdom in the shadow of Divine wisdom; understands and
experiences infinite goodness in the shadow of infinite goodness which surrounds it;[17] and so forth. Finally, it experiences the glory of God in the shadow of glory, which causes
it to know the nature and proportions of the glory of God
when all these pass by in bright and enkindled shadows
cast by these bright and enkindled lamps, all of which are
in one lamp of one single and simple Being of God, which
actually shines forth upon it in all these ways.

[13] Bg, C, P omit: 'of God.'
[14] Bg, P read: 'and, more correctly, it will be the same beauty
of God, in shadow, for the soul, although perfect, cannot comprehend it.'
[15] Bg, P omit this parenthetical clause.
[16] Bg: 'Divine omnipotence.'
[17] C omits: 'in the shadow . . . surrounds it.'

16. Oh, what the soul will feel here, when it experiences the knowledge and communication of that figure which Ezechiel saw in that beast with four faces, and in that wheel[18] with four wheels, when he saw that its appearance was as the appearance of kindled coals and as the appearance of lamps![19] The soul will see the wheel, which is the wisdom of God, full of eyes within and without, which are Divine manifestations of knowledge and the splendours of His virtues, and will hear in its spirit that sound made by their passage, which was like the sound of a multitude and of great armies,[20] signifying many grandeurs of God, of which the soul here has distinct knowledge in one single sound of God's passing through it. Finally, it will experience that sound of the beating of wings, which the Prophet says was as the sound of many waters and as the sound of the Most High God;[21] this indicates the vehemence of the Divine waters, which we have described, and which, at the beating of the wings of the Holy Spirit, overwhelm the soul and make it to rejoice in the flame of love, so that it now enjoys the glory of God in His likeness and shadow,[22] even as this Prophet says that the visions of that beast and that wheel were similitudes of the glory of the Lord.[23] And to what a height may this happy soul now find itself raised! How greatly will it know itself to be exalted! How wondrous will it see itself to be in holy beauty! How far beyond all telling! For so copiously does it become assailed by the waters of these Divine splendours that it is able to see that the Eternal Father, with bounteous hand,[24] has granted it the upper and the lower streams that water the earth, even as the father of Axa gave these to her when she

18 C: 'that cart.'
19 C has only: 'was as the appearance of coals.'
20 P: 'and of servants.'
21 [Ezechiel i, 15–25.]
22 Bg: 'likeness and the favour of His shadow.'
23 C: 'of the wheel of the Lord' [cf. Ezechiel i, 28].
24 Bg, P omit: 'with bounteous hand.'

longed for them,[25] for these irrigating waters penetrate both soul and body, which are the upper and the nether parts of man.

17. Oh, wondrous excellence of God that these lamps of the Divine attributes should be one simple being in which alone they are experienced, and yet that they should be distinctly seen,[26] each being as completely enkindled as the other and each being substantially the other! Oh, abyss of delights, that art the more abundant in proportion as thy riches are gathered together in the infinite simplicity and unity of Thy sole Being, so that each one is known and experienced in such a way that the perfect knowledge and absorption of the other is not impeded thereby, but rather each grace and virtue that exists in thee is light that comes from some other of thy grandeurs, so that through thy purity, oh, Divine wisdom, many things are seen in thee when one thing is seen, since thou art the store-house of the treasures of the Father, the splendour of eternal light, a stainless mirror and image of His goodness.[27] For in thy splendours are

The deep caverns of sense

18. These caverns are the faculties of the soul—memory, understanding and will—of which the depth is proportionate to their capacity for great blessings, for they can be filled with nothing less than the infinite. But considering what they suffer when they are empty we can realize in some measure the greatness of their joy and delight when they are filled with God, for one contrary can give light to another.[1] In the first place, it must be noted that these caverns of the faculties, when they are not empty and purged and cleansed from all creature affection, are not conscious of their great emptiness, which is due to their

[25] [Judges i, 15. Cf. p. 94, n. 18, above.]
[26] Bg, P: 'seen and experienced.' Bz: 'seen and enjoyed.'
[27] Wisdom vii, 26.
[1] [Cf. p. 46, n. 14, above.]

profound capacity. For in this life any trifle that remains within them suffices to keep them so cumbered and fascinated that they are neither conscious of their loss nor do they miss the immense blessings that might be theirs, nor are they aware of their own capacity.[2] And it is a wondrous thing that, despite their capacity for infinite blessing, the least thing suffices to cumber them, so that they cannot receive these blessings until they are completely empty, as we shall say hereafter. But, when they are empty and clean, the hunger and thirst and yearning of their spiritual sense become intolerable; for, as the capacities[3] of these caverns are deep, their pain is deep likewise, as is also the food that they lack, which, as I say, is God. And this great feeling of pain commonly occurs towards the close of the illumination and purification of the soul, ere it attain to union, wherein it[4] has satisfaction. For, when the spiritual appetite is empty and purged from every creature and from every creature affection, and its natural temper is lost and it has become attempered to the Divine, and its emptiness is disposed to be filled, and when the Divine communication of union with God has not yet reached it, then the suffering caused by this emptiness and thirst is worse than death, especially when the soul is vouchsafed some foresight or glimpse of the Divine ray and this is not communicated to it.[5] It is souls in this condition that suffer with impatient love, so that they cannot remain long without either receiving or dying.

19. With respect to the first cavern which we here describe—namely, the understanding—its emptiness is thirst for God, and, when the understanding is made ready for God, this is so great that David compares it to that of the hart, finding no greater thirst wherewith to compare it, for

[2] Bz omits the last clause.
[3] [*Lit.*, 'the stomachs.']
[4] Bg, P: 'wherein that spiritual appetite.'
[5] Bz: 'and the Divine, in union with God, is not communicated to it.' Bg, P: 'and God communicates not Himself to it.'

the thirst of the hart is said to be most vehement. 'Even as the hart (says David) desires the fountains of the waters, even so does my soul desire Thee, O God.'[6] This thirst is for the waters of the wisdom of God, which is the object of the understanding.

20. The second cavern is the will, and the emptiness thereof is hunger for God, so great that it causes the soul to swoon,[7] even as David says, in these words: 'My soul desires and faints for the tabernacles of the Lord.'[8] And this hunger is for the perfection of love to which the soul aspires.

21. The third cavern is the memory, whereof the emptiness is the melting away and languishing of the soul for the possession of God, as Jeremias notes in these words: *Memoria memor ero et tabescet in me anima mea.*[9] That is: With remembrance I shall remember, and I shall remember Him well and my soul shall melt away within me; turning over these things in my heart, I shall live in hope of God.

22. The capacity of these caverns, then, is deep; for that which they are capable of containing, which is God, is deep and infinite;[10] and thus in a certain sense their capacity will be infinite, and likewise their thirst will be infinite, and their hunger also will be infinite and deep, and their languishing[11] and pain are infinite death. For, although the soul suffers not so intensely as in the next life, it suffers nevertheless a vivid image of that infinite privation, since it is to a certain extent prepared to receive fullness; although this suffering is of another kind, for it dwells in the bosom of the love of the will, and this love does not alleviate the pain; for the greater is the love, the greater is

6 Psalm xli, 1 [A.V., xlii, 1].

7 C abbreviates: 'and the emptiness thereof causes the soul to swoon.'

8 Psalm lxxxiii, 3 [A.V., lxxxiv, 2].

9 Lamentations iii, 20–1.

10 S: 'is deep in infinite goodness.'

11 C: 'their swooning.'

the impatience of the soul for the possession of its God, for Whom it hopes continually with intense desire.

23. But, seeing it is certain that, when the soul desires God with entire[12] truth, it already (as Saint Gregory says in writing of Saint John[13]) possesses Him Whom it loves, how comes it, O God, that it yearns for Him Whom it already possesses? For, in the desire which, as Saint Peter says,[14] the angels have to see the Son of God, there is neither pain nor yearning, since they possess Him already; so it seems that, if the soul possesses God more completely according as it desires Him more earnestly, the possession of God should give delight and satisfaction to the soul. Even so the angels have delight when they are fulfilling their desire in possession, and satisfying their soul continually with desire, yet have none of the weariness that comes from satiety; wherefore, since they have no weariness, they continually desire, and because they have possession they have no pain. Thus, the greater is the desire of the soul in this state, the more satisfaction and desire it should experience, since it has the more of God and has not grief or pain.

24. In this matter, however, it is well to note clearly the difference that exists between the possession of God through grace itself alone and the possession of Him through union; for the one consists in deep mutual love, but in the other there is also communication. There is as great a difference between these states as there is between betrothal and marriage. For in betrothal there is only a consent by agreement, and a unity of will between the two parties, and the jewels and the adornment of the bride-to-be, given her graciously by the bridegroom. But in marriage there is likewise communication between the persons, and union. During the betrothal, although from time to time the bridegroom sees the bride and gives her gifts, as we have said, there is no

[12] Bz: 'intense.'
[13] Hom. XXX in Evang.
[14] 1 St. Peter i, 12.

union between them, for that is the end[15] of betrothal. Even so, when the soul has attained to such purity in itself and in its faculties that the will is well purged[16] of other strange tastes and desires, according to its lower and higher parts, and when it has given its consent to God with respect to all this, and the will of God and of the soul are as one in a free consent of their own,[17] then it has attained to the possession of God through grace of will, in so far as can be by means of will and grace; and this signifies that God has given it, through its own consent, His true and entire consent, which comes through His grace.

25. And this is the lofty state of spiritual betrothal of the soul with the Word,[18] wherein the Spouse grants the soul great favours, and visits it most lovingly and frequently, wherein the soul receives great favours and delights. But these have nothing to do with those of marriage, for the former are all preparations for the union of marriage; and, though it is true that they come to the soul when it is completely purged from all creature affection (for spiritual betrothal, as we say, cannot take place until this happens), nevertheless the soul has need of other and positive preparations on the part of God, of His visits and gifts whereby He purifies the soul ever more completely and beautifies and refines it so that it may be fitly prepared for such high union. In some souls more time is necessary than in others, for God works here according to the state of the soul. This is prefigured in those maidens who were chosen for King Assuerus;[19] although they had been taken from their own countries and from their fathers' houses, yet, before they were sent to the king's bed, they were kept waiting for a year, albeit within the enclosure of the palace. For one half of the year they were prepared with certain ointments

---

[15] S reads: 'nor is that the end.'
[16] S: 'is very pure and well purged.'
[17] Bg, P: 'in a consent that is ready and free.'
[18] P: 'with God the Word.' Bg: 'with the Word, God.'
[19] Esther ii, 12.

of myrrh and other spices, and for the other half of the year with other and choicer ointments, after which they went to the king's bed.[20]

26. During the time, then, of this betrothal and expectation of marriage in the unctions of the Holy Spirit, when there are choicest ointments[21] preparing the soul for union with God, the yearnings of the caverns of the soul are wont to be extreme and delicate. For, as those ointments are a most proximate preparation for union with God, because they are nearest to God and for this cause make the soul more desirous of Him and inspire it with a more delicate affection for Him, the desire is more delicate and also deeper; for the desire for God is a preparation for union with God.

27. Oh, how good a place would this be to warn souls whom God is leading to these delicate anointings[22] to take care what they are doing and into whose hands they commit themselves, lest they go backward, were not this beyond the limits of that whereof we are speaking! But such is the compassion and pity that fills my heart when I see souls going backward, and not only failing to submit themselves to the anointing of the spirit so that they may make progress therein, but even losing the effects of that anointing of God which they have received, that I must not fail to warn them here as to what they should do in order to avoid such loss, even though this should cause us to delay the return to our subject a little. I shall return to it shortly, and indeed all this will help us to understand the properties of these caverns. And since it is very necessary, not only for these souls that prosper on this way but also for all the rest who seek their Beloved, I am anxious to describe it.

28. First, it must be known that, if a soul is seeking God, its Beloved[23] is seeking it much more; and, if it sends after

[20] Bz omits: 'after which . . . bed.'
[21] Bg, P: 'when there are now the choicest ointments.'
[22] Bz: 'unions.'
[23] Bg, P: 'its Beloved, God.'

Him its loving desires, which are as fragrant to Him as a pillar of smoke that issues from the aromatic spices of myrrh and incense,[24] He likewise sends after it the fragrance of His ointments, wherewith He attracts the soul and causes it to run after Him. These ointments are His Divine inspirations and touches, which, whenever they are His, are ordered[25] and ruled with respect to the perfection of the law of God and of faith, in which perfection the soul must ever draw nearer and nearer to God. And thus the soul must understand that the desire of God in all the favours that He bestows upon it in the unctions[26] and fragrance of His ointments is to prepare it for other choicer and more delicate ointments which have been made more after the temper of God, until it reaches such a delicate and pure state of preparation that it merits union with God and substantial transformation in all its faculties.[27]

29. When, therefore, the soul reflects that God is the principal agent in this matter, and the guide of its blind self, Who will take it by the hand and lead it where it could not of itself go (namely, to the supernatural things which neither its understanding nor its will nor its memory could know as they are), then its chief care will be to see that it sets no obstacle in the way of Him that guides it upon the road which God has ordained for it, in the perfection of the law of God and faith,[28] as we are saying. And this impediment may come to the soul if it allows itself to be led and guided by another blind guide; and the blind guides that might lead it out of its way are three, namely, the spiritual director, the devil and its own self. And, that the soul may understand how this is, we will treat shortly of each of them.[29]

24 Canticles iii, 6.
25 Bz: 'are anointed.'
26 Bz: 'communications.' C: 'unions.'
27 Bg, P omit: 'in all its faculties.'
28 Bz: 'of the love of God and of the law and of faith.'
29 Bg, P: 'of each of these blind guides.'

30. With regard to the first of these, it is of great importance for the soul that desires to make progress in recollection and perfection to consider in whose hands it is placing itself; for, as is the master, so will be the disciple, and, as is the father, so will be the son. And let it be noted there is hardly anyone who in all respects will guide the soul perfectly along the highest stretch of the road, or even along the intermediate stretches, for it is needful that such a guide should be experienced as well as wise and discreet. The fundamental requirement of a guide in spiritual things is knowledge and discretion; yet, if a guide have no experience of the nature of pure and true spirituality, he will be unable to direct[30] the soul therein, when God permits it to attain so far, nor will he even understand it.

31. In this way many spiritual masters[31] do much harm to many souls, for, not themselves understanding the ways and properties of the spirit, they commonly cause souls to lose the unction of these delicate ointments, wherewith the Holy Spirit gradually anoints and prepares them for Himself, and instructs them by other and lower means which they have used and of which they have read here and there, and which are unsuitable save for beginners. They themselves know no more than how to deal with these—please God they may know even so much!—and refuse to allow souls to go beyond these rudimentary acts of meditation and imagination, even though God is seeking to lead them farther, so that they may never exceed or depart from their natural capacity, whereby a soul can achieve very little.

32. And in order that we may better understand the characteristics of beginners, we must know that the state and exercise of beginners is one of meditation and of the making of discursive exercises and acts with the imagination. In this state, it is necessary for the soul to be given material for meditation and reasoning, and it is well for it to make interior acts on its own account, and even in spiritual things

30 Bz: 'to examine' [*examinar* for *encaminar*].
31 Bg: 'fathers.'

to take advantage of the sweetness and pleasure[32] which come from sense; for, if the desire is fed with pleasure in spiritual things, it becomes detached from pleasure in sensual things and wearies of things of the world. But when to some extent the desire has been fed, and in some sense habituated to spiritual things, and has acquired some fortitude and constancy, God then begins, as they say, to wean the soul and bring it into the state of contemplation, which in some persons is wont to happen very quickly, especially in religious, because these, having renounced[33] things of the world, quickly attune their senses and desires to God, and their exercises become spiritual through God's working in them; this happens when the discursive acts and the meditation of the soul itself cease, and the first fervours and sweetness of sense cease likewise, so that the soul cannot meditate as before, or find any help in the senses; for the senses remain in a state of aridity, inasmuch as their treasure is transformed into spirit, and no longer falls within the capacity of sense. And, as all the operations which the soul can perform on its own account naturally depend upon sense only, it follows that God is the agent in this state and the soul is the recipient; for the soul behaves only as one that receives and as one in whom these things are being wrought; and God as One that gives and acts and as One that works these things in the soul, giving it spiritual blessings in contemplation, which is Divine love and knowledge in one—that is, a loving knowledge, wherein the soul has not to use its natural acts and reasonings,[34] for it can no longer enter into them as before.

33. It follows that at this time the soul must be led in a way entirely contrary to the way wherein it was led at first. If formerly it was given material for meditation, and practised meditation, this material must now be taken from it and it must not meditate; for, as I say, it will be unable

---

[32] C: 'the fervour, favour and pleasure.'
[33] S: 'abandoned.'
[34] Bz omits: 'and reasonings.'

to do so even though it would, and, instead of becoming recollected, it will become distracted. And if formerly it sought sweetness and love and fervour, and found it, now it must neither seek it nor desire it, for not only will it be unable to find it through its own diligence, but it will rather find aridity, for it turns from the quiet and peaceful blessings which were secretly given to its spirit, to the work that it desires to do with sense; and thus it will lose the one and not obtain the other, since no blessings are now given to it by means of sense as they were formerly. Wherefore in this state the soul must never have meditation imposed upon it, nor must it make any acts, nor strive after sweetness or fervour; for this would be to set an obstacle in the way of the principal agent, who, as I say, is God. For God secretly and quietly[35] infuses into the soul loving knowledge and wisdom without any intervention of specific acts, although sometimes He specifically produces them in the soul for some length of time. And the soul has then to walk with loving advertence to God, without making specific acts, but conducting itself, as we have said, passively, and making no efforts of its own, but preserving this simple, pure and[36] loving advertence and determination, like one that opens his eyes with the advertence of love.

34. Since God, then, as giver, is communing with the soul by means of loving and simple knowledge, the soul must likewise commune with Him by receiving with a loving and simple knowledge and advertence, so that knowledge may be united with knowledge and love with love. For it is meet that he who receives should behave in conformity with that which he receives, and not in any other manner, in order to be able to receive and retain it as it is given[37] to him; for, as the philosophers say, anything that is received is in the recipient according to the manner of acting

[35] Bz: 'secretly and in a hidden way.'
[36] S omits: 'simple, pure and.'
[37] Bz: 'as it was given.'

of the recipient. Wherefore it is clear that if the soul at this time were not to abandon its natural procedure of active meditation, it would not receive this blessing in other than a natural way. It would not, in fact, receive it, but would retain its natural act alone, for the supernatural cannot be received in a natural way, nor can it have aught to do with it. And thus, if the soul at this time desires to work on its own account, and to do aught else than remain, quite passively and tranquilly, in that passive and loving advertence whereof we have spoken, making no natural act, save if God should unite it with Himself in some act, it would set a total and effective impediment in the way of the blessings which God is communicating to it supernaturally in loving knowledge. This comes to pass first of all in the exercise of interior purgation wherein, as we have said above, it suffers, and afterwards in sweetness of love. If, as I say, and as in truth is the case, the soul receives this loving knowledge passively and after the supernatural manner of God, and not after the manner of the natural soul, it follows that, in order to receive them, this soul must be quite annihilated in its natural operations, disencumbered, at ease, quiet, peaceful, serene, and adapted to the manner of God; exactly like the air, which receives the greater clarification and heat from the sun when it is pure and cleansed from vapours and at rest. Therefore the soul must be attached to nothing—to no exercise of meditation or reasoning; to no kind of sweetness, whether it be of sense or of spirit; and to no other kind of apprehension.[38] For the spirit needs to be so free and so completely annihilated that any kind of thought or meditation or pleasure to which the soul in this state may conceive an attachment would impede and disturb it and would introduce noise into the deep silence which it is meet that the soul should observe, according both to sense and to spirit, so that it may hear the deep and delicate voice in which God speaks to the

[38] S: 'of operation.'

heart in this secret place,[39] as He said through Osee,[40] in the utmost peace and tranquillity, so that the soul may listen and hear the words of the Lord God to it, as David says,[41] when in this secret place He speaks this peace.

35. When, therefore, it comes to pass that the soul is conscious of being led into silence, and hearkens, it must forget even the practice of that loving advertence of which I have spoken, so that it may remain free for that which the Lord then desires of it; for it must practise that advertence only when it is not conscious of being brought into solitude or interior rest[42] or forgetfulness or attentiveness of the spirit, which, in order that it may be perceived, is always accompanied by a certain peaceful tranquillity and interior absorption.

36. Wherefore, whatever be the time or season, when once the soul has begun to enter into this pure and restful state of contemplation, which comes to pass when it may no longer meditate and is unable to do so, it must not seek to gather to itself meditations, neither must it desire to find help in spiritual sweetness or delight, but it must stand in complete detachment above all this and its spirit must be completely freed from it, as Habacuc[43] said that he must needs do in order to hear what the Lord should say to him. 'I will stand upon my watch,' he says, 'and I will fix my step upon my munition, and I will watch to see that which will be said to me.' This is as though he had said: I will raise up my mind above all the operations and all the knowledge that can be comprehended by my senses, and above that which they can keep and retain within themselves: all this I will leave below. And I will fix the step of the munition of my faculties,[44] not allowing them to advance

39 S: 'in this important secret place.'
40 Osee ii, 14.
41 Psalm lxxxiv, 9 [A.V., lxxxv, 8].
42 S: 'into solitude, with all interior rest.'
43 Habacuc ii, 1.
44 Bz: 'of the communication of my faculties.' S omits: 'of my faculties.'

a step as to their own operation, so that through contemplation I may receive that which is communicated to me from God. For we have already said that pure contemplation consists in receiving.

37. It is not possible that this loftiest wisdom and language of God, such as is contemplation, can be received save in a spirit that is silent and detached from sweetness and discursive knowledge. For this is that which is said by Isaias, in these words: 'Whom shall He teach knowledge and whom shall He make to hear its voice?'[45] Them that are weaned from the milk—that is, from sweetness and pleasures—and them that are detached from the breasts—that is, from particular apprehensions and knowledge.

38. Oh, spiritual soul, take away the motes and the hairs and the mists,[46] and cleanse thine eye, and the bright sun shall shine upon thee, and thou shalt see clearly.[47] Set the soul in peace, and draw it away and free it from the yoke and slavery of the weak operation of its own capacity, which is the captivity of Egypt, where all is little more than gathering straw to make bricks; and guide it, oh, spiritual director, to the promised land flowing with milk and honey, remembering that it is to give the soul this freedom and holy rest which belongs to His sons that God calls it into the wilderness. There it journeys adorned with festal robes, and with jewels of silver and of gold, having now left Egypt,[48] by which is meant the sensual part of the soul, and emptied it of its riches. And not only so, but the Egyptians[49] are drowned in the sea of contemplation, where the Egyptian of sense finds no support, or foothold, and thus is drowned, and sets free the child of God—that is, the spirit that has gone forth from the limits[50] and the slavery of the opera-

45 Isaias xxviii, 9.
46 Bz, C omit: 'and the mists.'
47 Bg, P omit: 'and thou shalt see clearly.'
48 Bg, C, P: 'having now despoiled Egypt.' Bz: 'Christ having now despoiled it' [or 'him'].
49 S: 'the giants.'
50 Bg, Bz, C: 'the narrow limits.'

tion of the senses (which is to say from its scant understanding, its lowly perception, and its miserable loving
and liking) so that God may give it the sweet manna, which,
though the sweetness thereof contains within itself all
these sweetnesses and delights for which thou desirest to
make the soul work, nevertheless, being so delicious that
it melts in the mouth, the soul shall not taste of it if it
desire to combine it with any other delight or with aught
else. Endeavour, then, when the soul is nearing this state,
to detach it from all coveting or spiritual sweetness, pleasure, delight and meditation, and disturb it not with care
and solicitude of any kind for higher things, still less for
lower things, but bring it into the greatest possible degree
of solitude and withdrawal. For the more nearly the soul
attains all this, and the sooner it reaches this restful tranquillity, the more abundantly does it become infused with
the spirit of Divine wisdom, which is the loving, tranquil,
lonely, peaceful, sweet inebriator of the spirit. Hereby the
soul feels itself to be gently and tenderly wounded and
ravished, knowing not by whom, nor whence, nor how. And
the reason of this is that the Spirit communicates Himself
without any act on the part of the soul.

39. And the smallest part of this that God brings to pass
in the soul in holy rest and solitude is an inestimable blessing, greater sometimes than either the soul itself, or he that
guides it, can imagine; and, although this may not be very
clearly realized at the time, it will in due course become
manifest. But the soul has at least been able[51] to attain
to a perception of estrangement and withdrawal from all
things, sometimes more so than at others, together with
an inclination to solitude and a sense of weariness with regard to all worldly creatures and a sweet aspiration of love
and life in the spirit. And in this state anything that does
not imply such withdrawal is distasteful to it, for, as they

[51] Bg, Bz, C, P add 'now.'

say, when a soul tastes of the spirit, it conceives a distaste for the flesh.

40. But the blessings that this silent communication and contemplation leave impressed upon the soul without its perceiving them at the time are, as I say, inestimable; for they are the most secret and therefore the most delicate anointings of the Holy Spirit, which secretly fill the soul with spiritual riches and gifts and graces; for, since it is God Who does all this, He does it not otherwise than as God.

41. These anointings, then, and these touches, are the delicate and sublime acts of the Holy Spirit, which, on account of their delicate and subtle purity, can be understood neither by the soul nor by him that has to do with it, but only by Him Who infuses them, in order to make the soul more pleasing to Himself. These blessings, with the greatest facility, by no more than the slightest act which the soul may desire to make on its own account, with its memory, understanding or will, or by the application of its sense or desire or knowledge or sweetness or pleasure, are disturbed or hindered in the soul, which is a grave evil and a great shame and pity.

42. Oh, how grave a matter is this, and what cause it gives for wonder, that, while the harm done is inconspicuous, and the interference with those holy anointings almost negligible, the harm should be more serious, and a matter for deeper sorrow and regret, than the disquieting and ruining of many souls of a more ordinary nature which have not attained to a state of such supreme fineness and delicacy! It is as though a portrait of supreme and delicate beauty were touched by a clumsy hand, and were daubed with coarse, crude colours. This would be a greater and more crying and pitiful shame than if many more ordinary portraits were besmeared in this way. For when the work of so delicate a hand as this of the Holy Spirit has been thus roughly treated, who will be able to repair its beauty?

43. Although the gravity and seriousness of this evil

cannot be exaggerated, it is so common and frequent that there will hardly be found a single spiritual director who does not inflict it upon souls whom God is beginning to draw nearer to Himself[52] in this kind of contemplation. For, whenever God is anointing the contemplative soul with some most delicate unction of loving knowledge—serene, peaceful, lonely and very far removed from sense and from all that has to do with thought—so that the soul cannot meditate or think of aught soever or find pleasure in aught, whether in higher things or in lower, inasmuch as God is keeping it full of that lonely unction and inclined to rest and solitude,[53] there will come some spiritual director who has no knowledge save of hammering and pounding with the faculties like a blacksmith, and, because his only teaching is of that kind, and he knows of naught save meditation, he will say: 'Come now, leave these periods of inactivity, for you are only living in idleness and wasting your time. Get to work, meditate and make interior acts, for it is right that you should do for yourself that which in you lies, for these other things are the practices of Illuminists and fools.'

44. And thus, since such persons have no understanding of the degrees of prayer or of the ways of the spirit, they cannot see that those acts which they counsel the soul to perform, and those attempts to make it progress along the path of meditation, have been made already, for such a soul as we have been describing has by this time attained to negation and silence of sense and discursive reasoning, and has reached the way of the spirit, which is contemplation,[54] wherein ceases the operation of sense and the soul's own discursive reasoning, and God alone is the agent and it is He that now speaks secretly to the solitary soul, while the soul keeps silence. And if, now that the spirit has achieved spirituality in this way that we are describing, such directors attempt to make the soul continue to walk

[52] [Cf. p. 109, n. 55, above.]
[53] S: 'full of that lonely rest and inclined to solitude.'
[54] Bg, P: 'the life of the spirit, which is the contemplative life.'

in sense, it cannot but go backward and become distracted. For if one that has reached his goal begins to set out again for it, he is doing a ridiculous thing, for he can do nothing but walk away from it.[55] When, therefore, through the operation of its faculties, the soul has reached that quiet recollection which is the aim of every spiritual person, wherein ceases the operation of these faculties, it would not only be a vain thing for it to begin to make acts with these faculties in order to reach this recollection, but it would be harmful to it, for it would cause it distraction and make it abandon the recollection that it already has.

45. Now these spiritual directors, not understanding, as I say, the nature and properties of the soul's spiritual solitude and recollection, in which solitude God effects these sublime anointings in the soul, superpose or interpose other anointings, which consist in more elementary spiritual exercises,[56] and make the soul work in the way we have described. There is as much difference between this and what the soul previously enjoyed as between any human operation and a Divine operation and between the natural and the supernatural; for in the one case God is working supernaturally in the soul and in the other case the soul alone is working naturally.[57] And the worst result is that, through the exercise of its natural operation, the soul loses its interior recollection and solitude and consequently spoils the wondrous work that God was painting[58] in it. It is thus as if the director were merely striking an anvil; and the soul loses in one respect and gains nothing in the other.

46. Let such guides of the soul as these take heed and remember that the principal agent and guide and mover

[55] Bg, P: 'but leave it.'
[56] Bg, P: 'which consist in more labour and spiritual exercises.'
[57] Bg, P: 'and in the other it is only itself working and its operation is no more than natural.' Bz reads similarly, but omits 'only.' C: 'for in the one case God is working and in the other only the soul itself is working and its operation is no more than natural.'
[58] S: 'was working.'

233

of souls in this matter is not the director, but the Holy Spirit, Who never loses His care for them; and that they themselves are only instruments to lead souls in the way of perfection by the faith and the law of God, according to the spirit that God is giving to each one. Let them not, therefore, merely aim at guiding these souls according to their own way and the manner suitable to themselves, but let them see if they know the way by which God is leading the soul, and, if they know it not, let them leave the soul in peace and not disturb it. And, in conformity with the way and the spirit by which God is leading these souls, let them ever seek to lead them into greater solitude, tranquillity and liberty of spirit and to give them a certain freedom so that the spiritual and bodily senses may not be bound to any particular thing, either interior or exterior, when God leads the soul by this way of solitude, and let them not worry or grieve, thinking that it is doing nothing; for, though it is not working at that time, God is working in it. Let them strive to disencumber the soul and to set it in a state of rest,[59] in such a way that it will not be bound to any particular kind of knowledge, either above or below, or be fettered by covetousness of any sweetness or pleasure or any other apprehension, but that it will be empty in pure negation with respect to every creature and will be established in poverty of spirit. It is this that the soul must do as far as in it lies, as the Son of God counsels, in these words: 'He that renounceth not all the things that he possesseth cannot be My disciple.'[60] This is to be understood, not only of the renunciation of all temporal things[61] with the will, but also of the surrender of spiritual things, wherein is included poverty of spirit, in which, says the Son of God, consists blessedness.[62] When in this way the soul voids itself of all things and achieves emptiness and

---

[59] S: 'of solitude and rest.'
[60] [St. Luke xiv, 33.]
[61] S: 'of all bodily and temporal things.'
[62] St. Matthew v, 3.

surrender of them (which, as we have said, is the part that the soul can play), it is impossible, if the soul does as much as in it lies, that God should fail to perform His own part by communicating Himself to the soul, at least secretly and in silence. It is more impossible than that the sun should fail to shine in a serene and unclouded sky; for as the sun, when it rises in the morning, will enter your house if you open the shutter,[63] even so will God, Who sleeps not in keeping Israel, still less slumbers,[64] enter the soul that is empty and fill it with Divine blessings.

47. God, like the sun, is above our souls and ready to communicate Himself to them. Let those who guide them, then, be content with preparing the soul for this according to evangelical perfection, which is detachment and emptiness of sense and of spirit; and let them not seek to go beyond this in the building up of the soul, for that work belongs only to the Father of lights, from Whom comes down every good and perfect boon.[65] For, if the Lord, as David says, builds not the house, in vain does he labour that builds it.[66] And since God is the supernatural artificer, He will build supernaturally[67] in each soul the building that He desires, if you yourself prepare it and strive to annihilate it with respect to its operations and natural affections, which give it no capacity or strength for the erection of the supernatural building, but at this season disturb rather than help. To prepare the soul thus is your office; and the office of God, as the Wise Man says,[68] is to direct the way of the soul—that is to say, to direct it to supernatural blessings, by ways and in manners which neither you nor the soul can understand. Say not, therefore: 'Oh, the soul is making no progress, for it is doing nothing!' For

[63] S: 'the window.'
[64] Psalm cxx, 4 [A.V., cxxi, 4]. This is the reading of S. The other MSS. repeat 'sleeps.'
[65] St. James i, 17.
[66] Psalm cxxvi, 1 [A.V., cxxvii, 1].
[67] S: 'naturally.'
[68] Proverbs xvi, 9.

if it is true that it is doing nothing, then, by this very fact that it is doing nothing, I will now prove to you that it is doing a great deal. For, if the understanding is voiding itself of particular kinds of knowledge, both natural and spiritual, it is making progress, and, the more it empties itself of particular knowledge and of the acts of understanding, the greater is the progress of the understanding in its journey to the highest spiritual good.

48. 'Oh,' you will say, 'but it understands nothing distinctly, and so it cannot be making progress.' My reply to you is that it would rather be making no progress if it were to understand anything distinctly. The reason of this is that God, towards Whom the understanding is journeying, transcends the understanding and is therefore incomprehensible and inaccessible to it; and thus, when it is understanding, it is not approaching God, but is rather withdrawing itself from Him. Therefore the understanding must withdraw from itself, and walk in faith, believing and not understanding. And in this way the understanding will reach perfection, for by faith and by no other means comes union with God; and the soul approaches God more nearly by not understanding than by understanding. Grieve not, therefore, at this, for if the understanding goes not backward (which it would be doing if it desired to occupy itself with distinct knowledge and other kinds of reasoning and understanding, and desired not to be at rest) it is making progress, for it is voiding itself of all that it could apprehend, nothing of which could be God; for, as we have said, God cannot be apprehended by the soul.[69] In this matter of perfection not to go backward is to go forward; it signifies the progress of the understanding, and a gradual increase of faith, and thus it is a progress in darkness, for faith is darkness to the understanding. Wherefore, since the understanding cannot know what God is, it must of necessity walk toward Him in submission and not by

[69] S: 'by the heart that is occupied.'

understanding;[70] and thus, what you are condemning in your penitent is fitting for his good—namely, that he should not occupy himself with distinct kinds of understanding, since by their means he cannot attain to God, but will rather embarrass himself in journeying to Him.

49. 'Oh,' you will say, 'but if the understanding understands not distinctly the will will be idle and will not love, since the will can only love that which is understood by the understanding; and this must always be avoided on the spiritual road.' There is truth in this, especially as regards the natural acts and operations of the soul, wherein the will loves only that which is distinctly understood by the understanding. But in the contemplation of which we are speaking, wherein God, as we have said, infuses Himself into the soul, there is no necessity for distinct knowledge, nor for the soul to perform any acts of the understanding, for God, in one act, is communicating to the soul light and love together, which is loving and supernatural knowledge, and may be said to be like heat-giving light, which gives out heat, for that light also enkindles the soul in love; and this is confused and obscure to the understanding, since it is knowledge of contemplation, which, as Saint Dionysius says, is a ray of darkness to the understanding. Therefore, as is intelligence in the understanding, so also is love in the will. For, as to the understanding this knowledge infused in it by God is general and dark, without distinction of intelligence, so the will also loves in a general way, without any distinction being made as to any particular thing that is understood. Now as God is Divine light and love, in the communication of Himself which He makes to the soul, He informs these two faculties (understanding and will) equally, with intelligence and love. And as He Himself cannot be understood in this life, the understanding is dark, as I say, and after the same fashion is love in the will; although sometimes in this delicate communication God

[70] S: 'in submission, and therefore walks not by understanding.'

communicates Himself more to the one faculty than to the other, and acts on the one more than on the other, the soul being at times more conscious of understanding than of love, while at other times it is more conscious of love than of understanding; at times, again, all is understanding, without any love,[71] and at times all is love and there is no understanding. Therefore I say that, as far as concerns the soul's performance of natural[72] acts with the understanding, there can be no love without understanding; but in the acts which God performs and infuses in the soul, as in those of which we are treating, it is different, for God can communicate Himself in the one faculty and not in the other. Thus He can enkindle the will by means of a touch of the heat of His love, although the understanding may have no understanding thereof, just as a person can be warmed by a fire without seeing the fire.

50. In this way the will may oftentimes feel itself to be enkindled or filled with tenderness and love without knowing or understanding anything more distinctly than before, since God is setting love in order in it, even as the Bride says in the Songs, in these words: 'The King made me enter the cellar of wine and set in order charity in me.'[73] There is no reason, therefore, to fear that the will in this state will be idle; for, if of itself it leave performing acts of love concerning particular kinds of knowledge, God performs them within it, inebriating it secretly in infused love, either by means of the knowledge of contemplation, or without such knowledge, as we have just said;[74] and these acts are as much more delectable and meritorious than those made by the soul as the mover and infuser of this love—namely, God—is better than the soul.

[71] Bg, P omit: 'at times, again, all is understanding, without any love.'
[72] S: 'interior.'
[73] Canticles ii, 4.
[74] Bz: 'infused love, or by means of the knowledge of simple contemplation, as we have just said.'

51. This love is infused by God in the will when it is empty and detached from other pleasures and particular affections, both higher and lower. The soul, therefore, must see to it that the will is empty and stripped of its affections; for if it is not going backward by desiring to experience some sweetness or pleasure, it is going forward, even though it have no particular perception of this in God, and it is soaring upward to God above all things, since it takes no pleasure in anything. It is going toward God, although it may be taking no particular and distinct delight in Him, nor may be loving Him with any distinct act, for it is taking greater pleasure in Him secretly, by means of that dark and general infusion of love, than it does in all things that are distinct, for it sees clearly in this state that nothing gives it so much pleasure as that solitary quiet. And it is loving Him above all things that can be loved, since it has flung from itself all other kinds of sweetness and pleasure which have become distasteful to it. And there is thus no reason to be troubled, for, if the will can find no sweetness and pleasure in particular acts, it is going forward; seeing that to refrain from going backward and from embracing anything that belongs to sense is to go forward towards the inaccessible, which is God, and thus there is no wonder that the soul has no perception thereof. Wherefore, in order to journey to God, the will has rather to be continually detaching itself from everything delectable and pleasant than to be conceiving an attachment to it. In this way it completely fulfils the precept of love, which is to love God above all things; and this cannot be unless it have detachment and emptiness[75] with regard to them all.

52. Neither is there any cause for misgivings when the memory is voided of its forms and figures, for, since God has no form or figure, the memory is safe if it be voided of form or figure, and it is approaching God the more nearly; for, the more it leans upon the imagination, the farther it

[75] Bg, P: 'and spiritual emptiness.'

is going from God, and the greater is the peril wherein it walks, since God is incomprehensible and therefore cannot be contained in the imagination.

53. These spiritual directors such as we have been describing fail to understand souls that are now walking in this solitary and quiet contemplation, because they themselves have not arrived so far, nor learned what it means to leave behind the discursive reasoning of meditations, as I have said, and they think that these souls are idle. And therefore they disturb and impede the peace of this quiet and hushed contemplation which God has been giving their penitents by His own power, and they cause them to follow the road of meditation and imaginative reasoning and make them perform interior acts, wherein the aforementioned souls find great repugnance, aridity and distraction, since they would fain remain in their holy rest and their quiet and peaceful state of recollection. But, as sense can perceive in this neither pleasure nor help nor activity, their directors persuade them to strive after sweetness and fervour, though they ought rather to advise them the contrary. The penitents, however, are unable to do as they did previously, and can enter into none of these things, for the time for them has now passed and they belong no more to their proper path; and so they are doubly disturbed and believe that they are going to perdition; and their directors encourage them in this belief and parch their spirits, and take from them the precious unctions wherewith God was anointing them in solitude and tranquillity. This, as I have said, is a great evil; their directors are plunging them into mire and mourning; for they are losing one thing and labouring without profit at the other.

54. Such persons have no knowledge of what is spirituality. They offer a great insult and great irreverence to God, by laying their coarse hands where God is working. For it has cost Him dearly to bring these souls to this place and He greatly esteems having brought them to this solitude and emptiness of their faculties and operations, that

He may speak to their hearts, which is what He ever desires. He has Himself taken them by the hand, and He Himself reigns in their souls in abundant peace and quietness, causing the natural acts of their faculties to fail wherewith they toiled all night and wrought nothing. And He has brought peace to their spirits without the work and operations of sense, for neither sense nor any act thereof is capable of receiving spirit.

55. How precious in His sight is this tranquillity and slumbering or withdrawal[76] of sense can be clearly seen in that adjuration,[77] so notable and effective, that He utters in the Songs, where He says: 'I adjure you, daughters of Jerusalem, by the goats and harts of the fields, that ye awaken not my beloved nor cause her to wake until she please.'[78] Herein, by introducing these solitary and retiring animals, He gives us to understand how much He loves that solitary[79] forgetfulness and slumber. But these spiritual directors will not let the soul have repose or quiet, but demand that it shall continually labour and work, that it may leave no room for God to work, and that that which He is working may be undone and wiped out through the operation of the soul. They have become as the little foxes which tear down the flowering vine[80] of the soul;[81] for which reason the Lord complains through Isaias, saying: 'You have devoured My vineyard.'[82]

56. But, it may possibly be said, these directors err with good intent, through insufficiency of knowledge. This, however, does not excuse them for the advice which they are rash enough to give without first learning to understand either the way that the soul is taking or its spirit. Not understanding this, they are laying their coarse hands upon things

76 Bg, Bz, P: 'annihilation.'
77 Bz: 'comparison.' P: 'conjunction.'
78 Canticles iii, 5.
79 Bg: 'voluntary.'
80 S: 'the flower of the vine.'
81 [Canticles ii, 15.]
82 Isaias iii, 14.

that they understand not, instead of leaving them for those who are able to understand them; for it is a thing of no small weight, and no slight crime, to cause the soul to lose inestimable blessings and sometimes to leave it completely confused[83] by rash counsel. And thus one who rashly errs, being under an obligation to give reliable advice—as is every man, whatever his office—shall not go unpunished, by reason of the harm that he has done. For the business of God has to be undertaken with great circumspection, and with eyes wide open, most of all in a case[84] of such great importance and a business so sublime as is the business of these souls, where a man may bring them almost infinite gain if the advice he gives be good and almost infinite loss if it be mistaken.

57. But if you will still maintain that you have some excuse, though for myself I can see none, you will at least be unable to say that there is any excuse for one who, in his treatment of a soul, never allows it to go out of his jurisdiction, for certain vain reasons and intentions which he best knows. Such a person will not go unpunished, for it is certain that, if that soul[85] is to make progress by going forward on the spiritual road, wherein God is ever aiding it, it will have to change the style and method of its prayer, and it will of necessity require instruction of a higher kind and a deeper spirituality than that of such a director. For not all directors have sufficient knowledge to meet all the possibilities and cases which they encounter on the spiritual road, neither is their spirituality so perfect that they know how a soul has to be led and guided and directed in every state of the spiritual life; at least no man should think that he knows everything[86] concerning this, or that God

---

[83] [The original has a stronger word: 'vitiated,' 'corrupted.' Cf. the energetic metaphor used in the first redaction (p. 118, n. 92, above).]

[84] S: 'in things.'

[85] Bg, P: 'if the soul that has come hither.'

[86] S: 'that he lacks nothing.'

will cease leading a given soul farther onward. Not everyone who can hew a block of wood is able to carve an image; nor is everyone who can carve it able to smooth[87] and polish it; nor is everyone that can polish it able to paint it; nor can everyone that is able to paint it complete it with the final touches. Each one of these, in working upon an image, can do no more than that with which he himself is familiar, and, if he tries to do more, he will only ruin his work.

58. How then, we may ask, if you are only a hewer of wood, which signifies that you can make a soul despise the world and mortify its desires;[88] or, if at best you are a carver, which means that you can lead a soul to holy meditations but can do no more: how, in such a case, will this soul attain to the final perfection of a delicate painting, the art of which consists neither in the hewing of the wood, nor in the carving of it, nor even in the outlining of it, but in the work which God Himself must do in it? It is certain, then, that if your instruction is always of one kind, and you cause the soul to be continually bound to you, it will either go backward, or, at the least, will not go forward. For what, I ask you, will the image be like, if you never do any work upon it save hewing and hammering, which in the language of the soul is exercising the faculties? When will this image be finished? When or how will it be left for God to paint it? Is it possible that you yourself can perform all these offices, and consider yourself so consummate a master that this soul shall never need any other?

59. And supposing that you have sufficient experience to direct some one soul, which perchance may have no ability to advance beyond your teaching, it is surely impossible for you to have sufficient experience for the direction of all those whom you refuse to allow to go out of your hands; for God leads each soul along a different road and there shall hardly be found a single spirit who can walk even

[87] C, S: 'to perfect.'
[88] [*Lit.*, 'appetites.'] Bg, P: 'its passions and appetites.'

half the way which is suitable for another. Who can be like Saint Paul and have the skill to make himself all things to all men, that he may gain them all? You yourself tyrannize over souls, and take away their liberty, and arrogate to yourself the breadth of evangelical doctrine, so that you not only strive that they may not leave you, but, what is worse, if any one of them should at some time have gone to discuss, with another director, some matter which he could not suitably discuss with you, or if God should lead him in order to teach him something which you have not taught him, you behave to him (I say it not without shame) like a husband who is jealous of his wife; nor is your jealousy even due to desire for the honour of God, or for the profit of that soul (for you must not presume to suppose that in neglecting you in this way he was neglecting God): it is due only to your own pride and presumption, or to some other imperfect motive relating to yourself.

60. Great is the indignation of God with such directors, whom He promises punishment when He speaks through Ezechiel and says: 'Ye drank of the milk of My flock and clothed yourselves with their wool and ye fed not My flock. I will require My flock at your hand.'[89]

61. Spiritual directors, then, ought to give these souls freedom, for, when they would seek to better themselves, their directors have an obligation to put a good face upon it,[90] since they know not by what means God desires such a soul to make progress, especially when the penitent dislikes the instruction that he is receiving, which is a sign that it is of no profit to him, either because God is leading him on farther, or by another way than that by which his director has been leading him, or because the director himself has changed his way of dealing with his penitents. The director, in such a case, should himself advise a change, since

[89] Ezechiel xxxiv, 2, 3, 10.
[90] C: 'when, in order to better themselves, they seek another director, their director has an obligation to put a good face upon it.'

any other advice springs from foolish pride and presumption or from some other pretension.

62. Let us now leave this question and speak of another more pestilential habit of such directors as these, which also belongs to others worse than they. For it may come to pass that God will be anointing certain souls with the unctions of holy desires and impulses to leave the world, to change their life and condition, to serve Him and despise the world (it is a great thing in His eyes that He should have succeeded in bringing them thus far, for the things of the world are not according to the will of God), and these directors, using human arguments or putting forward considerations quite contrary to the doctrine of Christ and His way of humility and despising of all things, place obstacles in their path or advise them to delay their decision, from motives of their own interest or pleasure, or because they fear where no fear is; or, what is still worse, they sometimes labour to remove these desires from their penitents' hearts. Such directors show an undevout spirit, and are clad, as it were, in very worldly garb, having little of the tenderness of Christ, since they neither enter themselves by the narrow gate of life, nor allow others to enter. These persons our Saviour threatens,[91] through Saint Luke, saying: 'Woe unto you that have taken away the key of knowledge, and enter not in yourselves nor allow others to enter.'[92] For these persons in truth are placed as barriers and obstacles at the gate of Heaven; they hinder from entering those that ask counsel of them, yet they are aware that God has commanded them, not only to allow and help them to enter, but even to compel them to enter. For God says, through Saint Luke: 'Insist, make them come in, that My house may be filled with guests.'[93] They, on the other hand, are compelling souls not to enter; such are blind guides who

91 Bg: 'admonishes.'
92 St. Luke xi, 52.
93 St. Luke xiv, 23.

can obstruct the life[94] of the soul, which is the Holy Spirit. This comes to pass with spiritual directors in many more ways than have been mentioned here; some do it knowingly, others unconsciously; but neither class shall remain unpunished, since, having assumed their office, they are under an obligation to know and consider what they do.

63. The second blind guide of whom we have spoken, who can hinder the soul in this kind[95] of recollection, is the devil, who, being himself blind, desires the soul to be blind also. When the soul is in these lofty and solitary places wherein are infused the delicate unctions of the Holy Spirit (at which he has heavy grief and envy, for he sees that not only is the soul gaining great riches, but is flying beyond him and he can in no wise lay hold on it), inasmuch as the soul is alone, detached and withdrawn from every creature and every trace thereof, the devil tries to cover this withdrawal, as it were, with cataracts of knowledge and mists[96] of sensible sweetness, which are sometimes good, so that he may entice the soul more surely, and thus cause it to return[97] to a different way of life and to the operation of sense, and to look at these delights and this good knowledge which he sets before it, and embrace them, so that it may continue its journey to God in reliance upon them. And herein he very easily distracts it and withdraws it from that solitude and recollection, wherein, as we have said, the Holy Spirit is working those great and secret things. As the soul is of itself inclined to sensible enjoyment, especially if these are the things which it is really desiring and understands not the road that it is taking, it is very easily led to cling to those kinds of knowledge and delights which the devil[98] is giving it, and withdraws itself from the solitude wherein God had placed it. For, it says, as it

[94] Thus P, S. The other authorities read: 'the way.'
[95] Bz: 'this business.'
[96] C: 'and particles.'
[97] Bg, P: 'to turn back.'
[98] Bz: 'the horned devil' [the adjective is depreciatory].

was doing nothing in that solitude and quiet of the faculties, this other state seems better, for now it is certainly doing something. It is a great pity that it cannot[99] realize how, for the sake of one mouthful—of some one delight or some particular kind of knowledge[100]—it is preventing itself from feeding wholly upon God Himself. This God effects in that solitude wherein He places the soul, for He absorbs it in Himself through these solitary and spiritual unctions.

64. In this way, with hardly any trouble, the devil works the gravest injuries, causing the soul to lose great riches, and dragging it forth like a fish, with the tiniest bait, from the depths of the pure waters of the spirit, where it had no support or foothold, but was engulfed and immersed in God. And hereupon he drags it to the bank, giving it help and support, and showing it something whereon it may lean, so that it may walk upon its own feet with great labour instead of floating in the waters of Siloe, that go with silence, bathed in the unctions of God. And to this the devil attaches such importance that it is a matter for great marvel; and, since a slight injury is more serious to a soul in this condition than is a serious injury to many other souls, as we have said, there is hardly any soul walking on this road which does not meet with great injuries and suffer great losses. For the evil one takes his stand, with great cunning, on the road which leads from sense to spirit,[101] deceiving and luring the soul by means of sense, and giving it sensual things, as we have said.[102] And the soul thinks not that anything is being lost thereby, and therefore fails to enter into the innermost chamber of the Spouse, but stands at the door to see what is happening outside in the sensual part. The devil, as Job says, beholdeth every high thing[103]—that

99 Bz: 'that it thinks it was doing nothing and cannot.'
100 Bg: 'of one mouthful and a particular delight.' P: 'of one mouthful of no such particular delight.'
101 Bg, P add: 'as is his invariable custom, so that the soul may not pass from sense to spirit.'
102 Bg follows the first redaction [p. 123, above] in this sentence.
103 Job xli, 25.

is to say, the spiritual high places of souls—that he may assault them. Therefore if perchance any soul enters into high recollection, since he cannot distract it in the way we have described, he labours so that he may at least be able to make it advert to sense[104] by means of horrors, fears or pains of the body, or by outward sounds[105] and noises, in order to bring it out and distract it from the interior spirit, until he can do no more and so leaves it. But with such ease does he corrupt these precious souls and squander their great riches, that, although he thinks this of greater importance than to bring about a heavy fall in many others, he esteems it not highly because of the facility with which it is done and the little effort that it costs him. In this sense we may understand that which God said to Job concerning the devil, namely: 'He shall drink up a river and shall not marvel, and he trusteth that the Jordan may run into his mouth—by the Jordan being understood the summit of perfection. In his eyes, as with a hook, shall he take him, and with stakes shall he bore his nostrils.'[106] That is, with the darts of the knowledge wherewith he is piercing the soul, he will disperse its spirituality; for the breath which goes out through his nostrils, when they are pierced, is dispersed in many directions. And later he says: 'The beams of the sun shall be under him and they shall scatter gold under him as mire.'[107] For he causes souls that have been enlightened to lose the marvellous rays of Divine knowledge, and from souls that are rich he takes away and scatters the precious gold of Divine adornment.

65. Oh, souls! Since God is showing you such sovereign mercies as to lead you through this state of solitude and recollection, withdrawing you from your labours of sense, return not to sense again. Lay aside your operations, for, though once, when you were beginners, they helped you to

104 Bz, C: 'to cause it to be diverted to sense.'
105 Thus Bg, P. The other MSS. [and P. Silverio] read 'senses.'
106 Job xl, 18–19 [A.V., xl, 23–4].
107 Job xli, 21 [A.V., xli, 30].

deny the world and yourselves, they will now be a great obstacle and hindrance to you, since God is granting you the grace of Himself working within you. If you are careful to set your faculties upon naught soever, withdrawing them from everything and in no way hindering them, which is the proper part for you to play in this state alone, and if you wait upon God with loving and pure attentiveness, as I said above, in the way which I there described (working no violence to the soul,[108] save to detach it from everything and set it free, lest you disturb and spoil its peace and tranquillity), God will feed your soul for you with heavenly food, since you are not hindering Him.

66. The third blind guide of the soul is the soul itself, which, not understanding itself, as we have said, becomes perturbed and does itself harm. For it knows not how to work save by means of sense and reasoning with the mind, and thus, when God is pleased to bring it into that emptiness and solitude where it can neither use its faculties nor make any acts, it sees that it is doing nothing, and strives to do something: in this way it becomes distracted and full of aridity and displeasure, whereas formerly it was rejoicing in the rest of the spiritual silence and peace wherein God was secretly exercising it.[109] And it may come to pass that God persists in keeping the soul in that silent tranquillity, while the soul also persists with its imagination and its understanding in trying to work by itself. In this it is like a child, whom its mother tries to carry in her arms, while it strikes out with its feet and cries out to be allowed to walk, and thus neither makes any progress nor allows its mother to do so. Or it is as when a painter is trying to paint a portrait and his subject keeps moving: either he will be

---

108 The MSS. show considerable divergences here, adding, as in the first redaction [p. 125, above], 'which must be when you have no desire to be attentive' (Bz). C, P omit 'no.' S [followed by P. Silverio]: 'which must be when you are not unwilling to not be attentive.' Bg reads similarly, but omits the second 'not,' thus reversing the sense.

109 Bg, G: 'was secretly giving it joy' [*a gusto* for *a gesto*].

unable to do anything at all or the picture will be spoiled.

67. The soul in this state of quiet must bear in mind that, although it may not be conscious of making any progress or of doing anything, it is making much more progress than if it were walking on its feet; for God is bearing it in His arms, and thus, although it is making progress at the rate willed by God Himself, it is not conscious of such movement. And although it is not working with its own faculties, it is nevertheless accomplishing much more than if it were doing so, since God is working within it. And it is not remarkable that the soul should be unable to see this, for sense cannot perceive that which God works in the soul at this time, since it is done in silence; for, as the Wise Man says, the words of wisdom are heard in silence. Let the soul leave itself in the hands of God and entrust itself neither to its own hands nor to those of these two blind guides;[110] for, if it remains thus and occupies not its faculties in anything, it will make sure progress.

68. Now let us return to the matter of these deep caverns of the faculties of the soul wherein we said that the suffering of the soul is wont to be great when God is anointing and preparing it with the most sublime[111] unctions of the Holy Spirit in order that He may unite it with Himself. These unctions are so subtle and so delicate in their anointing that they penetrate the inmost[112] substance of the depth[113] of the soul, preparing it and filling it with sweetness in such a way that its suffering and fainting with desire in the boundless emptiness of these caverns is likewise boundless. Here we must note this: if the unctions that were preparing these caverns of the soul for the union of the spiritual marriage with God are as sublime as we have said, what do we suppose will be the possession of intelligence, love and glory which understanding, will and memory attain in

[110] Bg: 'of the two other.'
[111] Bg, P: 'most subtle.'
[112] Bz, S: 'final.' P: 'infinite.'
[113] Bz: 'of the sense.'

the said union with God? It is certain that, even as was the thirst and hunger which characterized these caverns, so now will be the satisfaction and fullness and delight thereof; and, as was the delicacy of the preparations, even so will be the wonder of the possession of the soul and the fruition of its sense.

69. By the sense of the soul is here understood the virtue and vigour that belong to the substance of the soul that it may perceive and have fruition of the objects of the spiritual faculties by means of which it tastes the wisdom and love and communication of God. Hence in this line the soul calls these three faculties—memory, understanding and will—the deep caverns of sense; for by means of them and in them the soul has a deep perception and experience of the grandeurs of the wisdom and the excellences of God. Wherefore it is with great propriety that the soul here calls them deep caverns, for, as it perceives that they are able to contain the deep intelligences and splendours of the lamps of fire, it realizes that they have capacity and depth as great as are the various things which they receive from the intelligences, the sweetnesses, the fruitions, the delights, and so forth, that come from God. All these things are received and established in this sense of the soul, which, as I say, is the soul's virtue and capacity for perceiving, possessing and having pleasure in everything, and the caverns of the faculties minister this to it, even as to the ordinary sense of the fancy there flock the bodily senses, with the forms of their objects, and this sense is the receptacle and storehouse for them. This common sense of the soul, therefore, which has become a receptacle and storehouse for the grandeurs of God, is enlightened and made rich to the extent that it attains this lofty and glorious possession.

Which were dark and blind

70. That is to say, before God enlightened them and made them glorious. For the understanding of this it must be known that there are two reasons for which the sense of

sight may be unable to see: either it may be in darkness or it may be blind. God is the light and the object of the soul; when this light illumines it not, it is in darkness, even though its power of vision may be most excellent. When it is in sin, or when it employs its desires upon aught else, it is then blind; and even though the light of God may then shine upon it, yet, because it is blind, the light cannot be seen by the darkness of the soul, which is the ignorance of the soul. Before God enlightened it through this trans-formation, the soul was blind and ignorant concerning many good things of God, even as the Wise Man says that he was blind before Wisdom illumined him,[1] using these words: 'He illumined my ignorance.'[2]

71. Speaking spiritually, it is one thing to be in darkness and another to be in thick darkness; for to be in thick darkness is to be blind (as we have said) in sin; but to be in darkness only is something that may happen when one is not in sin. This may be in two ways: in the natural sense, when the soul has no light from certain[3] natural things; and in the supernatural sense, when it has no light from certain[4] supernatural things; and with regard to both these things the soul here says that its sense was dark before this precious union.[5] For until the Lord said: *Fiat lux*, thick darkness was upon the face of the abyss of the cavern of sense of the soul; and the deeper is this abyss and the more profound are its caverns, the more abysmal and profound are the caverns and the more profound is the thick darkness that is upon it with respect to the supernatural, when God, Who is its light, enlightens it not. And thus it is impossible for the soul to raise its eyes to the Divine light, or even to think of such light, for it knows not of what manner is this light, since it has never seen it; wherefore

[1] Bz: 'before [He] enlightened and illumined him.'
[2] Ecclesiasticus li, 26.
[3] Bg, P omit 'certain.'
[4] Bg, C, P omit 'certain.'
[5] C, S: 'precious unction.'

it cannot desire it, but will rather desire thick darkness, knowing what this is like; and it will go from one darkness to another, guided by that darkness, for darkness cannot lead to anything save to fresh darkness. Then, as David says: 'Day unto day uttereth speech, and night unto night showeth knowledge.'[6] And thus one abyss calls to another abyss; namely, an abyss of light calls to another abyss of light, and an abyss of thick darkness to another abyss of thick darkness; each like calls to its like and communicates itself to it. And thus the light of the grace that God had already given to this soul, wherewith He had enlightened the eye of the abyss of its spirit, opened it to the Divine light, and so made it pleasing to Himself, has called to another abyss of grace, which is this Divine transformation of the soul in God, whereby the eye of sense is so greatly enlightened and made pleasing to God that we may say that the light of God and that of the soul are both one, the natural light of the soul is united to the supernatural light of God and the supernatural light alone shines; even as the light created by God was united with that of the sun and the light of the sun alone now shines without the other failing.

72. And the soul was also blind inasmuch as it took pleasure in other things than God; for the blindness of the higher and rational sense is that desire which, like a cataract and a cloud, overlays and covers the eye of reason, so that the soul shall not see the things that are in front of it. And thus, for as long as the soul took any pleasure in sense, it was blind and could not see the great riches and Divine beauty[7] that were behind the cataract. For just as, if a man sets anything before his eyes, however small, this suffices to obstruct his sight so that he cannot see other things that are in front of him, however large they be, just so any small desire or idle act in the soul suffices to obstruct its vision

---

[6] Psalm xviii, 2 [A.V., xix, 2].
[7] Bg, P: 'the Divine riches and grandeurs.'

of all these great and Divine things, which come after the pleasures and desires for which the soul longs.

73. Oh, that one might describe here how impossible it is for the soul that has other desires to judge of the things of God as they are! For, in order to judge the things of God,[8] the soul must cast out wholly from itself its own desire and pleasure and must not judge them together with Him; else it will infallibly come to consider the things of God as though they were not of God and those that are not of God as though they were of God. For, when that cataract and cloud of desire covers the eye of judgment, the soul sees nothing but the cataract—sometimes of one colour, sometimes of another, just as it may happen to be; and the soul thinks that the cataract is God, for, as I say, it can see nothing beyond the cataract, which covers the senses, and God cannot be apprehended by the senses. And in this way desire and the pleasures of the senses hinder the soul from a knowledge of lofty things. This the Wise Man well expresses, in these words, saying: 'The deceit of vanity[9] obscureth good things, and the inconstancy of concupiscence transformeth the sense devoid of malice'—that is to say, good judgment.[10]

74. Wherefore those persons who are not spiritual enough to be purged of their desires and pleasures, but still to some extent follow their animal nature with respect to these, may think much of the things that are viler and baser to the spirit, which are those that come nearest to the sensual condition according to which they still live, and they will consider them to be of great importance; while those things that are loftier and more greatly prized by the spirit, which are those that are farthest withdrawn from sense, they will count of small importance and will not esteem them, and sometimes will even consider them to be folly,

---

[8] Bz abbreviates: 'to obstruct its vision of all these great things of God as they are. For, in order to judge the things of God aright.'
[9] C: 'of the will.'
[10] Wisdom iv, 12.

as Saint Paul well expresses it in these words: 'The animal man perceiveth not the things of God; they are to him as foolishness and he cannot understand them.'[11] By the animal man is here understood the man that still lives according to natural desires and pleasures. For, although certain pleasures of sense may be born in the spirit, yet, if a man desires to cling to them with his natural desire, they are no more than natural desires; it is of small importance that the motive or object of this desire should be supernatural if the desire proceeds from nature[12] and has its root and strength in nature; it does not cease to be a natural desire, for it has the same substance and nature as if it related to a natural matter and motive.

75. But you will say to me: 'It must follow, then, that, when the soul desires God, it desires Him not supernaturally and therefore its desire will not be meritorious in the sight of God.' I reply that it is true that that desire of the soul for God is not always supernatural, but only when God infuses it, and Himself gives it its strength, and then it is a very different thing from natural desire, and, until God infuses it, it has little or no merit. When you, of your own accord, would fain desire God, this is no more than a natural desire; nor will it be anything more until God be pleased to inform it supernaturally. And thus when you, of your own accord, would fain attach your desire to spiritual things,[13] and when you would lay hold upon the pleasure of them, you exercise your own natural desire, and are spreading a cataract over your eye, and are an animal being.[14] And you cannot therefore understand or judge of that which is spiritual, which is higher than any natural desire and sense. And if you are still doubtful, I know not what to say to you save to bid you read these words again, and then perhaps

---

[11] 1 Corinthians ii, 14. S: 'and it is very difficult for him to understand them.'

[12] Bg, P: 'from a natural motive.'

[13] Bg, P: 'attach your desire to spiritual things and taste them.'

[14] S: 'and you do not cease to be an animal being.'

you will understand them, for what I have said is the substance of the truth, and I cannot possibly enlarge upon it here any further.

76. This sense of the soul, then, which before was dark, without this Divine light of God, and was blind, because of its desires and affections, is now not only enlightened and bright in its deep caverns[15] through this Divine union[16] with God, but has even become as it were resplendent light in the caverns, which are its faculties.[17]

With strange brightness   Give heat and light together to their Beloved!

77. For, now that these caverns of the faculties are so wonderful, and so marvellously[1] infused with the wondrous splendours of those lamps, which, as we have said, are burning within them, they are sending back to God in God, over and above the surrender of themselves which they are making to God, since they are illumined and enkindled in God, those same splendours which the soul has received with loving glory; they turn to God in God, and become themselves lamps enkindled in the splendours of the Divine lamps, giving to the Beloved the same light and heat of love that they receive;[2] for in this state, after the same manner as they receive, they are giving to Him that receives and has given with the very brightness that He gives to them; even as glass, when the sun strikes it, sends out splendours likewise; although the former is after a nobler manner, because the exercise of the will intervenes.

78. 'With strange brightness' signifies that the brightness is strange in a way that is far remote from all common thought and all description and every way and manner.

---

[15] C adds: 'of sense.'

[16] S: 'through this most high and Divine union.'

[17] Bg, P add: 'so much so, that they.'

[1] Bg, P: 'so wonderfully and marvellously.' Bz has 'greatly mortified' for 'wonderful.'

[2] Bg, P add: 'from Him.'

For the brightness with which God visits the soul is like to the brightness wherewith the understanding receives Divine wisdom and is made one with the understanding of God; for one cannot give save in the way wherein is given to him. And like to the brightness wherewith the will is united in goodness[3] is the brightness wherewith the soul gives to God in God the same goodness; for the soul receives it only to give it again. In the same way, according to the brightness wherewith the soul has knowledge of the greatness of God, being united therewith, it shines and gives heat of love. According to the brightness of the other Divine attributes which are here communicated to the soul—fortitude, beauty, justice, etc.—are the manners of brightness wherewith the sense, having fruition, is giving to its Beloved, in its Beloved—that is to say, giving that same light and heat that it is receiving from its Beloved; for, since in this state it has been made one and the same thing with Him, it is after a certain manner God by participation; for, although this is not so as perfectly as in the next life, the soul is, as we have said, as it were a shadow of God. And in this way, since the soul, by means of this substantial transformation, is the shadow of God, it does in God and through God that which He does through Himself in the soul, in the same way as He does it; for the will of these two is one and thus the operation of God and that of the soul are one. Therefore, even as God is giving Himself to the soul with free and gracious will, even so likewise the soul, having a will that is the freer and the more generous in proportion as it has a greater degree of union with God, is giving God in God to God Himself, and thus the gift of the soul to God is true and entire. For in this state the soul sees that God truly belongs to it, and that it possesses Him with hereditary possession, with rightful ownership,[4] as an adopted child of God, through the grace

3 C: 'united with the Divine will.'
4 Bz: 'with rightful ownership and possession.'

that God gave to it, and it sees that, since He belongs to it, it may give and communicate Him to whomsoever it desires of its own will; and thus it gives Him to its Beloved, Who is the very God that gave Himself to it. And herein the soul pays God all that it owes Him; inasmuch as, of its own will, it gives as much as it has received of Him.

79. And since, in making this gift to God, it gives it to the Holy Spirit, with voluntary surrender, as that which is His own, that He may be loved therein as He deserves, the soul has[5] inestimable delight and fruition, for it sees that it is giving to God that which is His own and which becomes Him according to His infinite Being. For, although it is true that the soul cannot give God Himself to Himself anew, since He in Himself is ever Himself, yet, in so far as the soul is itself concerned, it gives perfectly and truly, giving all that He had given to it, to pay the debt of love.[6] And this is to give as has been given to it, and God is repaid by that gift of the soul—yet with less than this He cannot be paid. And this He takes with gratitude, as something belonging to the soul that it gives to Him, and in that same gift He also loves the soul, as it were, anew,[7] and so at this time there is formed between God and the soul a reciprocal love in the agreement of the union and surrender of marriage, wherein the possessions of both, which are the Divine Being, are possessed by each one freely, by reason of the voluntary surrender of the one to the other, and are possessed likewise by both together, wherein each says to the other that which the Son of God said to the Father in Saint John, namely: *Omnia mea tua sunt, et tua mea sunt et clarificatus sum in eis.*[8] That is: All My possessions are Thine, and Thine are Mine, and I

---

[5] Bg, P: 'has as it were.'

[6] [*Lit.*, 'to pay the love.'] C, S: 'to gain the love.'

[7] Bg: 'that it gives to Him, and in that surrender of God the soul also loves as it were anew, and He gives Himself freely to the soul anew and therein loves the soul.'

[8] St. John xvii, 10.

am glorified in them. In the next life this happens without any intermission in the perfect fruition thereof. But in this state of union this comes to pass when God brings about[9] this act of transformation in the soul, although not with the same perfection as in the life to come. And it is evident that the soul can make that gift,[10] although it is greater than its capacity and its being; for it is evident that one who possesses many peoples and kingdoms as his own, which are much greater in importance,[11] can give them to whom he desires.

80. This is the great satisfaction and contentment of the soul, to see that it is giving to God more than it is in itself and is in itself worth,[12] with that same Divine light[13] and Divine warmth which He gives to it; this[14] comes to pass in the next life through the light of glory, and, in this life, through most enlightened faith. In this way, the deep caverns of sense, with strange brightness, give heat and light together to their Beloved. The soul says 'together,' because the communication of the Father and of the Son and of the Holy Spirit in the soul are made together, and are the light and fire of love in it.

81. But here we must make a brief observation on the brightness wherewith the soul makes this surrender. Concerning this it must be noted that, as the soul enjoys a certain image of fruition caused by the union of the understanding and the affection with God, being delighted and constrained by this great favour, it makes the surrender, of God and of itself, to God, in wondrous manners. For, with respect to love, the soul presents itself to God with strange brightness; and equally so with respect to this shadow of

9 Bg: 'when God excites.'

10 Bg, P: 'that so great gift.' [This text has *el*, not *al*, like that of the first redaction. Cf. p. 134, n. 17, above.]

11 Bg adds: 'than himself.'

12 Bg adds: 'giving God to Himself with such great liberality, as that which is its own.'

13 C: 'Divine light and brightness.'

14 S: 'Divine warmth and solitude; this, etc.'

fruition; and likewise with respect to praise, and, in the same way, with respect to gratitude.

82. With regard to the first of these, the soul has three principal kinds of love which may be called brightnesses. The first is that the soul now loves God, not through itself, but through Himself; which is a wondrous brightness, since it loves through the Holy Spirit, even as the Father and the Son love One Another, as the Son Himself says, in Saint John: 'May the love wherewith Thou hast loved Me be in them and I in them.'[15] The second kind of brightness is to love God in God; for in this vehement union the soul is absorbed in the love of God and God surrenders Himself to the soul with great vehemence. The third kind of love which is brightness is that the soul here loves Him for Who He is; it loves Him not only because He is bountiful, good, glorious,[16] and so forth, with respect to itself, but much more earnestly, because He is all this in Himself essentially.

83. And with regard to this image of fruition there are also three other principal kinds of brightness, no less wonderful.[17] The first is that the soul in this state has fruition of God through God Himself, for, as the soul in this state unites understanding with omnipotence, wisdom, goodness, and so forth, albeit not so clearly as it will do in the next life, it delights greatly in all these things, understood distinctly, as we have said above. The second principal brightness belonging to this delight is that the soul delights itself duly in God alone, without any intermingling of creatures. The third delight is that it enjoys Him for Who He is alone, without any intermingling of its own pleasure.

84. With respect to the praise which the soul offers to God in this union, there are three kinds of brightness here also. First, the soul praises God as a duty, for it sees that He created it to offer Him praise, as He says through Isaias:

[15] St. John xvii, 26.
[16] Bg, C, P: 'good, glory.'
[17] S adds: 'and precious.'

'I have formed this people for Myself; it shall sing My praises.'[18] The second kind of brightness of this praise comes from the blessings which the soul receives and the delight that it has in offering Him praise. The third is that it praises God for that which He is in Himself; even if to do so caused the soul no delight at all, it would still praise Him for Who He is.

85. With respect to gratitude, again, there are three kinds[19] of brightness. First, there is gratitude for the natural and spiritual blessings and the benefits which the soul has received. Secondly, there is the great delight which the soul has in praising[20] God, because it is absorbed with great vehemence in this praise. Thirdly, the soul praises God because of what He is, and this praise is much more profound and delectable.

STANZA IV

How gently and lovingly thou awakenest in my bosom,
    Where thou dwellest secretly and alone!
And in thy sweet breathing, full of blessing and glory,
    How delicately thou inspirest my love!

EXPOSITION

HERE the soul turns to its Spouse with great love, extolling Him and giving Him thanks for two wondrous effects which He sometimes produces within it by means of this union, noting likewise in what way He produces each and also the effect upon itself which in each case is the result thereof.

2. The first effect is the awakening of God in the soul, and the means whereby this is produced are those of gentle-

18 Isaias xliii, 21.
19 Bg, P: 'three principal kinds.'
20 S: 'in loving.'

ness and love. The second effect is the breathing of God in the soul and the means thereof are in the blessing and glory that are communicated to the soul in this breathing. And that which is produced thereby in the soul is a delicate and tender inspiration of love.

3. The stanza, then, has this meaning: Thine awakening, O Word and Spouse, in the centre and depth of my soul, which is its pure and inmost substance, wherein alone, secretly and in silence, Thou dwellest as its only Lord, not only as in Thine own house, nor even as in Thine own bed, but intimately and closely united as in mine own bosom—how gentle and how loving is this![1] That is, it is exceedingly gentle and loving; and in this delectable breathing which Thou makest in this Thine awakening, delectable for me, filled as it is with blessing and glory, with what delicacy dost Thou inspire me with love and affection for Thyself! Herein the soul uses a similitude of the breathing of one that awakens from his sleep; for in truth, the soul in this condition feels it to be so. There follows the line:

How gently and lovingly thou awakenest in my bosom,

4. There are many ways in which God awakens in the soul: so many that, if we had to begin to enumerate them, we should never end. But this awakening of the Son of God which the soul here desires to describe, is, as I believe, one of the loftiest and one which brings the greatest good to the soul. For this awakening is a movement of the Word in the substance of the soul, of such greatness and dominion and glory, and of such intimate sweetness,[1] that it seems to the soul that all the balms and perfumed spices and flowers in the world are mingled and shaken and revolved together to give their sweetness; and that all the kingdoms and dominions of the world and all the powers[2] and virtues of Heaven are moved. And not only so, but all

---

[1] Bg, P: 'is this awakening!'
[1] Bz: 'such immense sweetness.' C: 'such great sweetness.'
[2] Bg, P: 'all the creatures, powers.'

the virtues and substances and perfections and graces of all
created things shine forth and make the same movement
together and in unison. For, as Saint John says,[3] all things
in Him are life, and in Him they live and are and move, as
the Apostle says likewise.[4] Hence it comes to pass that,
when this great Emperor moves in the soul, Whose kingdom, as Isaias says, is borne upon His shoulder[5] (namely,
the three spheres, the celestial, the terrestrial and the
infernal, and the things that are in them; and He sustains
them all, as Saint Paul says, with the Word of His virtue[6])
then all the spheres seem to move together. Just as, when
the earth moves, all material things that are upon it move
likewise, as if they were nothing, even so, when this Prince
moves, He carries His court with Him, and the court carries
not Him.

5. Yet this comparison is highly unsuitable, for in this
latter case not only do all seem to be moving, but they also
reveal the beauties of their being, virtue, loveliness and
graces, and the root of their duration[7] and life. For there
the soul is able to see how all creatures, above and below,
have their life and strength and duration in Him, and it
sees clearly that which the Book of the Proverbs expresses
in these words: 'By Me kings reign, by Me princes rule
and the powerful exercise justice and understand it.'[8] And
although it is true that the soul is now able to see that these
things are distinct from God, inasmuch as they have a
created being, and it sees them in Him, with their force,
root and strength, it knows equally that God, in His own
Being, is all these things, in an infinite and pre-eminent
way,[9] to such a point that it understands them better in
His Being than in themselves. And this is the great delight

[3] St. John i, 3.
[4] Acts xvii, 28.
[5] Isaias ix, 6.
[6] Hebrews i, 3.
[7] Bz: 'detraction.'
[8] Proverbs viii, 15.
[9] [*Lit.*, 'with infinite eminence.'] S: 'with infinite immensity.'

of this awakening: to know the creatures through God and not God through the creatures; to know the effects through their cause and not the cause through the effects; for the latter knowledge is secondary and this other is essential.

6. And the manner of this movement[10] in the soul, since God is immovable, is a wondrous thing, for, although in reality God moves not, it seems to the soul that He is indeed moving; for, as it is the soul that is renewed and moved[11] by God that it may behold this supernatural sight, and there is revealed to it in this great renewal that Divine life and the being and harmony of all creatures[12] in it which have their movements in God, it seems to the soul that it is God that is moving, and thus the cause takes the name of the effect which it produces, according to which effect we may say that God is moving, even as the Wise Man says: 'Wisdom is more movable than all movable things.'[13] And this is not because it moves itself, but because it is the beginning and root of all movement; remaining in itself stable, as the passage goes on to say, it renews all things. And thus what is here meant is that wisdom is more active than all active things. And thus we should say here that it is the soul that is moved in this motion, and is awakened from the sleep of its natural vision to a supernatural vision, for which reason it is very properly given the name of an awakening.

7. But God, as the soul is enabled to see, is always moving, ruling and giving being and virtue and graces and gifts to all creatures, containing them all in Himself, virtually, presentially and substantially; so that in one single glance the soul sees that which God is in Himself and that which He is in His creatures. Even so, when a palace is thrown open, a man may see at one and the same time the

---

[10] Bz, C: 'knowledge.'
[11] Bz: 'is moved and guided.'
[12] Bg, P: 'of all things and creatures.'
[13] Wisdom vii, 24. Bz has 'causes' for 'things.'

eminence of the person who is within the palace and also what he is doing. And it is this, as I understand it, that happens upon this awakening and glance of the soul. Though the soul is substantially in God, as is every creature, He draws back from before it some of the veils and curtains which are in front of it, so that it may see of what nature He is; and then there is revealed to it, and it is able to see[14] (though somewhat darkly, since not all the veils are drawn back) that face of His that is full of graces. And, since it is moving all things by its power, there appears together with it that which it is doing, and it appears to move in·them, and they in it, with continual movement; and for this reason the soul believes that God has moved and awakened, whereas in reality that which has moved and awakened is itself.

8. For such is the lowly nature of this kind of life which we live[15] that we believe others to be as we are ourselves; and we judge others as we are ourselves, so that our judgment proceeds from ourselves and begins with ourselves and not outside ourselves. In this way the thief believes that others steal likewise; and he that lusts, that others also are lustful like himself;[16] and he that bears malice, that others bear malice, his judgment proceeding from his own malice; and the good man thinks well of others, his judgment proceeding from the goodness of his own thoughts; and so likewise he that is negligent and slothful thinks that others are the same. And hence, when we are negligent and slothful in the sight of God, we think that it is God Who is slothful and negligent with us, as we read in the forty-third Psalm, where David says to God:[17] 'Arise, Lord, why sleepest Thou?'[18] He attributes to God qualities that are in man; for though it is they that are asleep and have

14 Bz: 'to descry.'
15 Bz: 'of our consideration.'
16 S: 'that others are of his condition.'
17 Bg adds: 'in our name.'
18 Psalm xliii, 23 [A.V., xliv, 23].

fallen, yet it is God Whom he bids arise and awaken, though He that keepeth Israel never sleeps.

9. But in truth, though every blessing that comes to man is from God, and man, of his own power, can do naught that is good, it is true to say that our awakening is an awakening of God, and our uprising is an uprising of God. And thus it is as though David had said: Raise us up and raise us up again[19] and awaken us, for we are asleep and we have fallen in two ways. Wherefore, since the soul had fallen into a sleep, whence of itself it could never awaken, and it is God alone that has been able to open its eyes and cause this awakening, it very properly describes it as an awakening of God, in these words: 'Thou awakenest in my bosom.' Do Thou awaken us, then, and enlighten us, my Lord, that we may know and love the blessings that Thou hast ever set before us, and we shall know that Thou hast been moved to grant us favours, and that Thou hast been mindful of us.

10. That which the soul knows and feels in this awakening concerning the excellence of God is wholly indescribable, for, since there is a communication of the excellence of God in the substance of the soul, which is that breast of the soul whereof the lines here speak, there is heard in the soul an immense power in the voice of a multitude of excellences, of thousands upon thousands[20] of virtues of God, which can never be numbered. In these the soul is entrenched and remains terribly and firmly arrayed among them like ranks of armies and made sweet and gracious in all the sweetnesses and graces of the creatures.

11. But this question will be raised: How can the soul bear so violent[21] a communication while in the weakness of the flesh, when indeed there is no means and strength in it to suffer so greatly without fainting away, since the mere sight of King Assuerus on his throne, in his royal

19 [*Lit.*, 'Raise us up twice.']
20 P, S: 'of thousands.' Bz: 'of millions upon thousands.'
21 [*Lit.*, 'so strong.']

apparel and adorned with gold and precious stones, caused Queen Esther such great fear when she saw how terrible he was to behold that she fainted away, as she confesses in that place where she says she fainted away by reason of the fear caused by his great glory, since he seemed to her like an angel and his face was full of grace.[22] For glory oppresses him that looks upon it if it glorifies him not. And how much more should the soul faint here, since it is no angel that it sees, but God, Whose face is full of graces of all the creatures and of terrible power and glory and Whose voice is the multitude of His excellences? Concerning this Job enquires, when we have such difficulty in hearing a spark, who shall be able to abide the greatness of His thunder.[23] And elsewhere he says: 'I will not that He contend and treat with me with much strength, lest perchance He oppress me with the weight of His greatness.'[24]

12. But the reason why the soul faints not away and fears not in this awakening which is so powerful and glorious is twofold. First, being, as it now is, in the state of perfection, wherein its lower part is throughly purged and conformed with the spirit, it feels not the suffering and pain that are wont to be experienced in spiritual communications by spirit and sense when these are not purged and prepared to receive them; although this suffices not to prevent the soul from suffering when it is faced with such greatness and glory; since, although its nature be very pure, yet it will be corrupted because it exceeds nature, even as a physical faculty is corrupted by any sensible thing which exceeds its power, in which sense must be taken that which we quoted from Job. But the second reason is the more relevant: it is that which the soul gave in the first line—namely, that God shows Himself gentle.[25] For, just as God shows

22 Esther xv, 16.
23 Job xxvi, 14. P: 'of His face.'
24 Job xxiii, 6.
25 Bg adds: 'kind and loving.'

the soul greatness[26] and glory in order to comfort and magnify it, just so does He grant it grace so that it receives no suffering, and protect its nature, showing the spirit His greatness, with tenderness and love, without the natural senses perceiving this, so that the soul knows not if it is in the body or out of the body. This may easily be done by that God Who protected Moses with His right hand that he might see His glory. And thus the soul feels the gentleness and lovingness of God proportionately to His power and dominion and greatness, since in God all these things are one and the same. And thus the delight of the soul is strong, and the protection given to it is strong in gentleness and love, so that it may be able to endure the strength of this delight; and thus the soul, far from fainting away, becomes strong and powerful. For, when Esther swooned, this was because the King showed himself to her at first unfavourably; for, as we read in that place, he showed her his burning eyes and the fury of his breast. But when he looked favourably upon her, stretching out his sceptre[27] and touching her with it and embracing her, she returned to herself, for he had said to her that he was her brother and she was not to fear.

13. And thus, when the King of Heaven has shown Himself as a friend to the soul, as its equal and its brother, the soul is no longer afraid; for when, in gentleness and not in wrath, He shows to it the strength of His power and the love of His goodness, He communicates to it the strength and love of His breast, and comes out to it from the throne (which is the soul) even as a spouse from his bridal chamber where he was hidden. He inclines to the soul, touches it with the sceptre of His majesty and embraces it as a brother. The soul beholds the royal apparel and perceives its fragrance—namely, the wondrous virtues of God; it observes the splendour of gold, which is charity; it sees the glittering of the precious stones, which are knowledge of

26 Bg: 'this greatness.'
27 Bz: 'his wand.'

created substances, both higher and lower; it looks upon the face of the Word, which is full of graces that strike this queen (which is the soul) and likewise clothe her, so that she may be transformed in these virtues of the King of Heaven and see herself a queen indeed, and thus she may say of herself truly that which David says in the Psalm, namely: 'The queen stood at Thy right hand in apparel of gold and surrounded with variety.'[28] And, since all this comes to pass in the inmost substance of the soul, it adds next:

Where thou dwellest secretly and alone!

14. The soul says that He dwells secretly in its breast, because, as we have said, this sweet embrace is made in the depth of the substance of the soul. That is to say that God dwells secretly in all souls and is hidden in their substance; for, were this not so, they would be unable to exist. But there is a difference between these two manners of dwelling, and a great one. For in some He dwells alone, and in others He dwells not alone; in some He dwells contented and in others He dwells displeased; in some He dwells as in His house, ordering it and ruling everything, while in others He dwells as a stranger in the house of another where He is not allowed to do anything or to give any commands. Where He dwells with the greatest content and most completely alone is in the soul wherein dwell fewest desires and pleasures of its own; here He is in His own house and rules and governs it. And the more completely alone does He dwell in the soul, the more secretly He dwells; and thus in this soul wherein dwells no desire, neither any other image or form or affection of aught that is created, the Beloved dwells most secretly, with more intimate, more interior and closer embrace, according as the soul, as we say, is the more purely and completely withdrawn from all save God. And thus He dwells secretly,

28 Psalm xliv, 10.

since the devil cannot attain to this place and to this embrace, neither can the understanding of any man attain to a knowledge of the manner thereof. But He dwells not secretly with respect to the soul which is in this state of perfection, for it feels[1] this intimate embrace within it. Yet this is not always so, for, when the Beloved causes these awakenings to take place, it seems to the soul that He is awakening in its bosom, where aforetime He was, as it were, sleeping; for, although it felt and enjoyed His presence, it experienced it as that of the Beloved asleep in its bosom;[2] and, when one of two persons is asleep, the understanding and love of them both are not mutually communicated, nor can they be until both have awakened.

15. Oh, how happy is this soul that is ever conscious of God resting and reposing within its breast! Oh, how well is it that it should withdraw from all things, flee from business and live in boundless tranquillity, lest anything, however small,[3] or the slightest turmoil, should disturb or turn away[4] the bosom of the Beloved within it. He is there, habitually, as it were, asleep in this embrace with the bride, in the substance of the soul; and of this the soul is quite conscious, and habitually has fruition of Him, for, if He were for ever awake[5] within it, communicating knowledge and love to it, it would be already living in glory. For, if one single awakening of God within the soul, and one glance from His eye, set it in such bliss, as we have said, what would its condition be if He were habitually within it and it were conscious of His being awake?[6]

16. In other souls, that have not attained to this union,

[1] Bg: 'which ever feels.'
[2] Bz, C, S: 'the Beloved sleeping in slumber.'
[3] [Lit., 'lest the very smallest speck,' a stronger expression than in the first redaction.] Bg, Bz read '[manifestation of] knowledge' [noticia] for 'speck' [motica]. P reads 'sign.'
[4] Bg: 'or move.'
[5] Bg: 'awakening.'
[6] [Lit., 'within it, for it well awake.'] Bg, Bz: 'for it well prepared.'

He dwells secretly likewise; and He is not displeased, since after all they are in grace, though they are not yet perfectly prepared for union. Such souls are not as a rule conscious of His presence save when He effects certain delectable awakenings within them, but these are not of the same kind or quality as that other awakening, nor have they aught to do with it. This awakening is not so secret from the understanding, or from the devil, as that other,[7] for something can always be understood concerning it by means of the movements of sense, inasmuch as sense is not completely annihilated until the soul attains to union, but still preserves certain actions and movements pertaining to the spiritual element, for it is not yet absolutely and wholly spiritualized. But in this awakening which the Spouse effects in this perfect soul, everything that happens and is done is perfect; for it is He that is its sole cause. Thus it is as if[8] a man awakened and breathed; the soul is conscious of a rare delight in the breathing of the Holy Spirit in God, in Whom it is glorified and enkindled in love. Therefore it utters the lines following:

**And in thy sweet breathing, full of blessing and glory,
How delicately thou inspirest my love!**

17. Of that breathing of God, which is full of blessing and glory and of the delicate love of God for the soul, I should not wish to speak, neither do I desire now to speak; for I see clearly that I cannot say aught concerning it, and that, were I to speak of it, it would not appear as great as it is.[1] For it is a breathing of God Himself into the soul, wherein, through that awakening of lofty knowledge of the Deity, the Holy Spirit breathes into the soul according

---

[7] Bg, Bz, P have confused renderings of this passage. Bz also reads: 'the understanding of man,' and Bg, P: 'another's understanding.'

[8] Bg: 'And then that aspiration and awakening are as if.'

[1] So Bg, P. The other authorities [followed by P. Silverio] read: 'it would appear that it is.'

to the understanding and knowledge which it has had of God, wherein He most profoundly absorbs it in the Holy Spirit, Who inspires it with Divine delicacy and glory, according to that which it has seen in God; for, His breathing being full of blessing and glory, the Holy Spirit has filled the soul with blessing and glory, wherein He has inspired it with love for Himself, which transcends all description and all sense, in the deep things of God, to Whom be[2] honour and glory. Amen.[3]

[2] Bg, P: 'be given.'

[3] So S. Bg, C, P: 'and glory *in sæcula sæculorum*. Amen.' Bz: 'and glory in the ages of the ages. Amen.' Bg, P add: '*Laus Deo*.'

OTHER IMAGE BOOKS

OTHER IMAGE BOOKS

OTHER IMAGE BOOKS

HOW TO BE REALLY WITH IT – Guide to the Good Life – Bernard Basset, S.J.

THE HUMAN ADVENTURE – William McNamara, O.C.D.

THE IMITATION OF CHRIST – Thomas à Kempis. Ed., with Intro., by Harold C. Gardiner, S.J.

IN SEARCH OF THE BEYOND – Carlo Carretto

INTERIOR CASTLE – St. Teresa of Avila – Trans. and ed. by E. Allison Peers

IN THE CHRISTIAN SPIRIT – Louis Evely

IN THE SPIRIT, IN THE FLESH – Eugene C. Kennedy

INTRODUCTION TO THE DEVOUT LIFE – St. Francis de Sales. Trans. and ed. by John K. Ryan

INVITATION TO ACTS – Robert J. Karris

INVITATION TO JOHN – George MacRae

INVITATION TO LUKE – Robert J. Karris

INVITATION TO MARK – Paul J. Achtemeier

INVITATION TO MATTHEW – Donald Senior

THE JESUS MYTH – Andrew M. Greeley

THE JOY OF BEING HUMAN – Eugene Kennedy

KEY TO THE BIBLE – Wilfrid J. Harrington, O.P.
    Vol. 1 – The Record of Revelation
    Vol. 2 – The Old Testament: Record of the Promise
    Vol. 3 – The New Testament: Record of the Fulfillment

THE LADDER OF MONKS AND TWELVE MEDITATIONS – Trans. with an Intro. by Edmund Colledge, O.S.A., and James Walsh, S.J.

LIFE AND HOLINESS – Thomas Merton

LIFE FOR A WANDERER – Andrew M. Greeley

LIFE IS WORTH LIVING – Fulton J. Sheen

LIFE OF CHRIST – Fulton J. Sheen

LIFE OF TERESA OF JESUS: THE AUTOBIOGRAPHY OF ST. TERESA OF AVILA – Trans. and ed. by E. Allison Peers

LIFT UP YOUR HEART – Fulton J. Sheen

LILIES OF THE FIELD – William E. Barrett

LITTLE FLOWERS OF ST. FRANCIS – Trans. by Raphael Brown

LIVING FLAME OF LOVE – St. John of the Cross. Trans., with Intro., by E. Allison Peers

LIVING IN HOPE – Ladislaus Boros, S.J.

LOVE AND SEXUALITY: A CHRISTIAN APPROACH – Revised Edition – Mary Perkins Ryan and John Julian Ryan

LOVE IS ALL – Joseph and Lois Bird

OTHER IMAGE BOOKS